THE

# LIFE OF DAVID.

BY

JOHN M. LOWRIE, D.D.,

AUTHOR OF "A WEEK WITH JESUS," "THE HEBREW LAWGIVER," "THE TRANSLATED PROPHET," &c., &c.

PHILADELPHIA:
PRESBYTERIAN BOARD OF PUBLICATION,
No. 821 CHESTNUT STREET.

Westcott & Thomson,
Stereotypers, Philada.

# PREFACE.

THE two volumes which immediately preceded this one—viz., "*The Translated Prophet*" and "*Elisha the Prophet*"—were the last of the Author's which he was himself permitted to prepare for the press. Though designed for ultimate publication, the present volume, as left by the Author at his decease, needed some revision before being sent to the public. These lessons had all been enforced from the pulpit. Much that is pertinent and necessary before a congregation would be out of place in a volume like this; the MS. has, therefore, been carefully revised, and the attempt has been made to do this work in accordance with the known plan of the Author in preparing his lectures for publication—with how much embarrassment the reader may well imagine.

With the hope that this book may meet a like acceptance with those already issued—that through it the works of the blessed dead may follow him, and above all that the blessed gospel of the Son of David may be widely proclaimed through its instrumentality—it is now given to the public.

M. B. L.

# CONTENTS.

## CHAPTER VIII.



## CHAPTER IX.



## CHAPTER X.



## CHAPTER XI.



## CHAPTER XII.



## CHAPTER XIII.



## CHAPTER XIV.



## CHAPTER XV.



## CHAPTER XVI.



## CHAPTER XVII.



## CHAPTER XVIII.

# INTRODUCTION.

It has been said, perhaps with truth, that the well-written and truthful memoir of any man that ever lived would be profitable for any other man to read. Close observers of men and manners have said that they could learn lessons of wisdom from every one they met; and while it is wisdom rather earthly-minded than pure that has immortalized for man the celebrated line of an English poet, yet we will acknowledge its profundity and wisdom if we are but allowed to alter a single brief word—

A "proper study of mankind is man."

It may indeed be said that man cannot be studied properly without rising to the Creator, with the knowledge of whom man's best interests are thoroughly identified; yet it is true, certainly, that thousands admire the poet's apothegm, and feel no obligation from it to study God or their duties to him; and we need to be admonished that the study of the lower branches of science does not so fairly include the higher as the study of the higher includes the lower. You can find many a man who has studied the alphabet and the multiplication table without knowing anything of rhetoric or algebra; but you cannot find any man that has studied oratory and algebra who yet is ignorant of letters and numbers. You may find many men who study human nature and natural things around them, while they think but little of God; but no man ever studies the character of God, understands his law and loves his service, who is willing to be ignorant of what man is, or to be indolent in what he should do toward man. We would change the poet's line, and say,

"The proper study of mankind is" GOD.

Yet much of our studies concerning God is through man, and practically bears upon the duties of life around us. The philosophy of human feeling and action we do well to study: and we have many lessons to learn through our fellow mortals. The human race is a unit, not only as descended of one man, but as inheriting the same characteristics, necessities and obligations. The temptations to which men are subject are greatly alike; the principles of duty in every land and in every age are substantially the same; and the peculiarities which arise from the individual disposition, from the age to which he belongs, from the education he has received and from the circumstances with which he comes in contact, do only serve to impart interest to the lessons taught us in his life. Of course the life of many a man, fairly written, would be profitable only from its lessons of deep and solemn warning, as we erect a tall and brilliant lighthouse upon the deceitful and dangerous rock where a noble ship has foundered. For it is obvious to every thoughtful mind that the lessons we get from biographies as they are written are not without their dangers. The *first* danger is from the partial views they present to us of the truth. The characters of their subjects are not fairly drawn; the good in them is exaggerated; the evil in them is palliated, perhaps even applauded and vindicated, and made the dangerous allurement to lead others astray. The profitable influence of any character implies its just exhibition. The memoir of a bad man must but make his vices attractive; the biography of a good man should not make him faultless, and thus lift him above the level of true humanity. As we know in our own experience that history, while it has its real interest and profit in the barest annals, yet derives its attractions largely from the historian—while, without impeaching their veracity, we find a great difference between two narrators of the same historical events, and while we know that familiar events acquire a new and absorbing interest from the graphic pen of a new delineator—so almost as much, for the profit of any biography, depends upon the writer as upon the subject of it. The elements of value in any life may be overlooked by the unskilful biographer, but will be discerned and presented by a wise writer. But besides the danger arising from partial views of truth, there is a *second* danger in biography that the readers, especially the youthful ones, may be led servilely to copy the examples held up for their imitation. And the tendency is to copy defects rather than excellences—errors rather than virtues.

Yet there are means by which these and other dangers may be avoided; and there are certainly many advantages in religious biographies, as we now speak especially of them, which we ought to secure. No man should ever be a close copyist of any other man. In God's works of creation and providence scarcely anything is more remarkable than that infinite diversity by reason of which no two things are ever exactly alike. No one man is exactly like any other man, but every one has his peculiarities that are individual to himself alone; and he will likely be the most successful in everything, as he will certainly be the happiest and the most useful, who acts just like himself. Let us study others to learn PRINCIPLES; to see dangers and avoid them; to discern duties and practice them; not to copy their manners, nor to suppose that the plans we should adopt have been stereotyped in past experience. The principles we need for our instruction are more interesting and more impressive when set forth in a good example than otherwise; and there is an insensible growth in likeness to those whom we study and admire. We must learn to distinguish, to avoid errors and to follow virtues, but also carefully observe times and circumstances, propriety and adaptedness. Perhaps it was to meet the exact necessities of human instruction that the scriptural writers give us so many biographies. It is our wisdom to study these, and to tarry upon them long enough to make our just practical reflections. Here, by the unerring pen of inspiration, have we given to us faithful exhibitions of men "of like passions with ourselves:" they have their faults, and these are not hidden; their virtues are not magnified; and in their study we have only to guard against this danger—which is common to all our efforts to interpret divine teachings—that we are liable to misconceive the facts and principles here brought before us.

We perhaps too seldom reflect upon the fact, that in all the departments of knowledge, in earthly as well as in heavenly matters, even divine teachings to the soul of man labour under great disadvantages, arising from the ignorance and stupidity of the scholar. Unless the very nature of things was altered in the present state of our existence, capacity and aptness in the scholar are as needful to instruction as wisdom in the teacher. God is ever teaching men, yet, as a race, how little do we learn! Divine lessons are written upon the stars above us, upon the hills and valleys and plains around us, upon the earth and in the waters beneath us, and upon our own hearts within us. Divine lessons have been taught by Providence in all man's history; are taught now in the commerce and travel, in the progress and decay, in the peace and war of nations; yet how few are competent to read correctly and to interpret wisely the lessons taught! Astronomy spreads above us the spangled banner of her wide domains, and the stars have been set for ages upon its azure folds, yet how few men are astronomers! Metaphysics have exhibited their phenomena within himself to every living man, yet how rare are mental philosophers! Men have used the fruits of the earth since the day that God planted a garden in Eden; for ages they have enjoyed the light and heat and air of heaven; for generations they have wondered at the disturbed strata of the earth's surface and at the scattered remains of past revolutions that are so often found; and the ceaseless swellings of human ambition and covetousness have placed before them the lessons of history and political economy; and yet, with all this, how few among men have been intelligent in these things!—how few have been botanists, geologists, political economists, philosophers or historians! Men often wonder why so many different teachings are drawn from the Bible, and they even use the cavil as an argument against its divine authority. But, unless we fall into blank atheism, we should as well wonder that God teaches men every other thing so obscurely that the human learners of this Divine Teacher have opinions as widely diversified upon every other subject. God teaches men law, medicine, philosophy, history, geology, astronomy; *i. e.*, every true student notices, classifies and endeavours to comprehend the facts as they appear, draws just principles from them, and thus the sciences are elaborated. God made the heavens and orders them; man studies God's work, and just so far as he comprehends it he is an astronomer. God places before us in this fallen world certain phenomena of disease; just so far as man understands these, in their causes, symptoms and cures, he is a physician. So he who observes and classifies wisely the proper facts and principles for human government is a jurist; he that properly understands the laws of nature is a philosopher; he that knows what are the earth's strata, and can justly explain the occurring phenomena, is a geologist. Now look at the crude and clashing opinions upon all these matters in all the earth. The lessons have been the same substantially in all ages and climes, except as some ages and nations have wrought out for themselves better advantages of studying them. But are men agreed? Have they always been agreed to understand alike the lessons they taught? Are even the most intelligent and scientific jurists, physicians, geologists agreed upon more than elementary principles in the matters they study most? Now, in this state of things whom are we to blame? Is the fault in the Great Teacher of all knowledge or in the vast variety of foolish scholars? Men everywhere mistake God's true teachings, and he wisely demands that only the humble and diligent shall become truly wise. If we inquire into this matter candidly, we will find that in the Bible we have God's very plainest teachings to the sons of men. Here men may most easily learn what he designs to teach; here the earnest and sincere learners are less liable to mistake than anywhere else in God's teachings. The instructions of this holy volume have their analogies to God's teachings elsewhere. He designs to educate the souls of men. He wishes to make men think. A Bible so plain that we need not even study it would be a calamity, if, indeed it is possible for man to learn any truth without exercising his faculties. But the cause of different and jarring opinions upon matters here taught with sufficient plainness is rather to be sought in the aversion, carelessness and prejudices of man as a student of the Bible. It requires but little observation to prove that the diversities among men around us spring more from the neglect of the Bible than from the study of it; and many a man has settled religious opinions, and is strenuous to maintain them, when he knows little or nothing of the book which God has given. Possibly the time is far distant when thoughtful men will learn to take the same views upon any subject, but certainly religious people will think more alike when they less intermingle human devices with divine teachings; as we may easily discern now that the careful, humble, devotional students of what God teaches here, though circumstances may have thrown them into different worshipping societies, are yet generally very close together, both in their faith and love toward God their common Father and in their zealous efforts to live a godly life among their fellow-men. Nor are men ever afraid to trust the integrity of any one when they judge that he honestly believes and truly loves the Bible.

The sacred biography that we now take up is that of one of the remarkable men of the Bible. The patience and forbearance of the reader may sometimes be taxed, as scenes of minor interest occur in every man's life; but these, though they may occupy less attention and space, cannot be omitted, for the sake of the connection. But the general train of such a life should give us much interesting instruction; and we look the more for this, because his life and history take up more of the inspired pages than any other, excepting Moses and the incomparable history—that of our Lord Jesus Christ himself.

THE

# LIFE OF DAVID.

## CHAPTER XIX.



## CHAPTER XX.



## CHAPTER XXI.



## CHAPTER XXII.



## CHAPTER XXIII.

# LIFE OF DAVID.

## CHAPTER I.

### *DAVID CHOSEN FOR THE THRONE.*

AS we are first introduced to David, the son of Jesse, he is a shepherd lad upon the plains of Bethlehem; he passes thence to become a leader of no small renown in the armies of Israel; and then, after a fiery ordeal through the king's envy and jealousy, he passes on, having achieved a moral triumph more honourable than any he ever won by his sword, to take his firm seat upon the throne in the most flourishing days of the Jewish monarchy. A poet is here—the sweet singer of Israel—inferior to none that have ever held the lyre in the celebrity of his poetry, in the influence that his sacred songs have exerted, or in the immense multitudes that have adopted them as eminently fitted for the expression of their religious emotions. It is no exaggeration to say that the Psalms of David have been sung by more voices, have excited more feeling, and have been more truly loved and admired, than any other poems ever written. This very hour they form the basis of divine praise in thousands of Christian assemblies all around the earth; and the growth of numbers in the Church of Christ is but the increase of those that sing the praises of God in the words of David. A warrior also is here, whose first conflict was Israel's signal deliverance; and who never actually lost a battle from that day forward, but was uniformly successful, save when once a guilty father abandoned for a season his palace and his capital to a rebellious son—a warrior who firmly established his kingdom, gave it rest from its enemies on every side, and full of wealth and peace, and honour and prosperity, handed it quietly down to his wise successor. A king, moreover, is here, of renown in his own day, the founder of a long line to rule over the covenant people, whose kingdom is the scriptural exemplar of Christ's everlasting kingdom, and from whom especially the Messiah was to descend. The name of David is one famous in the annals of the kingdom of Christ: such expressions in the Scriptures as the throne of David, and the house of David, and the sure mercies of David should make every believer desirous of an acquaintance with the life and character and times of this shepherd-poet—this warrior-king.

Tekel, the significant expression of a later prophet, was already written against the name of Saul—"Thou art weighed in the balance and art found wanting." The aged Samuel yet mourned for his perverseness while he stood aloof in obedience to the divine directions. But now he was told to take his horn of oil and go and anoint one of the sons of Jesse at Bethlehem. The jealousy of Saul, however, was now so aroused that such a service publicly performed would have provoked the death of Samuel and of any man whom he would venture to anoint. We cannot think that Samuel would use untruthful means to conceal the object of his visit to Bethlehem—much less that he would be divinely directed so to do. But if it is manifestly proper to do things which we do not wish were known publicly, so it is right to ward off the suspicion of our chief designs by allowing minor matters to become public. Samuel did attend a sacrifice in Bethlehem: this was well known. Whatever else he did there, he designed to do more privately. The elders of the city *trembled* at his coming. As the prophet was now old, and had been relieved of his cares as a civil ruler, perhaps he seldom went abroad except to correct some existing abuse. But he came now to sacrifice; and all he himself knows as yet of the person that most is concerned in his visit is, that the family of Jesse must be summoned. There were eight sons and two daughters, though perhaps one of the sons died not long after this, since the names of but seven are recorded in 1 Chron. ii. 13. Of these, David was the youngest, and was held in so little estimation—doubtless on the mere account of his youth—that his father did not even call him to the sacrifice. The ideas of Samuel were as they were when Saul was chosen, and he looked for one of fine personal appearance; and perhaps, supposing that the reign of Saul would come to an end sooner, he had no thought that the choice of the Lord would fall upon one so young. He was ready to pour the oil of consecration upon the stately form of Eliab. But the Lord had not chosen him.

It is difficult to understand, in this entire transaction, how publicly the actual anointing was performed, and how much of its purport was understood at the time. We think clearly that the prophet's thought, "Surely, the Lord's anointed is before me;" and the several answers, "The Lord hath not chosen this," were not words spoken aloud, but the Lord's communing with the mind of Samuel. As it was needful to send off for David, the day passed well on before they sat down to eat, and the company may have dispersed before he was anointed; or as Samuel had sent the servant away, and anointed Saul when no witnesses were by, so now may it have been in the case of David. If this was so, we may read verse 13 differently. He anointed David *from* the midst of his brethren; or, if this anointing was public, perhaps it was not understood by any one there. It was customary to anoint prophets and priests as well as kings; and it may have been thought, and in part it was really so, that the shepherd-poet of Jesse's family was now anointed a prophet by the aged man so soon to need a successor. The facts which occur afterward; the little esteem in which David continued to be held; the reproof which his elder brother gave him in the camp of Israel; the remarkable facts that no one ever accused David before Saul, and that Saul betrayed no jealousy for this anointing as treason against his throne; and finally the fact that David was again anointed before he ascended the throne,—all these things seem to imply either that this anointing was not understood, or that it was a private matter between David and the prophet, as before between Samuel and Saul.

Although in this transaction the personal appearance of David is spoken of rather slightingly, yet it is said he was of a beautiful countenance and goodly; and we believe, as he was then but a growing lad, that in the course of a few years he did not lack the accomplishments of a kingly presence. Yet we lay the less stress upon what we may judge of these things because of the express testimony concerning him, in words which may properly be weighed in every age: "Man looketh on the outward appearance, but the Lord looketh upon the heart."

A captious infidelity, which delights to find occasion to revile the sacred volume, even upon the most frivolous pretexts, has selected as a mark for its poisoned arrows the expression of Samuel upon Saul's rejection, "The Lord hath sought a man after his own heart." An outcry is therefore made, not against the general character of David, but against that dark and shameful sin which disfigures a later period of his history. It may not be improper for us, then, to tarry a little upon this expression of the Lord's regard for this newly-chosen king of Israel. We need not, indeed, understand, when David is called a man after God's heart, that any reference is had to his individual character. It may place his choice as king in contrast with that of Saul. Saul was made king at the urgent solicitation of the people, but God chose David of his own mind, without any wish expressed on the part of the people, and against the thoughts both of Jesse and Samuel. Or it may refer to God's approval of David's efficient character, in contrast with the vain, fickle and unfaithful Saul. Saul was rejected for not carrying out the divine will, while David steadfastly adhered to the discharge of his official duties in the control of the kingdom. But without excluding these thoughts, we judge that the expression refers to the personal character of David. He was not a perfect servant to God, God has no such servants upon earth. But he was a man of real piety. Taking the character of this man as a whole, there have been few such upon earth—of early piety, of amiable disposition, of lofty genius, of refined poetic taste. We may look at his courage as a soldier, his kindness as a man, his constancy as a friend, his justice as a ruler, his magnificence as a king, his faith as a believer or his fervour as a worshipper; and we may justly decide that here is a man of exalted excellence. Even from his lamentable fall we may derive just thoughts to elevate his general character, and to vindicate the Lord's condescending love toward such a servant. If any man can so impose upon his own mind and conscience as to believe that the mention of this sin implies the approval of it, in any degree or shape, by the writers of the Scriptures or by the believers in the Bible, or on the part of David himself, much less on the part of God, such a conclusion is reached not only against the nature of religion, but in defiance of the facts as mentioned, and of the explicit expressions of the sacred writings. "The thing which David had done displeased the Lord," is the express record in the case: this is followed by many similar expressions of the divine displeasure, and by repeated judgments upon the household of the sinner, and by penitent acknowledgments and long and deep mourning on the part of David himself. The sin of David is aggravated by the high position he had previously occupied as the friend of God; but surely it magnifies our ideas of God's condescending mercy that he forgave such an offender. And if David is no example for our imitation as he thus departs from the usual rectitude of his character, even here is he not without his redeeming trait. Not many who sin as David did, repent as he did. We may look upon David as a penitent sinner after his lamentable fall; and while we admire God's pardoning mercy to the chief of sinners, let us take courage to return from our far wanderings to Him who is ready to forgive.

It was by the Lord, who looketh upon the heart, that David was now chosen. This does not indeed exclude the idea of the divine sovereignty. It does not exclude the call of David to piety through God's sovereign mercy; nor does it forbid the supposition that God's omniscience may have discerned, or God's grace have raised up in Israel, other instruments as fit as he to fulfil the divine will. But primarily the expression teaches us that David was prepared by eminence in piety for eminent service in the Church of God. And as we think it just and proper through all the life of David to learn the state of his mind, in his various emergencies, from the expression of his thoughts in his Psalms, so far as we can ascertain the occasions on which they were composed, so may we learn his early character from the Psalms which we judge were earliest written. Some of those Psalms—*e. g.*, the eighth—seem to have been composed as he watched his flocks by night, and while no mention is made of the sun or the green fields around him, the mind of the thoughtful lad is deeply impressed with the contrast between the magnificence of the starry hosts above and the insignificance of man, for whom yet God cares: "When I consider the heavens, the work of thy fingers, the moon and stars which thou hast ordained, what is man?" On the other hand, the nineteenth Psalm seems to have been composed as the long watch is closing, as the shadows of night are fleeing and as day is beginning to dawn upon the earth. It begins with wondering at the glory of God in the starry heavens; it proceeds with admiring the glory of God in the rising sun, coming forth from the chambers of the east; but as the light spreads around, and he is able to read the parchment roll of God's covenanted mercy, the devotional shepherd turns from God's works to God's word, and finds greater evidences of God's glory in the perfect law that converts the soul.

Doubtless the engagements of a shepherd were in many respects favourable for the formation of a pious character and for the cultivation of religious feelings. Piety has indeed flourished, and may again flourish, under many disadvantages, and an earnest and resolute mind may refuse to bend to the most untoward circumstances. Yet is it proper and wise for every man to secure the best advantages he may. The earlier periods of life are always more favourable than the later for the instruction of the mind in religious truths and for the formation of pious habits. This indeed depends upon the very constitution of the human mind; and it is as true in other matters as it is in religion. When any wise teacher can select his own pupils, he wishes the young and the unprejudiced. A physician desires his student not only to be young in years, but untrammelled also by the vicious teachings of an erroneous school. A pupil of bad habits and erroneous teachings is far harder to instruct than one who is ready to learn and has nothing to unlearn. As man grows up, he must have moral habits and religious views of some kind; and the younger he is the better when he learns the salutary lessons and feels the wholesome emotions of true piety. He keeps thus from much evil, and learns and loves good more easily and thoroughly.

True piety implies self-communion. In all ages it is an affair of the heart. The basis of religion is thoughtfulness. "I thought on my ways and turned my feet unto thy testimonies." Men are seldom irreligious through deliberate thoughtfulness, and perhaps never are men systematically impious in erroneous views until the practical impiety of life has prepared them for the acceptance of impious doctrines. The general truth, undoubtedly, is, men are irreligious through carelessness. A spirit of serious thought in any man usually precedes his decided piety, for piety will bear thought, and the more we think about it the more reasonable it is. The busy, bustling age in which we live is one dangerous to the souls of men, because we are too prone to let other things crowd religion from our thoughts. In spite of all earthly engagements, man must think about salvation or he must be lost. Youth is a favourable time for thought, because the mind is then less occupied than it ever again will be. And there are occupations which give greater leisure than others. Every man has his sabbaths, or wrongs his own soul if he gives them up. But many have more than this. As a shepherd, David had time for meditation, and we cannot question that his thoughts ran much upon the law of the Lord. Not once alone, but many a time, we may believe, he passed a sleepless night, and thoughts of what God had done for man filled his soul. Not one, but many a bright day, passed he in reading the volume of divine truth and in treasuring up its lessons of wisdom. Little dreamed he then that he treasured up these thoughts to order the life of Israel's greatest king. Little thought he then that his influence would pass down in the Church for so much good through so many generations. No man can tell what coming ages will eat the sweet or the bitter fruit of the good or evil tree which his hand has planted, nor how many trees may be multiplied, nor how much fruit may be increased, from the seeds his planting may scatter. It was not in vain for the good of his own heart, not in vain for the great blessing of his people, that David made the plains of Bethlehem resound with the sweet notes of his harp, and sang his midnight song to those echoes which awaked, a thousand years later, at the birth of David's greater Son, to hear the chant of angelic voices, "Peace on earth; good-will toward men."

But let us not make the mistake of supposing that the life of a shepherd was effeminate or indolent; or the grosser error of supposing that a life of idleness is favourable to the formation of a religious character. As true piety is to be exercised among the useful duties of life, so it is best formed among life's useful duties; and he is a wise man who strikes the proper balance between the attention he should give to the things of time and the things of eternity. Neither should be neglected; it is easy to judge what is of superior importance, and a just regard to either will help rather than hinder a just regard for the other. Religion is not passing out of the world, nor away from the world's affairs; it fits us for the world, and its most important influences may be secured while we are not slothful in our worldly concerns. The life of a shepherd had its hours of leisure, but it had its seasons of laborious toil; few Eastern occupations exceeded it in its exposures to the seasons, and none but that of a warrior had more dangerous encounters to expect. So Jacob describes the life he led in Laban's service in terms like these: "In the day the drought consumed me, and the frost by night, and my sleep departed from mine eyes." Gen. xxxi. 40. The range of their flocks was large; they must often be led to other and distant pasturage; they must pass sometimes through dangerous defiles and the rough rocks wounded the flock, or the fierce wild beast lay in wait for them. The good shepherd would not stand back from the peril that threatened the flock: and we are informed that David had his fierce but successful encounters with the strongest beasts of the forest. His was a character formed by wise contemplation, but settled also by the toil he endured, and rendered firm by the energy of the efforts he must needs put forth.

## CHAPTER II.

### *THE VICTORY OVER GOLIATH.*

THE condition of the unhappy king of Israel grew more and more wretched and miserable as he brooded over the judgments which God had denounced against his sins. How frequently are we taught in the history of the world that no sinner is the master of his own happiness! God has written it almost as plainly upon the pages of providence as upon the pages of revelation. There is no peace to the wicked. Men are often, indeed, careless in their sins; they often find pleasure in the indulgence of them. But this is in God's forbearance. When God lets loose upon any man the terrors of his own awakened conscience, then flee away from him all carelessness and all peace. No sinner needs more to make him wretched beyond all earthly relief than the awakening of his own conscience at the bidding of God: all the past memories of life may throng unexpectedly upon him, and fill him with anguish and horror; and in his happiest hours he is liable to an inward awakening which would make him forget every surrounding joy, and overwhelm him with unspeakable terror. The mind of Saul was filled with indefinable fears. He knew that God had rejected him; he knew that a successor was designed for the throne; but he knew not whom the Lord had chosen, nor when the revolution should begin that would cast him down; nor by what bloody tragedy, ending in his own sudden and violent death and the extermination of his family, it might be consummated. Judging, perhaps, by the usual changes in the governments of other nations; filled with the various and perplexing agitations which excite a man's worst fears as he looks forward to the unknown future; fearing to trust the men of his own household lest the elements to overthrow his family might be gathering at the very foot of the throne itself; not knowing friend from foe, nor which way to turn; forsaken of God and therefore distrustful of man,—can we well imagine a more distressing condition than that of Saul? and can we wonder that he became jealous, gloomy, despondent, or that perhaps reason staggered upon her seat and the king of Israel was a deranged man?

Yet Saul had around him faithful and sympathizing and attached friends. The loyalty of his people, even the loyalty of the anointed David, was firmly exhibited long after this. Even the divine displeasure against him did not deprive him of every support; and though we hardly think it was so, yet it may even have been that he was forsaken of God simply in his official character, and thus, after his irrevocable rejection from the throne, there may have been opportunity yet given in the divine mercy for Saul's personal humiliation and repentance and return to God.

In the despondency of the king means were used to relieve his malady. We will not dwell upon this part of the history. In all ages the power of music to relieve mental distresses has been recognized, and many instances of it are recorded in history. Among the most remarkable is the relief given to Philip V. of Spain by a musician named Farinelli, about a hundred years ago. By this time, David the son of Jesse had acquired considerable reputation, in his own neighbourhood, at least, as a young man of courage and of remarkable musical talents. Though he is called a "man of war," we can hardly suppose that he had been in any battle with the enemies of his country. The attacks made upon his flocks by wild beasts, or perhaps by predatory incursions from the neighbouring tribes, may have been met by him with a promptitude and courage which gave him reputation among those that knew him. As Gibeah, where Saul dwelt, was not over ten or twelve miles from the abode of Jesse, it is not surprising that the young man was known to some around the king. He was therefore sent for. His playing had the desired effect upon Saul's mind, and though he had returns of his morbid melancholy at times, yet it may be said that, as far as the nature of the case admitted, a cure was effected through this means.

We may notice here, in passing, one of the providential preparations which fit David for the throne. The young shepherd lad is introduced into the king's house, sees what is the state of a king, and has the opportunity of learning how business is there transacted. But the chief matter needing our attention in these incidents is the strange fact that Saul now loved David and made him his armour-bearer, and yet afterward did not seem to know him at all when he appeared in the camp and volunteered to fight the giant of Gath. The first remark we may make upon this apparent inconsistency is this, that the writer of the sacred pages does not attempt to explain it at all! This seems to imply that the reconciliation is easy. When an intelligent and truthful writer makes a plain statement upon one page and upon the next page a statement equally plain, and these two do not seem to agree together, yet without manifest contradiction, we may easily judge that they would agree if we had his explanation, and that he sees no need of reconciling the two, for certainly he would not allow a plain inconsistency to go without remark.

Some have supposed that in the interval David had grown to more mature manhood, at which time a great change often takes place in the personal appearance. Perhaps that when he came the first time to Saul he was beardless; and certainly a full beard makes a wonderful change from a smooth face. Others suppose that the king, having many persons around him, could easily forget a youth who had held but the nominal office of armour-bearer in a time of peace, or at least when Saul was not personally engaged in war. But why may not the whole matter be solved by remembering the nature of Saul's disease? David perhaps remained at court no longer than the king's recovery, and it is certainly no uncommon thing for deranged persons, when their malady takes a despondent turn, to forget, upon their recovery, the persons they have seen and the events that have occurred during the time of their despondency.

The next scene in the life of David is the one where he slew Goliath of the Philistines. A new war had sprung up, and the opposing armies, stationed upon opposite hills, were watching each other. While neither army seemed willing to leave its strong position to advance to a disadvantageous attack, and both were kept thus in suspense for some time, a single champion of the Philistines came forth between the two hosts and challenged any man in all the army of Israel to meet in single combat. It was no uncommon thing in ancient warfare for champions to be selected to fight, either to decide the issue of the entire conflict in their persons, or as preliminary to the general battle and as exerting a great influence upon it. The reader of Roman history will readily recall the famous triple combat, when the superiority of the Romans over the Albans was decided by three brothers on each side—the Horatii and the Curatii—five of whom fell in the battle, and the sixth was but spared from the hand of justice for an act of flagrant wickedness done in the flush of his victory. Even as late as the battle of Bannockburn, Robert Bruce himself put his life and his throne in peril by venturing upon a single combat between the two armies with Sir Henry de Bohun. Such combats belong to the ancient style of warfare; then personal strength often gave success, now secured rather by superior arms or superior skill. The champion of the Philistines upon this occasion was Goliath of Gath, distinguished for his extraordinary height. This was six cubits and a span. We do not definitely know the length of the scriptural cubit. It was, perhaps, from eighteen to twenty-one inches of our measurement, and thus the height of Goliath was from nine to eleven feet. We have no good reason to believe that for ages back, if ever, the average height of the human race has decreased. There is a disposition among men to slight the present age in comparison with the past, and this in respect of physical strength and firm health, as well as in other matters. Yet the tables of mortality denote rather a lengthening of human life, and men grow about as tall as they ever did. Yet we have many accounts in history of the existence of very large men—some of them altogether fabulous, some exaggerated and others authentic. There seems to have been a family of gigantic race in Canaan, of whom mention is frequently made in the sacred narratives. The spies sent up by Israel from the wilderness brought back the report from the promised land that there were giants there; and long after this time even we find David and his heroes fighting against the kindred of Goliath.

The armour of this gigantic champion is particularly described, and thus is the more remarkable because it is the first description of armour that we find in the Scriptures. Perhaps defensive armour was now gradually coming into use among these tribes. Saul also, we learn, had armour; but it is likely that the coat of mail of Goliath was very superior for the age, and thus he had more than the mere advantage of superior personal strength. It is interesting to know that among the ruins of ancient Assyria, Mr. Layard has disinterred not only the figures of warriors in armour made of scales, but has actually found some of the scales that composed this armour. They are generally of iron, but some are inlaid with copper, and seem to have been fastened upon a kind of coarse shirt, so that the person would be completely covered, while yet the motion would be comparatively easy. It was between the scales or joinings of armour like this that the arrow entered that slew Ahab. The other parts of the armour are also described, but we will not delay upon the description. We may only say that similar pieces of armour are found portrayed in the remains of Egypt and Assyria.

The appearance of this champion on the field between the two armies struck dismay into the hosts of Israel. His immense height and his complete equipment prevented any man from daring to meet him. Even the brave and pious Jonathan, who had shown his courage and capacity upon a former occasion, at Michmash, shrunk back from the opportunity now afforded. We are told that for forty days the challenge was repeated and was not accepted, but that no conflict took place between the armies: that the exulting Philistines, with the giant at their head, made no advance to scatter the disheartened hosts of Israel was doubtless owing to the fact that the latter occupied too strong a position to be easily forced.

The long delay rendered it needful that the people of Israel should send supplies of food to the camp of Saul. Accordingly, Jesse, who had three sons there, sent David with provisions for them and a present for their captain; yet, doubtless, with no other thought than that he should perform his errand and return peacefully to his home. He found the camp in great agitation and the challenge of Goliath in every mouth. The indignation of the young man was roused that any enemy of Israel should be allowed to defy the armies of God's people; and, doubtless in a good deal of excitement, he talked freely about the matter to every man he met. His eldest brother, Eliab, who had perhaps never learned to regard him as anything more than a child, and who thought his stout words mere youthful vaunting or perhaps a reflection upon his own courage, roughly rebuked him; and yet implies that he knew well his daring and bold character, that he desired to be present when the battle came on. David firmly contends that he had come there in obedience to his father's orders, and that certainly there was good cause for his present zeal, in the fact that not only Israel, but the God of Israel, had been insulted by this bold challenger. The whole affair created so much stir among the Israelites that Saul heard of David's words and sent for him. By this time David is ready to offer himself as the champion of Israel. It is not an easy thing for us to decide in advance concerning the rashness or the faith of an offer like this. In this case the result proves that David was right; but it seemed to ordinary eyes a rash undertaking indeed, and we are rather surprised that Saul should consent to allow him to go forth as Israel's representative against such an one as Goliath. Yet it seems often true that the ventures of faith are *assisted, even when not prompted*, by desperate circumstances and the reflection that this is all that can be done. Yet this is not the feeling of David. No one would have thought him lacking in courage or faith had he now stood aloof from the contest. No man in the camp could do it more honourably than he; perhaps no one was as little thought of to do this thing as he. A youthful shepherd sent merely to carry bread to his brethren, armed only with his staff and a sling, and not even attached to the army, he might come and go without remark. God often employs a feeble instrumentality to carry out great purposes. No member of a congregation is so insignificant that his or her faith may not prove a blessing to the entire Church of God. Faith in God can do wonders. It is David's striking characteristic that he gives the honour to God of all that he is able to secure. It is not through vain-glory that he relates to Saul the deeds he was able to accomplish in his shepherd life. He tells his victories over the lion and the bear only to give proof that he is not wholly unacquainted with danger; and he is careful to say that he then experienced a divine deliverance. But this is a case where he may more reasonably expect the divine aid, for this champion had defied God's people, and the honour of Jehovah himself seemed involved. In no case can we more confidently expect God's blessing than when we most directly aim at his glory.

Saul accepted David as the champion of Israel. We can hardly think that the armour with which he thought to clothe him was Saul's personal armour: this would hardly fit the youth. But it was armour from Saul's armory. Yet, as David had never been accustomed to wear anything of the kind, he declined to go in it, and would venture forth in his usual dress. This circumstance gives natural rise to the reflection that men ever think and act effectively only when they act naturally. Had David gone out in Saul's armour, he could not have used the sling at all—certainly not with the usual freedom; and he could have contended safely with the giant with no different weapon. Let every man follow out his own character, and let every effort at self-improvement and every aim to do good be without the servile imitation of any other. Our principles may be exactly like those of other good men, yet every man has his own natural peculiarities, which may be wisely preserved while carrying out correct principles.

We may imagine the breathless interest with which the hosts of Israel saw the young David step forth from their ranks and go toward the camp of the Philistines. There were doubtless conflicting opinions upon the matter—some judging it the extreme of rashness to send out such an one; others blaming themselves, as veterans in warfare, that, since the issue must be tried, they had not been bold enough, and are now put to shame by the courage of a stripling; and a few, perhaps, hoping in the blessing of Israel's God. Yet we can easily judge that all the confidence in the issue lay in the Philistines, and David was the forlorn hope of Israel. But he himself went forth cheerfully and full of courage. As he passed the brook in the valley, the dividing line between the two armies, he selected five smooth stones and put them in a coarse bag in his hand. The use of the sling has been common in many lands and ages. Every one is perhaps sufficiently acquainted with it to judge of the great force with which a stone may be sent from such an instrument; and the precision which practice gives is astonishing. We are told in one place of a regiment of Benjamites who could sling a stone and scarce swerve the breadth of a hair in their aim, and this too with the left hand. Rather, perhaps, they were ambidexters, and could throw equally well with either hand.* The Egyptians, Assyrians and Persians all used the sling, and the ball was sometimes lead rather than a stone.

Yet, as this weapon was despised by the heavy-armed troops, Goliath was galled by the double insult—that a boy should be sent against him, and that he should be armed with a staff and a sling. As they drew near each other, he began to curse David and to threaten him. What we would regard as the most arrant braggadocia was the very common language of ancient heroes. The speeches which Homer puts into the mouth of his heroes can hardly be read without a smile at the abuse they heap upon each other before they begin

* 1 Chron. xii. 2.

the battle. The modern Chinese, with other features of antiquity, retain this ancient mode of warfare. To see two Chinese wrangling upon the street we would hardly think they could separate without bloodshed, and yet they rarely come to blows. The recent wars of the people with civilized nations show also the same temper in their gravest public documents. The speech of Goliath is nothing more than would be uttered by any of these heroes, especially one who felt insulted by the meanness of his antagonist.

On the other hand, the speech of David is characterized by humility and piety. It does not lack in boldness; there is not a sign of an intimidated spirit. But his dependence upon the God of Israel is clearly avowed, and proclamation clearly made that his appeal is to the divine Arm.

It seems likely that as Goliath came on he left open the vizor of his helmet—doubtless through contempt of his feeble foe. It is the folly of many men to despise their enemies—to think too lightly of the trials they are to meet. Vain confidence has been the temporal and eternal ruin of multitudes of souls. True courage is never foolhardy. Lord Wellington is said to have made this remark upon an officer whom he saw turn pale as he marched against a battery: "That is a brave man; he understands the danger, but he does not flinch from it." True courage makes no needless ventures. We can secure every valuable end, and yet never allow ourselves to be boastful or presumptuous. Even a sling might have had no effect had the stone struck the strong helmet of the giant. As he came on, David hasted and ran to meet him. He took a well-chosen stone from his shepherd's bag, and delivered it from his sling with such precision and force that the single stroke sufficed for his victory. The haughty champion of the Philistines sank lifeless to the earth. Then, amidst the shoutings of Israel and the dismay of the enemy, he ran forward, drew forth the great sword of the giant and smote off his head as the trophy of the great occasion. In the mean time, the hosts of Israel ran forward to the battle, and the Philistines fled and were pursued to the very gates of their own cities. The victory was decided and important in its influence; and from this time forward David was one of the chief terrors of the Philistine armies.

In the Septuagint version of the Book of Psalms, and in the Syriac, Ethiopic and Arabic versions, there is an additional Psalm to the number of the Psalms in the Hebrew, and the subject of this one hundred and fifty-first Psalm is David's victory over Goliath. It is a very ancient production, but lacks internal and external evidences of its genuineness. It has never been received as authentic, is not found in the Hebrew, and possesses nothing of the excellences of David's writings. It may be mentioned, as a mere matter of curiosity, that such a psalm exists, but neither the style nor the contents of it are worthy of the trouble of quoting entire. But while we give no credit to this as a psalm of David upon that memorable day, we are quite unwilling to think that David gained that great victory without returning his grateful thanks to that God who had given him power over his foe. He ventured to fight with Goliath because the cause was the cause of the Lord of hosts, and the thanksgiving after the victory was too consonant with the tone of David's piety to be omitted. We do not know that the youthful champion pressed on in the pursuit; let us rather adopt the idea of a modern poet:

"The carnage moved on, and alone in the vale
The shepherd knelt down by the dead in his mail;
And there, with his arm on that still reeking sword,
Poured forth his thanksgiving in prayer to the Lord.
"CAPRICES."

It would be an easy thing for us to *allegorize* the chief scene we have regarded, and to take the champion of Gath as an exemplar of many a gigantic evil with which we are called to contend in the world. The points of analogy are neither few nor trifling. For it seems that evil all around us, more easily than good, attains to a giant's strength and stature; that good men stand back too often appalled at its great strength and its weapons of defensive armour; and that there are not wanting Eliabs in the camp of

Israel to rebuke the forwardness of the humble piety that is jealous for the honour of God. But there is one lesson of more importance than any other which we may draw from that eventful conflict. The lesson is this, that the bold virtues of an humble, earnest faith in God are nowhere upon these sacred pages discouraged or put to shame. The triumphs of faith are here recorded, and the defects of unbelief are here rebuked. But amidst all the bold efforts which men have made to serve God; with all their wonderful reliance upon his promises in the most discouraging cases; with all their hopes directed toward him in their deepest distress; with all the trials to which faith itself is sometimes subjected to test its strength and genuineness,—we find nothing designed to hinder, but everything to foster, our faith in God. As God himself is infinite in excellence, and as our holy love and reverence cannot possibly outstep the boundaries which his nature justifies, so our reasons for trusting him are to be bounded and regulated by the infinite excellency of his own nature. It is recorded in praise of Abraham, that "against hope he believed in hope;" and the most extraordinary act of his life was faith in the command of God in apparent contradiction to God's promises. The history of redemption is the history of the triumphs of faith; and we learn from it that it is a sin to despair while God is gracious, and that all things are possible to him that believeth.

But let us understand that the faith thus highly commended is faith in God—in his character, his covenant, his word and his promises. We must carefully guard against the delusive idea, prevalent in many minds, that faith is the firm persuasion that God will do for us what we ask of him. This is no definition of faith. If this is faith, then God is under the government of man—not man under the government of God. Faith is the belief of truth respecting God, and the belief of a falsehood he will not respond to. It would be dishonouring to God and calamitous to man if God should do, at man's request, that which the divine truth and goodness and wisdom do not approve. If a man asks that which God cannot consistently do, because forbidden by his truth or his holiness or his justice, no confident expectation will secure that such a thing must be done. And as faith must thus be conformed to God's character, and as it is presumption, and not faith, which expects him to do an unholy or an unwise thing, so faith must be conformed to the word and covenant and promises of God. We do not say, indeed, that the thing which we hope for from God must be expressly named in his word before we are justified in believing that it will be granted. But we are certainly never right in believing that God will grant a desire whose very character is opposed to his covenants, his truth and his promises. If he has promised to save only the believing and the obedient, then it cannot be faith, but presumption, which trusts and expects the salvation of the unbelieving, the prayerless and the disobedient. Faith need not depend upon an express pledge in the word of God that what we ask shall be granted. On the contrary, some of its most exemplary actings have been when no such pledge existed. The parents of Moses had no express promise that the life of Moses would be spared, when, by faith, they laid him by the margin of the Nile. Esther had no express promise that her life would be spared when she ventured in before the king. Our Lord commends the faith of Gentiles who came with urgent requests that depended upon no invitation. But faith, if not depending upon a direct promise, must ever ask things consonant with the divine character and the covenant and promises of God.

Thus the faith of David when he ventured forth against Goliath accorded with the covenant and the promises of God. God had promised good to his people; he was jealous of his honour; he had ever been ready to help Israel. David took up this quarrel as one that would vindicate the honour of God and secure a blessing to the covenant people.

Our believing prayers and efforts for the blessing of God upon the souls of men around us depend in general upon God's promises for enlarging his Church, but for their individual application they are called forth and encouraged by their consonance with the divine word and character. God has not promised definitely to convert this or that soul, but he has encouraged our prayers for such things, and it is far from being presumptuous to plead earnestly and believingly for those whom we love. Often he says, According to your faith, so be it unto you. Let us be reverent; let us study the principles upon which he answers prayer; let us rather rejoice when an unwise petition remains unanswered, and we may rely with unbounded confidence upon God's willingness to bless.

But let sinful men rejoice to draw near to God and exercise toward him that earnest faith which becomes the soul's salvation. The faith exercised by a soul that hears the gospel and lays hold upon its blessings unto everlasting life is a faith warranted not only by God's holy character, but by the express and plain pledges of God's own word. The question, Is a sinner justified in believing the gospel to his soul's salvation? is one answered not only by the direction of the gospel commission, "TO EVERY CREATURE," not only by the express promise itself, "He that believeth shall be saved," but also by the solemn assurance of that threatening which shuts every soul up to this imperative duty, "He that believeth not shall be damned."

There is not a living sinner who hears the gospel message who is not by its own terms warranted immediately to receive it. The man that says now, "I am a lost sinner; I know that Christ came to save; I know that if I believe not I must perish;

I cast away my sins at his bidding; I renounce every other dependence; I have confidence in his ability; I trust in his gracious promise; I will yield myself to his service; I long for his salvation"—this man is a believer in Christ; his humble faith is accepted of Christ; he shall never be confounded.

## CHAPTER III.

### *DAVID'S TROUBLES FROM SAUL.*

THERE are two important ends which are secured by the varying and severe trials of life. One is, they tend *to form* the character; the other is, they tend *to test* it. A piece of counterfeit coin or a fraudulent bank-note may pass currently from hand to hand for a long time, until it meet the eye of a competent judge, when its worthlessness is immediately detected. Or possibly the ring of the true metal may be so nearly secured in a base piece that it must be broken or melted down before it is fully known. It is the character of a good coin that it will abide any test, even that of the crucible; and he who knows his own honesty in passing money is not afraid of the most rigid scrutiny. Now we may say, in regard to character, that only is a virtuous character which will abide the test of severe examination. He is truly honest who is so not only upon ordinary occasions, but when motives of gain and secresy are strongest to tempt him aside. He only is a true patriot who abides by his duty in the most trying times and when most poorly supported by those who should stand by him. He only is a true Christian who maintains his place and piety when the current of irreligion sets all away from truth and the Church of God, and who finds reason to be more earnest in the very fact that many around him are remiss in their duties. But while we thus reason abstractly of what ought to be the principles of a stable character, we should not overlook the important fact that character is the result of growth. As perhaps no human character is ever perfectly firm and proof against all temptation—as certainly we cannot admit that any man is safe without the supportings of divine grace, so those characters that are now the firmest have not always possessed their present strength of principle. Even though in earlier life the principles of a man may be as sincere and as upright as ever they shall be, they are not as well established. We may admire the giant oak on the mountain's brow as it spreads its brawny arms and defies the fiercest storms, but that oak is now what it once was not. There was a time when it could have been pulled out of the ground by the hand of a passing stranger, or when its very trunk could have been easily snapped in two. It was an oak then as truly as now, but it needed growth. And had its subsequent growth been in the shelter of a conservatory, though it might have grown more rapidly and to a larger size, it could not have attained its present firmness and strength. Planted among the rocks, exposed to every storm, obliged to send out its tendril roots to seek for the meagre soil in every crevice, during all the life of that tree there has been a wonderful proportion, arranged by the providence of God, between the tempests to which it was exposed and the strength it had to endure them. Even if we should say that the winds swept as fiercely over that mountain exposure when the tree was a sapling as when it was older, we must still remember that the tree felt the violence of the storm just in proportion to its size, and that before it spread its arms so wide its roots were equally spread to fasten it in the soil, and its trunk and branches had their symmetry of strength with the growth of the whole. Now, just as it is hard to decide for how much of its strength the oak is indebted to its exposed position, and yet easy to judge that it has greater strength because it grew there, so it is difficult to say for how much of his strength of character any man is indebted to the trials and temptations of life. We do not pretend to say that the analogy between the man and the tree is a perfect analogy; we do not decide that the character of a child ought to be exposed to temptation that it may be formed to resist it; but as we judge that a healthy and hardy plant is not to be reared in a hot-house, so we judge that a decided and worthy character is best formed by a healthy exposure to cold as well as heat—to the storm as well as the sunshine. We fear to have the young enter into temptation; we warn them against it. Especially we fear for those whose principles are less firmly established. But the needful exposure involved in their providential position in life we ought not to fear. Watchful we may be; watchful we may urge them to be; but so timid as to shrink back from the path of duty, so fearful that they may not venture forth to grapple with the trials of life, we should neither be for them nor wish them to be for themselves. If in mature life we may speak of temptations as testing the character, perhaps we ought to consider the trials of earlier life as serving to form the character. The young man who contends successfully and righteously with the trials he now meets will be prepared to endure the harder trials which life may yet bring to him. Few men have ever been great in goodness who have not been schooled for their public position by a long course of trials, which, while they have searched and proved them, have served also to develop and strengthen their powers for the duties which Providence has designed for them.

The early life of David had been so spent as to give him the advantage of learning the principles of righteousness from the sacred word of God. The value of these years of retirement and of early instruction it is impossible to estimate; and happy, indeed, was it for the young man as he ventured forth into the world that already he was a lover of God's law and an humble servant of the Lord.

This was David's safeguard, as now his bark crept no longer along the shores of his early associations, but stood boldly out for the rough and stormy sea of life. We must go with him now, and see how these trials and difficulties at once prove his uprightness and prepare him for more important duties of the distant future.

How strange it is that as some of the sweetest consolations and enjoyments of this our mortal life grow out of our severest sorrows, so our deepest troubles sometimes spring out of our highest triumphs! So one of our evangelical poets truly writes:

> "The brightest things below the skies
> Give but a flattering light;
> We should suspect some danger nigh
> When we possess delight."

David is no longer now the youthful shepherd, but the champion of Israel; he is no longer the little esteemed of the house of Jesse, but his name has honourable mention in all the families of the land; the noble Jonathan gives him substantial tokens that he loved him as his own soul; he is the idol of the army; and as they come home from the triumphant campaign, the cities of Israel pour out their glad processions of daughters with songs and dances, ascribing the merited honours in thankful language—"Saul hath slain his thousands and David his ten thousands." Happy deliverer of his people! The new and flattering strain fell gratefully on his ear; and the heart of David, while it swelled with thankfulness toward God, felt perhaps also a proud happiness as he stood the chief object of observation among the crowds of his fellow-citizens. But the very height of his triumph was the source of his danger. The words uttered so cheerfully by the daughters of the land—the words that fell so pleasantly on his ear—awakenèd far different feelings in the mind of Saul. This unhappy monarch, rejected of God, forewarned that the kingdom was to be taken from him, and ignorant of the time and person through whose means he was to be cast down, had become jealous of those around him; and while perhaps he formed no definite suspicions of David for some time after this, he took up immediately the expressions of the grateful people and made them the ground of an envious hostility to the young man. Though he now owed to David the most illustrious victory that had occurred in his reign, it seemed as nothing to the dangerous popularity which it seemed to have secured to the youthful hero. "What can he have here but the kingdom?" is an expression which seems sufficiently to indicate the turn which Saul's suspicions took; and this feeling—certainly not without its just grounds—laid the foundation for all the unhappy intercourse of these two men from that day on. We have no reason to judge that David had any improper aspirations for the kingdom. Even though he had been before anointed—and this he knew well, if no one else did—yet we can discern in David from this time onward not a word or thought of disloyalty toward Saul so long as he was king, not a symptom of impatience, as though he longed to wear the crown himself. And now we have no reason to think that David at all understood the jealousy and suspicion of Saul toward him. The unhappy passions of envy, jealousy and suspicion are the tormentors of those that indulge them. The same events that give delight to others around them fill them with wretchedness, and the gladness of others makes them more gloomy. That night Saul revolved the praises of David in his envious breast, and by the morning he had a return of his former malady. Yet even in his madness he knew well where to strike, and David was twice obliged to avoid the stroke of a javelin, by which Saul would have rewarded his services to himself and to Israel.

And now begin the checkered scenes of David's earlier public life, while for a time he is alternately courted and persecuted by the king, and afterward driven out from society to wander a fugitive or an exile. At first, Saul, having no plausible pretext for his hostility, did not venture to cast him off, much less to show open enmity. The service rendered had been too great, the love of the people had been too plainly shown, and the merit of the young man was too eminent, not to make open hostility unpopular and possibly dangerous to Saul himself. The very things which provoked him most in David were yet the things which obliged him to move cautiously against him. But he carefully evaded fulfilling the promise he had made that the slayer of Goliath should be son-in-law to the king. If he suspected that David was to be his successor, it might be a step upon his path to the throne to become the king's son-in-law even in a kingdom where no lawful queen ever held the sceptre. But what Saul keeps back from David as too dangerous an honour in spite of his royal promise, he is willing to hold out to him as a snare to secure his destruction. Knowing his public zeal and ready valour, he gave him to understand that by victories over the Philistines he could secure his daughter for a wife; and though in the very midst of the negotiations he exhibited his faithlessness by marrying his eldest daughter to another man, he took immediate occasion to renew his proposals upon learning that his youngest daughter bore an affection for David. We might almost understand the meekness of David as a want of spirit to resent the insults of the king, but we are not to interpret his conduct by the usages of our own times. Better, at all events, the meekness of David than a temper of proud defiance. It will perhaps seldom be found in any man's experience that the meek endurance of personal slights has been much cause of subsequent regrets, while hasty resentments often cause bitter and permanent sorrow. The snare of Saul was set in vain. David gave evidence that he had slain double as many of the enemy as the king had required. No possible excuse could be alleged, and the son of Jesse became the son-in-law of Saul.

And now David is in the family of the king, and two members of that family at least are warmly attached to him. These were Michal, his wife, and Jonathan, his brother-in-law. This position did not abate the jealousy of Saul, but it rendered it needful for him to move cautiously in his schemes of mischief. But in seeking for those that might render him the service of killing David, Saul happily mentioned the matter to his eldest son. Doubtless he thought that Jonathan would have much the same reasons with himself for wishing David out of the way. But among all the characters drawn upon these sacred pages there are few that command more our esteem and respect than Jonathan. Hardly a greater contrast could be instituted than we may find between the father and the son; and if we allow ourselves to conjecture what would have been the state of Israel had the natural succession gone on, and Jonathan reigned in the room of Saul his father, we can hardly anticipate a sceptre in his hands less exalted and righteous than the rule in the hands of David. If we vindicate the downfall of Saul upon principles of divine rectitude, we must rather regard the transfer of sceptre from Saul's family to that of David as a display of divine sovereignty, which, while not inconsistent with righteousness, yet rests rather upon His will who raiseth up kings or casts them down as he pleases. The upright and loving Jonathan had no sympathy with the dark schemes of his envious father. He not only informed David of the plots formed against him, but devised measures to defeat them. We have no reason to charge Jonathan with any breach of confidence toward his father. No worker of mischievous schemes has any right to make a confidant of an upright man, and then expect that he will at least favour them so much as to keep silent about them. Let every good man guard against being ensnared by any promises of secresy in evil things; let him judge that no righteous principles can bind him to the complicity of silence or indifference, and if wicked men must have confidants, let them be men of their own stamp. We may very properly listen to righteous schemes, and keep sacredly the confidence reposed in us when we are expected so to do; but we are under no obligations to keep silence respecting wickedness because its actors have presumed upon our co-operation and have made us confidants of their plans. Jonathan did not even so far comply with his father's plans as to keep silent while he explained them. As he divulged them to David, so he expostulated with his father against them. He so arranged an interview that David was allowed to listen and learn for himself in what danger he stood. At this time Jonathan, with the warmth of disinterested friendship, set before his father the wickedness of his purposes, and their especial ingratitude in view of the eminent services which David had rendered. There was, perhaps, no living man who could better venture this remonstrance with Saul or better make it successful. Jonathan was as deeply interested in the regular succession of the crown as Saul was; he had gained a high reputation for wisdom, piety and valour, and he doubtless had as much influence over Saul as any one. We cannot, indeed, decide that he awakened some of the better feelings in his father's nature and made him ashamed of his suspicions. Two things were against the safety of David, which even Jonathan could not explain away. *First*, the evil instincts of Saul were really upon the right track; and however unjust he was to David or unwise toward God to attempt to thwart the declarations of the prophet, this really was the man to whom his throne was to descend. *Secondly*, the morbid envy and jealousy of Saul were too deeply-seated, evil had too full possession of him, to give way at any expostulations, or even to yield long to any convictions. Perhaps it is not just to surmise that Saul hypocritically gave an apparent consent to Jonathan's views, with the design still to pursue his schemes of malice. Bad a man as he was, he might perhaps start back from the sin of perjury.

But in pretence or in sincerity, a promise, even if sealed by an oath, binds very slightly the conscience of a suspicious and wicked man. The king solemnly swore that David should be safe, but it amounted to nothing. He returned to his duties in the royal presence, and perhaps for a little time no plots were formed against him. But war sprang up again between Israel and the Philistines, and David's precarious position could easily be discerned. He was in danger whichever way turned the tide of battle. If he defeated the Philistines, he incurred anew the jealousy of Saul; if he was defeated by them, they would take their vengeance for Goliath's death, and Saul would have made his defeat a pretext for his murderous schemes. The success of his arms began afresh the plans of the king. He endeavoured again to strike him with the javelin, and as David again avoided him—and now this was an open declaration of his feelings—Saul was excited to energetic measures and David was fully upon his guard. An attempt was made that night to secure him in his own house. A watch was set around it to prevent his escape, and but for the care of his wife the plot might have succeeded. She warned him of it, assisted him to escape, and used measures to delay the pursuit as long as possible. She placed an image in his bed and feigned that he was sick. So the messengers returned to Saul and told that David was sick. Perhaps Michal thought that the report of his illness would change the current of her father's thoughts—possibly lead him to abandon his attempts, at least until the issue of the sickness was known. But the delay occasioned was perhaps several hours after the departure of David. Of course we offer no justification of the falsehoods of his wife in securing his escape. Her language toward her father is widely different from the bold stand and the frank expostulations which her brother Jonathan would have used in such a case.

The escape of David gave occasion to his composing the fifty-ninth Psalm, and we may mention this to contrast his character with the falsehood of his wife. He ascribes his safety to the watchful providence of God, and relies with unshaken confidence upon the divine protection, while he describes his pursuers as a disappointed pack of dogs round the walls of the city, hungry for their prey, yet unable to reach it.

The refuge of David was with Samuel. This was a natural movement upon his part, but perhaps it was as dangerous a step as he could have taken, unless he had already given up all hope of a reconciliation with Saul. For if the king's persecutions arose from his suspecting that David was to be his successor, these suspicions would be confirmed by the intimacy of David with the venerable prophet through whose lips Saul had learned his own rejection. But it may be that now David preferred an open outbreak to the insidious plots which up to this time had been formed against him. He knew how to guard against open violence; against secret machinations he knew not how to protect himself. Samuel took him to Naioth, where was established a school of the prophets, which would prove a protection against the designs of the king. But Saul had no regard for the sanctity of places when his revenge urged him on. He sent a first and a second and a third band of messengers to tear him away, even from the presence of Samuel. But these messengers returned not to him. Each band of them, as they came before the prophet and among the sons of the prophets, was seized by an uncontrollable divine impulse, listened to the prophesyings of the young men and began themselves to prophesy. Saul seems to have been in a transport of rage as he heard of these things, and, bent upon his wicked purpose, he resolved to go himself for the arrest of the fugitive. But his coming was equally ineffectual. Even the wicked king of Israel, when he came among the sons of the prophets, was influenced beyond his own will. He stripped off his royal robes and lay down naked all that day and all that night. The expression *naked* is not to be literally understood. It means simply that he took off his upper garments—those that were the emblems of his royal estate. We cannot pretend to explain the nature of the influence which rested upon Saul and his messengers. It excited great surprise, and revived the proverb to which a former occurrence in his life had given origin, "Is Saul also among the prophets?" It expresses the wonderful nature of the change that had passed upon such a man to make him appear among those that testify for God. It may be applied to two distinct classes of religious experience which we sometimes see: 1st. We may wonder at the extraordinary spiritual influences which at different times have affected entire communities. In the great religious excitements which prevailed in Kentucky and Tennessee at the beginning of the present century, there were some affections for which we are unable to account upon any known principles in physiology, metaphysics or religion. That there was much genuine religious experience at these times of religious interest cannot be questioned, for the fruit was long tested in the Church, and at this very hour one of the most useful men in the Presbyterian Church is an elder who was a subject of these peculiar exercises, and whose piety has been tested since by half a century of devotion to the service of Christ. But "enthusiasm is the counterfeit of true religion," and where the genuine much abounds the copy will rarely be entirely absent. So there was much at that time that was spurious mixed up with the genuine, and the bodily effects of the excitements were shared alike by the willing and the unwilling. Instances are recorded of men who had resolutely resolved they would not be influenced, and who had kept out of the way, yet affected against their wills. "It affected the good and the bad alike," writes an eye-witness of the scenes—"the aged and the young. It was entirely involuntary, dreaded and hated and even cursed by some, while it was desired and courted and highly prized by others." So, again, "It was not confined to the public assembly; it invaded the private circle, while engaged in domestic business or travelling on the road. The same individual was frequently the subject of it; young and old, male and female, refined and unrefined, the pious and the wicked were alike under its operations." There is no real piety in any of these things, but the point of our present notice is, that they exist alongside of influences that are really religious. And we have other examples in the sacred Scriptures besides this of Saul to show that the influences of the prophetic spirit fell sometimes upon unwilling and wicked men. So Balaam was a wicked man, but a prophet. So Caiaphas, unconsciously to himself, testified concerning Christ's death. We do not pretend to explain all these things; we cannot accurately draw the line between spurious and genuine religious influences; but we do as did the Israelites in that day—we stand and wonder and exclaim, "Is Saul also among the prophets?" When we see wicked men continuing in their wickedness, yet compelled to acknowledge the genuineness of religion, we do not judge that the mixture of evil in their views and feelings destroys the value of their testimony, but we take what they confess as the verdict of their consciences to the truth. When we see ungodly men upon a sick bed asking for the prayers of the pious and longing for the death of the righteous, we do not judge that their unrighteous lives, after a sudden restoration, is proof that all their views were wrong. We take the testimony of their consciences in an honest hour in favour of the true excellence of religion even in their esteem. When we discover in the unguarded or the unwilling testimony of men who have no religious predilections proof corroborative of the evidences of Christianity, and find even our enemies bearing witness that God is with us, we regard it as the finger of God bringing good out of evil and calling light out of darkness. In all those cases we ask, "Is Saul also among the prophets?" As God held his hook in the jaws of even the rejected king to restrain him at his pleasure, so often he causes the wrath of man to praise him and restrains the remainder thereof.

But, 2d. This proverb may apply, not only when men experience religious influences that have no transforming and permanent effect upon their characters, but with yet more force when the entire man is changed by the renewing power of God the Holy Spirit. Do we wonder that Saul, the king of Israel, should be constrained by a power he could not resist to utter words of prophecy and to stand back from the revenge he meditated? We may be yet more surprised that the Spirit of God long afterward arrested another and a greater Saul as he was on a fiercer errand against the greater Son of David—that Saul of Tarsus, so much aside from his thoughts, should be smitten down at noonday, and after three days of blindness and perplexity be led as a humble follower of Jesus to spend years of earnest and holy labours for the good of his race! We may be surprised that the Spirit of God should take a man like John Bunyan and transform the profane soldier, the wicked, Sabbath-breaking tinker, into the devoted preacher, the inimitable dreamer for the rich instruction of Christian people in all after ages. Perhaps we have met in our own experiences instances of the most surprising changes wrought in the most sovereign and remarkable manner as to the persons, the time, the means and the important results. But it is really true that every genuine conversion of a soul through the power of the Spirit may excite our thankful wonder. Strange that any sinful soul should be so changed by the influences of the Divine Spirit! The change that makes any man truly pious is the effect of divine power. As it occurs in many persons who have been trained all their lives to observe many precepts of religion, it is less striking in its external results, and therefore the evidences of it are not so apparent. But a thorough change in the man results from it. It produces an entire change in his relations to God, and involves the most glorious prospects beyond this life. The effect upon Saul, to make him lay aside his revenge for a season, is not worthy of comparison with the influence of religion upon David, to produce meekness and patience and trust in God in the midst of these unprovoked persecutions.

The varieties of human experience are as great in religion as they are in other matters. As each one of us has a past history peculiarly his own, however much it may be *like* another man's life, so each one may expect the future to differ from all we have heretofore felt and known. Every day of life has its lessons, and the profit we derive from them may not at all be proportionate to the importance we now attach to them. The period of David's life at which we now look is one of very great importance in fitting him for his future duties, and he here shows some of the most quiet yet most valuable and difficult virtues of piety. He here shows meekness amidst his provocations, and a forbearing and forgiving temper amidst unprovoked persecutions. In all ages piety has required that the heart be schooled, and the showy accomplishments which men have admired have been of low esteem in the sight of God. He that hath no rule over his own spirit is like a city that is broken down and without walls. As God had said before that David was chosen for the throne of Israel, not because of his noble bearing, but because of the virtues of his heart, so will we see that these virtues shine brightly in these early times of David's unjust persecutions from Saul.

Every young man especially is wise when he regards himself in his providential lot as undergoing those trials which tend at once to test and to form the character. We must not decide that only in adversity are men tried. If we are surrounded by all that heart can wish, we should fear lest our prosperity should prove our snare. If we have difficulties to contend with, let the overcoming of these give us strength for future tasks. But overlook not what too many regard as the trifles of life. If we decide that a man's principles of truth and honesty can be tested by trifles; if we judge that he is a liar who wilfully tells a single falsehood—that he is dishonest who wilfully defrauds another of a single penny; if we claim that the dereliction of principle is aggravated by meanness when a man consents to be a liar or a thief for a trifle's sake,—when we say that we cannot prejudge how far the man may go astray who has thus begun, we should transfer all these decisions to other matters of conduct and character. Nothing is a trifle that is right or wrong. The spark of anger that is stricken out from our rough contact with a neighbour cannot be safely allowed to burn, or the little fire may kindle a great matter. Err on the side of forgiveness, not of revenge; of meekness, not of impatience; of suffering, rather than of inflicting evils—if there can be any error in fostering good or in suppressing evil. The hasty word let go cannot be recalled; how often we have wished it could! The unholy thought indulged often increases to more ungodliness. Every day we need to watch; we are not safe in any hour of carelessness. We have no greater matters to attend to than the care of our own spirits, especially in reference to those cardinal principles which regard our eternal well-being. Yet let us not neglect the chief of these things—the reconciling of our simple hearts themselves to God through the mediation of Jesus Christ. For we have often heard his question of unanswerable emphasis, "What is a man profited if he gain the whole world and lose his own soul?" The man who has practically neglected the great matter has reason to judge that his past experience has found him wanting, and has reason to fear that the longer he allows this to be so, the danger increases that he will rank with Saul rather than David—be rejected rather than accepted. What care we, indeed, for any of our duties without the divine blessing and assistance? How mad to decline the needful aid which the Holy Spirit of God proffers! How cheerfully should we hear and obey his voice, and harden not our hearts!

To refuse to repent this hour, though we know that our sins and the voice of God call us to the duty, is a peril from the venturing of which every immortal soul should earnestly shrink back.

## CHAPTER IV.

### *THE FRIENDSHIP OF DAVID AND JONATHAN.*

"A FRIEND loveth at all times, and a brother is born for adversity." These are the words of the wisest of mortals. To say that they commend themselves to our common experience is but to recognize that the wisdom of Solomon was practical, and that his most valuable thoughts seem to express only what every one else could utter. It may be that Solomon learned many of the truths he uttered concerning friends and friendship from the remarkable attachment between his father and the eldest son of Saul. If any one wishes to know what true friendship is, and to see how firm and abiding are its attachments, let him study what the sacred pages tell us of the intercourse of David and Jonathan. As if to sustain David in the unjust and unexpected trials to which he was exposed from his first entrance upon public life until the death of Saul, Providence raised up for him a friend of the most tender attachment, of the most disinterested affection and of the most enduring constancy. It is not possible, perhaps, for us to explain fully the grounds of a genuine friendship.

It is not mere esteem, for we may esteem one for whom we have not this peculiar attachment; it is not mere congeniality of temper, for, though friendship can exist only between kindred spirits, it is such congeniality as admits of wide diversity of age, culture, engagements and even tastes. It would rather seem that true friendship, like some other attachments of life, springs in a large degree out of inexplicable sympathies between the parties. There may be rational grounds of esteem toward one who still does not hold the place of a friend in the intimate sense of that word; there may be kindred tastes and dispositions without this relation; so that, however proper these things may be to form a wise basis of friendship, they are not the sole grounds. No friendship can be true or lasting that is not supported by those proper qualities in the parties which justify the claims it makes upon them; but it arises also from promptings of natural sympathy, which direct these kind affections toward this or that person, while others, quite as worthy of the sentiment, are not the objects of it. As we often see ill-assorted marriages, and wonder how these parties could ever be drawn together—while yet we must confess that they love each other truly—so we find it difficult to explain many attachments of friendship. The cases are not parallel, we may admit, but they are sufficiently so to illustrate the point before us. Let friendship be founded upon estimable qualities; let there be congeniality of mind.

We need more than this; we need a certain sympathetic bond of union, which draws men together as friends more than mere esteem or mere congeniality can alone do.

In ancient writings, and in the writings of later times, much is said of friendship—its nature and claims and its excellences. The most celebrated instances of friendship in ancient history and poetry are Damon and Pythias, Nisus and Euryalus, Scipio and Læbius, David and Jonathan. It would indeed be a defect in the sacred Scriptures if, as a celebrated infidel insinuates, they made no inculcation of this virtue. The charge is as bold and as false as if one should venture to charge it upon the sun that he did not shine. Nowhere are truer friendships fostered than under the influence of Christian piety. If, as Cicero very properly urges, true friendship must be subservient to true virtue, we may as properly urge that mutual virtue is an important preparative for the sentiment of friendship; and surely the prospect of permanent companionship, as held forth by Christianity, is an aid to these social attachments which Paganism was wholly incapable of affording. And so we find not only that the Great Master of Christianity was susceptible of the delights of friendship, but that his followers have ever cultivated it. In reading the life of Dr. Chalmers, there are few chapters that do more honour to the nobler feelings of the heart than that which gives us an account of his tender attachment—interrupted, indeed, by an early death—to a young man named Thomas Smith.

But let us consider the instance here brought before us—the friendship of David and Jonathan.

It was not the mutual friendship of two persons upon an equality with each other. We judge that Jonathan was older than David, as he was also superior in rank. He was the king's son, and was already a hero of tried experience in battle before David is ready to go forth in the armies of Israel. It is not needful that friends should stand upon an equality. It may even be that one is able and willing to bestow large favours upon the other, though a mercenary expectation of such favours as the bond of attachment is inconsistent with true friendship in the dependent party. But it deserves to be considered that, while favours may be received by a friend without indulging such a mind as leaves us chargeable with selfishness, the power of granting favours may be an important test of disinterested feeling in the giver. So we see it in this case. David and Jonathan are warmly attached to each other, but so long as they both lived all the sacrifices which we find mentioned are sacrifices on the side rather of Jonathan than of David. The subsequent history of David makes him appear the prominent character, but if we judge of them during the period of their attachment, we must decide that Jonathan is David's superior in age, in social position, in the sacrifices which his friendship makes, in the bestowment of kindness, and apparently also in the exhibition of strong feeling. The soul of Jonathan was knit toward David even when he was comparatively unknown in Israel, while Jonathan was the king's eldest son. Doubtless it is but justice to acknowledge that David deserved his warmest esteem and affection, but it was a rare mind indeed that was willing to bestow such affection in such a case. One of the strongest of the bad passions of men is jealousy, and few are more easily roused in the mind. And when we see the bad feeling so keenly awakened toward David in the breast of Saul, it seems the more strange that a son of Saul should be so entirely free from it. If ever a man had reason to be jealous of another, Jonathan had reason to be jealous of David. Men are usually tenacious of their military standing; and just at the period when Jonathan seemed the most promising leader in Israel's armies, David stood forth and by his victory over the giant of Gath became Jonathan's military rival. When the hearts of the people were turned toward the eldest son of Saul, the son of Jesse became a new object for their warm affection. It is yet more to be noticed that at a time when a venerable prophet had predicted the downfall of his father's family, when the heir of the throne might well look with a scrutinizing eye upon any man that would be likely to come between him and the right of his inheritance, Jonathan should fix his esteem and exhibit his tender attachment toward the very man who was to take his place and wear the crown that by natural descent belonged to him. Nor are we doing justice to the character of Jonathan if we suppose that he gave his warm affections to David because he was ignorant of the rival claims which he thus held. It may be, indeed, that in the beginning of their friendship he foresaw little or nothing of these things; but it is very certain that he abated nothing of his love at a later period, when both he and his father were well persuaded that David would be the future king. So we are told that during the time that David hid himself from Saul, Jonathan "arose and went to David in the wood and strengthened his hand in God; and he said unto him, Fear thou not: for the hand of Saul my father shall not find thee; and thou shalt be king over Israel, and I shall be next unto thee, and that also Saul my father knoweth."

We have here exhibited, then, a wonderful degree of disinterested feeling in the friendship of Jonathan for David. Admire as we should the qualities in David that called this forth, let us give that honour to Jonathan which his noble conduct deserves. Friendship has ever been noted for the sacrifices it is willing to make, but the history of the race affords no more excellent example than this. See how easy a thing it would have been for Jonathan to remove out of his way a dangerous rival, whose success he had such good reason to anticipate. He did not need to strike a blow himself. Had Jonathan but stood out of the way and allowed the malice of his father to act, David would have been slain. And men are often willing to allow that to be done which they would not venture to do themselves; and they allow their minds to be at ease for crimes at which they have but connived. No upright mind will ever reason so; no one whose heart is truly interested for another will be any more ready to see an evil befall him which he can prevent than himself to inflict it. The true reasoning is,

> "He that declines to ward it, gives the blow."

We may neither do evil, nor, if we can prevent, may we suffer it to be done. A heart that feels right is the soundest casuist. Jonathan loved David, and he allowed none of the conflicts of interest to excite his jealousy. But in order to a fair understanding of their mutual attachment, it becomes us to notice that it had its firm foundation in piety. Every good writer upon this subject acknowledges that virtue is necessary to the firm and just esteem and affection inspired by true friendship. It is interesting to notice, in Cicero's treatise upon Friendship, in how strong terms he condemns the thought that any one for friendship's sake should be willing to do an unrighteous thing. It is no excuse for a fault that it was committed for the sake of a friend, for friendship cannot exist when we depart from virtue. It is asking too much of any friend to demand that he should support or aid us in wrong. It is not in the nature of things that we can put confidence in one who would so do, for he who is willing to wrong truth and justice can hardly be faithful to anything else; and he can easily judge that one who wishes him so to do would not scruple to do the same. The attachments of wicked men are liable to be easily sundered when policy or advantage seems to demand this. A true and reliable friendship rests upon the solid foundation of virtuous principles.

The friendship of David and Jonathan was eminently a pious friendship. There is not a vestige of any feeling on the part of either which does not seem to breathe the true spirit of piety, and this of an exalted nature. Look first at the conduct of David through the whole period—from the first mention of this extraordinary attachment until the death of Jonathan—and he voluntarily gives his friend not a single occasion for jealousy or unkind feeling. It is true David did seem to take the lead of Jonathan from his battle with Goliath onward. He was in high esteem among the people, and every act seemed to increase his popularity. It is also true that David became king of Israel, and that he was the proper person for Jonathan to fear in regard to Samuel's prophecy. But to do David full justice in the case, it is also true that none of these things came to pass through his scheming;

that he was as loyal to Saul as a subject could be—as loyal to Jonathan as a friend could be; that in no single instance did he wrong his friend or plot against his king. When Saul was inflicting upon David the grossest injuries, when he separated him from his wife, exiled him from the land, banished him from the ordinances of Israel's worship and hunted him for his life "as a partridge upon the mountains," there was not a moment of the whole period in which David was betrayed to a word or act hostile to Saul or traitorous to Israel. We may find fault with some of his sayings or doings in these times of trial and persecutions, but not touching these things—his friendship to Jonathan and his loyalty to Saul. Though provoked by Saul's injustice, grieved by his cruelty in putting to death the Lord's priests, and doubtless convinced of his growing incompetency to govern the kingdom, David took not the slightest step toward the kingdom which might justly have excited the jealousy of Saul or his son. Nor can we say he had no opportunity. Saul was twice at least in his power, and self-defence would in both cases have been a plausible plea for freeing himself from his malicious persecutions. If, as we shall presently see, their friendship cost Jonathan many sacrifices, we may judge also that it cost David a vast deal of forbearance.

But let us look next at Jonathan's side of the matter. We have already seen that it was not in ignorance of the dangers to his interest which lay couched beneath David's advancement that Jonathan continued his warm attachment. The matter gradually became clear to him that the God of Israel designed David to sit upon the throne. His own father called his attention to this evident tendency of things, and urged him, for his own sake as the heir of the throne, to join in the efforts for David's destruction. And he saw for himself, from the rising influence of David and the plain working of God's providence, that this must be the issue. And we greatly misjudge this noble-minded prince of Israel if we suppose that through tameness of spirit he consented to pass below David and take the second place in the kingdom, where his own birthright bade him look for the first. We account for this conduct of Jonathan upon the noblest principles. It was not a weak mind becoming subject to a stronger; nor was it the sacrifice which a friend will make to gratify a friend, since such a principle might justly make David keep his own place and retain Jonathan's esteem, while he also maintained his. We account for Jonathan's submission to David's prospective prosperity in this way: that he was a pious child of Israel's covenant, who meekly acquiesced in the decision of Israel's God, and who would not allow himself to resist the movements of his providential will. Having no fault to find with David and his conduct, he will not take occasion to find fault for the workings of God's providence in David's behalf. Indeed he calmly recognizes the tendencies of Providence for David's advancement, furthers them by his advice and protection, makes a solemn covenant with his friend, in the details of which not a trace of envious feeling can be found, and cheerfully acquiesces in the sacrifices which he is thus called to make.

All this was simply the duty of Jonathan as a pious man. Since God evidently exhibited this favour toward David, it would have been folly and madness for him to resist the divine will. But we honour the man who does his duty, especially when he departs widely from the course which men generally adopt, and when his conduct is in wide contrast with those whom he might be expected to imitate. The dealings of Saul toward David are widely different from the line of conduct in his pious son. Saul had as good reason to judge well of David; he had given him no cause for enmity; he was his faithful servant. But the king of Israel acted toward David in violation of every sacred duty, and made use of the most violent and wicked means to secure his death. Not content with aiming directly at his life and with stirring up the members of his family against him; not content with laying snares in his very fidelity and bravery; not content with breaking his own royal promise for his safety, the king even massacred a whole village of the Lord's priests where David had been entertained, and went forth himself to pursue the fugitive when he feared that his own troops might fail in fidelity or in energy. In short, whether we make the contrast between the forgiving temper of David and the implacable malice of Saul, or between the meek submission of Jonathan to the divine indications and the restive rebellion of his father, we may equally discern the piety of the two friends, and see that their mutual attachment is strengthened by the common bond of an earnest faith in God. The favour of God shown to David is for Jonathan no cause of alienation.

The two friends upon one occasion made a solemn covenant with each other with reference to future matters. Doubtless this originated in the anxiety of Jonathan respecting the events he anticipates. He has gradually come to recognize that his friend, and not himself, is to be the king of the land; and knowing well the changes which power often produces and the cruelties which often attended a change of kings, he desires to secure his own safety and that of his family. In this interview David exhibits more fear of Saul, for Jonathan would naturally judge leniently of his father's designs, and from such a son Saul would be likely to conceal much, while Jonathan exhibits more faith and foresight respecting the plans of providence. He made David swear, not only to show him kindness while he lived, but also to continue his kindness to his children afterward. To give David assurance of the peaceful designs of Saul, he promised to bring the matter up for conversation between him and his father, and ascertain definitely and tell his friend the truth of the case. It resulted as David had anticipated; and Jonathan, true to his friendship, told David the whole. Perhaps they had not designed to see each other if Jonathan's report was unfavourable for their mutual safety, lest Saul should know that his son was more closely drawn toward David, lest his anger should be kindled against Jonathan, lest it should be less in his power to discover the plans devised against David. But their warm affection could not obey these urgings of policy. They were now about to separate, and but once after this did they ever meet again. David came forth from the place of concealment, where he had heard all that Jonathan desired to communicate, and the two met in warm and tearful embrace. The solemn covenant in the presence of God was renewed, and they parted. Doubtless in the subsequent wanderings of David he received many tokens of sympathy from his friend. He was supported in his trials by knowing that one heart even in Saul's house beat in kindly unison with his. We hear little more of this noble-minded man from this time forward, save the simple record of his death upon the battle-field of Gilboa. He went into that battle perhaps with sad presentiments, because the jealousy of his father had driven off Israel's most illustrious warrior; and though doubtless Jonathan fought bravely until he lost his own life in the vain effort to retrieve the fortunes of Israel, yet even he would have struck harder blows for victory if the arm of David, which had never turned back from the foe, had been with him in the battle. The hope of success is often the chief means of securing success.

If David, though separated from his friend Jonathan after this, yet held him in the most affectionate remembrance, and never forgot the solemn covenant they had made, we can easily judge that it was far better for the advancement of providential designs that Jonathan should die in the great battle which proved fatal to Saul. The people in general were yet loyal to the family of Saul, as appears evident from the fact that they put one of his sons upon the throne. If Jonathan had been alive, he would have been made a rival king to David—an event that might have been deeply disastrous to the interests of all the tribes. But the lamentation of David over his early death is sincere and truthful, in entire keeping with the tenor of his life as faithful to his friend. And many years after this David remembered his covenant in behalf of the house of Jonathan. When Jonathan died upon Mount Gilboa, he left behind him one son, then five years of age. Through the fright of his nurse, who caught him up to escape when the sad tidings came of Israel's defeat, the poor child became a helpless cripple for life. For this son, now grown to maturity, David made ample provision; and though afterward he seems to have judged of him too hastily upon the doubtful report of an interested informer, yet the provision he made for Mephibosheth was such as to render him comfortable for life. We might indeed say that the unfortunate condition of this son of Jonathan appealed to his sympathy; but let us not forget that Mephibosheth was the son of the heir of the throne, and thus, notwithstanding his infirmity, might have many friends in the kingdom, to the endangering of David's prosperity; and we may see the king's generosity and faithfulness. Nor is this an idle suggestion of a thought that David did not weigh. When Ziba treacherously accused Mephibosheth to David, this is the very charge he made against him: "To-day shall the house of Israel restore me the kingdom of my father." David did for the son of Jonathan only what the covenant with Jonathan bade him do, and what his warm friendship might otherwise prompt. But, considering the frail tenure of monarchy in the East and the usual jealousy of monarchs, he did otherwise than many would have done in his place. As he had received favours from his friend when Jonathan had the power to bestow them, so he is willing to make his sacrifices when the power belongs to him. That only is true friendship which abides the test of changing fortunes, and which forgets not to cherish its warm attachments, and to make its cheerful sacrifices when death has made its separation between the parties, and time has filled the survivor with new and pressing cares.

There was also another occasion when the friendship of David for Jonathan, and the covenant they had made together, were the means of saving the life of Mephibosheth. The crime of Saul in persecuting the Gibeonites had brought a judgment upon the land, which could only be averted by giving some satisfaction to that injured people. They demanded that seven of the descendants of Saul should be delivered into their hands as reparation of the injury. The transaction will be more fully considered hereafter. We mention it now only to bring to view the kindness of David toward the son of Jonathan. He selected seven other descendants of Saul to suffer death, and for the sake of his covenant spared Mephibosheth.

We remark, by the way, that the sacredness of an oath is shown plainly in this transaction. Though the Israelites had been deceived in covenanting with Gibeon, and though four hundred years passed before the oath was violated, the breach of such an oath and after so long a time was severely punished. In the light of this transaction, as well as urged by his own friendly feelings toward Jonathan and his family, well might David be willing to remember his covenant and spare the son of his early friend.

Upon the general subject of friendship, we may remark that there are two classes of friends. The *first* includes the large circle of persons with whom we maintain kindly intercourse—this circle is smaller than the number of our acquaintance—for the indulgence of kindly feelings toward all men, even toward the hostile, the injurious and the wicked, is fully consistent with our refraining from all dangerous and unprofitable company. Though we may be willing to do good to any man, there are men whose society we may avoid; and there are many into whose company we may often be thrown, with whom yet we cultivate little intercourse. Many are profitable as acquaintances and general friends who do not wish any intimate relation to us, and with whom we need but to exchange those courtesies and kindnesses which make up so much of the enjoyment of life. The *second* class includes those whom we receive to intimate friendship. Some of these are more closely drawn to us than others. But a few may be very near and dear. They are our counsellors in perplexity, our supporters in adversity, our comforters in sorrow. They share our delights, and we are truly glad in their prosperity. It is proper for every one to have special friends. Let them be carefully selected, let the intercourse we have with them be frank, sincere and faithful, and never should any mere changes of worldly condition affect our attachment to them.

But, above all, for the sake of the permanency and the real excellence of our friendship, let it be founded on virtuous principles. If a heathen philosopher, uninstructed in the great teachings of divine revelation, should "lay it down as a primary law concerning friendship that we expect from our friends only what is honourable, and do for our friends what is honourable,"* if such an one could say, "Virtue both wins friendship and preserves it,"† much more should those that are taught in the sacred Scriptures desire to make true piety the substantial basis of every friendship. We may find those that love us, those that form sincere attachments to us, those that are willing to do much for us, and those to whom we have formed strong attachments, where piety is wanting. And yet there is an important matter lacking when the heart is not right before God. Can we be entirely true to man when we are faithless toward God? If you knew a man to be a faithless husband or a disobedient and unkind son, could you fully trust him as a faithful friend? Is it not a more dangerous lack of principle when the duties we owe to God are forgotten?

But true piety is the firmest basis of friendship, because it alone promises a permanent attachment. There is a sense in which the best delights of earth are the deepest sources of trouble to an ungodly mind. We are liable to lose our best treasures in

* Cicero, De Amicitia, § viii. † Ibid., § xxvii.

any passing moment. These enjoyments of friendship, how soon may they be lost! Death, unpitying Death, steps in to sever us from those we have loved, and we soon know them no more. Oh what a poor consolation is that to which the philosophic mind of Cicero turned upon a friend's decease!—"If this be rather the truth, that the death of the soul and of the body is one and the same, and that no consciousness remains, as there is no advantage in death, so certainly there is no evil." If we lose a friend, the loss is irreparable. This is Paganism. Upon Christian principles the separation of ungodly friends is more dreadful indeed; but we have the most precious supports and comforts when friendship is associated with piety. If we love each other as Christian friends, then the principles of the gospel hold out to us the animating prospect of everlasting and happy companionship. The ties that bind us together are not only more tender and delightful in their very nature, but they grow more precious as they grow older; death separates us from a large circle of friends, but it also introduces us to a much larger circle. Everything that can endear us to each other is provided for in the promises of the gospel, and the everlasting bliss of heaven is the completion of all. Surely those who prize the delights of friendship should desire to sanctify it with the privileges of piety.

It is obvious that the highest honour to which any man can aspire is to be the friend of God.

Here is a friendship where indeed the parties stand not upon an equality. There is infinite condescension on his part to ask our friendship. Do we wonder at Jonathan, the king's son, desiring the friendship of the shepherd boy—stripping off his own clothing to adorn him, and willing to descend from the very throne that his friend may be crowned a king? All these are feeble analogies to the grace of the Lord Jesus Christ. The Son of the Eternal King left his throne of glory to raise us to immortal crowns; left his robes of light to clothe us in garments of righteousness; and died a shameful death that we might live for ever. No comparison drawn from mortal scenes can adequately present the condescension of his grace. Can we hold back when he calls us to share his friendship? It is by our sins we are at enmity with him—at enmity with God; and to atone for these he shed his priceless blood. Here is a Friend worth having indeed. Can immortal minds be called to the enjoyment of a higher privilege? "There is a Friend that sticketh closer than a brother." If the expression may apply to those we know here, how much rather is it applicable to him? The dignity of this great Friend, the infinite excellence of his character, the abundant resources of his wealth and his willingness to bless us with the largest benefits, are all reasons why we should desire his love. Blessed are all they who put their trust in him!

## CHAPTER V.

### *DAVID'S FLIGHT TO NOB AND GATH.*

THROUGH the disinterested faithfulness of Jonathan, David is now fully aware that all hopes are at an end of any reconciliation with Saul; and though conscious of his own loyalty, he can easily understand that no care or pains would be spared by Saul to secure his destruction; especially if there is likelihood that Saul now had heard of his anointing by Samuel. David therefore resolved to seek refuge in a foreign land. This was a sad alternative for a Jew, but not without its examples in other cases, and even by divine direction. When the prophet Elijah was in necessitous circumstances, and could not venture to seek relief among his own people, he was directed to go to a widow woman in the neighbouring country of Zidon, where he remained for over two years. If we had nothing else to charge against David except his seeking refuge among the Philistines in this period of persecution, his conduct could be better vindicated.

The tabernacle seems at this time to have been at Nob. It is sad proof—if we needed further evidence than that furnished by the life of Saul—

of the low estate of religion in Israel that we cannot even trace the wanderings of the tabernacle. It is at one time in one place, at one time in another; and if here said to be at Nob, the place of its sojourn was so insignificant that we cannot fully decide where it was. It was evidently a small city, perhaps belonging entirely to a few families of priests. After parting with Jonathan, David came to this city first in his flight. It would seem that he arrived there on the evening before the Sabbath. The Jewish day was reckoned from sunset to sunset. He came there on Friday evening, and, as the Jewish law forbade travelling upon the Sabbath, he expected to remain there till the sacred day was past. The proof that he was there on the Sabbath lies chiefly in this, that the shew-bread was changed upon the day he came there, and the law expressly made the priests change it on the Sabbath.* This is corroborated by the fact that Doeg, the Edomite, was that day *detained before the Lord*—*i. e.*, he was not allowed to travel upon that day—and that David and his men were compelled to eat the shew-bread. The necessity arose not so much from the fact that in his hasty flight they could not wait till food was prepared, but from the fact that upon the Sabbath-day it was not lawful to kindle a fire or make even the hasty preparation of a meal. It is said that David escaped *that day*. This seems to tell us that he did not remain there

* Levit. xxiv. 8; 1 Chron. ix. 32.

over the Sabbath. The sight of Doeg there, with whose character he was doubtless well acquainted, alarmed him lest tidings of his route and delay should reach the ears of Saul. He had good reason to fear that the unscrupulous king would pay but little regard to the Sabbath, and he felt himself justified in continuing his journey, even on the sacred day.

The high priest, Ahimelech, was greatly surprised to see David alone, unarmed and no man with him. He was not indeed entirely alone. He had young men with him, as the narrative plainly declares. But he was the son-in-law of the king and one of the chief officers in the army, and for him to come with so small a retinue was to be "alone." Alas! David departs widely from the character he has usually maintained, and answers the inquiry of the high priest, and this too at the tabernacle of God, with deliberate falsehood. There is no reason why, on the one hand, we should think to vindicate David in this thing, or, on the other, palliate his sad offence by considerations which subvert the very foundations of pure morality, as some that rank among Christian moralists are willing to do. Here is the first important stain upon the character of David; he was doubtless betrayed into it by an improper, unbelieving and exaggerated sense of personal danger. We cannot say, with Archdeacon Paley, that it is no wrong to lie to save your life or your property, or where little inconvenience will result from the falsehood, for in a matter of plain right and wrong the results of an action are not to determine their moral quality. The Bible never teaches us that we may do evil that good may come. Let Jesuits say, "The end justifies the means." We have no such maxim. Yet, if even Christian moralists, at so late a day teach that a falsehood is sometimes justifiable, we may recognize that the prevailing sentiments of any particular age often carry good men along with them to judge and allow things that are not really right. A hundred years ago things were not thought wrong in the Church which more enlightened piety now abhors. A great change has taken place in reference to many matters. A century ago, good men were engaged in the slave-trade, and within that period churches have been erected from the proceeds of the drawings of lotteries; and a great change has taken place in the views and practices of Christian people upon the subject of temperance. Now, if we argue upon these things abstractly, we must allow that the standard of right and wrong is of unchangeable excellence. What was right a thousand years ago is right now, and what was then wrong has not become virtuous by the lapse of years. Yet the guilt of a transgressor is to be judged by the light upon his mind, and by the influences against which he sins. In a certain sense, the sin was the very same for a man to destroy himself by intemperance a hundred years ago as for a young man to do it in our own age. In another sense, the sin is very different; it is almost a perfect contrast. So many influences then favoured intemperance that the wonder is how a young man could escape from forming the wretched habit; now, on the contrary, though there are many insidious influences favouring the spread of intemperance, every young man can escape who wishes to do so; and the sin of forming the habit of drinking intoxicating liquors in an age when so much has been said upon the subject is very great. Thus we see that men are to be judged not simply by the immutable laws of morality, but by the light and sentiments of their own age. The reasoning may, perhaps, be less applicable to falsehood than to many other things. What is thought wrong in one age is not thought erroneous in another. It is our duty for the government of our own hearts and lives to secure and follow, as nearly as we may, the true standard of morality, but when we are judging of others, true justice and true charity alike require us to understand the true state of the case and to make every proper allowance. David is to be judged according to the age in which he lived.

It does not seem to be true that the character of David as an inspired prophet is to be reckoned as lifting him above the imperfections of the age in which he lived, and as therefore placing him at least upon a level with us. For certainly the inspired character of the Old Testament prophets did not put them in the same rank—as to clearness of intelligence—with the New Testament apostles, and in neither of them did the inspired authority of their public ministry free them from errors in their private capacity.* The fall of Peter, upon two occasions at least, is proof enough of this.

These thoughts may enable us to form a more correct idea of the sin of David upon this occasion. We have no desire to apologize for him, but we have no wish to exaggerate his offence. The sin of falsehood is always a great sin. No virtue that is ever understood, appreciated or cultivated among men is more important in itself and in its influence upon the character, and in its influence over others, than the love of truth. No volume ever known on earth is so truthful, is of so much power to make men love the truth, as the Bible. The law of truth in all its fulness and integrity is here set before us, the inflexibility of its demands is clearly explained, and the most powerful motives, drawn from the character of a holy God and the infinite rewards of heaven and hell, are presented to impress upon us the value of this great virtue. This is a world of lies indeed, but against every inroad of falsehood this holy volume lifts up its opposing standard. If there be any two things needful to the estate of man as a reasonable and responsible being, they are knowledge and conscience; and both these demand our unchanging adherence to the truth. No man can be intelligent except as he is able to rely upon the truth—the belief of a falsehood is not knowledge—and without truth neither wisdom nor virtue can effect any valuable results.

David told Ahimelech that he had been despatched upon the king's business, that it was a secret matter, and that he was to meet his suite at an appointed place. This was all deliberately untrue. There is no sin of which a man can be more fully aware that it is committed in violation of right than lying. We are not, indeed, to regard it as lying when a man declares that which he believes to be true, if even his words are false. Every man should use carefully and diligently the best sources of information in his power; should endeavour to separate the false from the true, the doubtful from the certain, and should avoid all deceitful and exaggerated representations. But with all the caution that a man can use he is liable to be deceived. With all sincerity of aim and motive, such a man may then deceive others. It is possible that even unintentional falsehood may not pass through a man's mind without leaving its influence to darken the understanding; as a quenched coal, though it does not burn the hand, may leave its black mark upon it. Yet we do not lose our confidence in the moral character of a man who has deceived us when we are assured that he himself was equally deceived, and had no design to speak untruthfully. We make this plain distinction: that a *falsehood* is the assertion of that which is not true, be the motives of him who speaks what they may; while a *lie* is a falsehood, with the additional vice that he who utters it is aware that it is false. Such lies may be greatly aggravated by the motives that prompt them or by the results that flow from them; but in its very lightest form knowingly to utter that which is not true, with the design or result of deceiving another for any reason, is a sin against the clearest dictates of conscience, and of such a nature that no virtuous man should ever be willing to extenuate it. The word of God upon no page gives its sanction to this dangerous vice, but it places among its closing warnings an enumeration of the characters who shall never enter the glorious presence of a truth-loving God; and there let the guilty read this prominent description, Whosoever loveth and maketh a lie.

This sin of David had not truly the common plea of necessity. He doubtless felt that he was in danger of his life as he fled from the vengeance of Saul, and it may be that he pleaded this necessity at the bar of his own conscience as an excuse for his bare falsehoods; but it does not seem evident that he needed to say these things. The rule of sincerity, which ought to govern every man, does not forbid us to be silent in regard to the truth or give partial and evasive information where the design is not to deceive, but to conceal. So Samuel concealed the main design he had at Bethlehem when he allowed it to be known that he came there to sacrifice. We are never allowed, indeed, to use falsehood for the purpose of evading inquiries, but when it is proper or important to conceal the truth we may be silent, or we may avoid curious and dangerous questions by partial information. It does not seem in this case that the priest inquired so curiously into the business of David as to give him even the appearance of necessity for the story he framed. Had he simply said that he did not feel free to tell his errand, it ought to have been enough. It was not a case where any duty called upon him to declare his business. Concealment was his privilege. Any undue pressing of the inquiry would have been improper meddling on the part of his interrogator; but in no case of all these can we justify his deliberate untruthfulness.

Nor would we vindicate the conduct of David as recorded in the latter part of the chapter, as it may be proper to consider that point here. When David left Nob, he went to Gath and took refuge there with Achish, the Philistine king. It was indeed a bold venture for the man who slew Goliath to go thus to the very city where the giant belonged. Perhaps he thought it safer to go among a people at war with Saul, rather than among the peaceful nations around, who might be disposed to deliver him up at Saul's demand. Perhaps he thought that his standing in the armies of Israel might be the cause of his glad reception among the Philistines—as long afterward the Volscians received Coriolanus, the Persians Themistocles, and the Bithynians Hannibal. But this only involves David in deeper deception, as we shall see that at a later period he did appear to favour the Philistines, while he had no design to turn his hand against Israel, but was simply consulting his own safety. Nor had he been long at Gath before he found that the battle with Goliath was not forgotten against him. He heard them speak of him not only as the victor over their champion, but as the very king of the land; that is, doubtless, the man to whom had been ascribed honours even superior to those ascribed to Saul. These whisperings alarmed David, and he began to meditate his escape. His stratagems again take the form of deceit. In the East the person of a deranged man is sacred. No matter what kind of excesses are committed by a lunatic, no attempt is made to restrain him. If this was the custom in those lands, as it is now, we may easily see the reason for David's assuming that character, and account for the success of his stratagem. The Philistine king, it would seem, at first did lay his hand upon him, but after this he even drove him away from his presence. (See Psalm lvi., *title.*)

But to return to the falsehood of David to the high priest: let us notice, further, that his falsehood was one of very serious mischief. It is but slight justification for an act of wrong in any case that no harm was meant by it. We do not intend to say that a thoughtless falsehood is in itself as heinous as a malicious lie, nor that a man is as fully to be charged with evil results as if he had designed them. But, as the common proverb runs, "A liar should have a good memory," because false statements made at various times are almost certain to be inconsistent with each other; so a sinner ought to be able to cast his thoughts far forward and over a wide territory, lest the time may come when his evil deed will bring forth far larger and more mischievous fruit than he would wish to gather. The man who plants good seed is never afraid of too large a harvest, but the man who plants thistles may find them spread faster than he desires, and may heartily wish some day he could root them all up. David did not design the mischief he wrought that day. But we cannot hold him guiltless; his own conscience held him not guiltless of the sad consequences of that day's falsehood.

The painful result will be noticed again. We cannot properly dismiss what we say of his falsehood without adverting to the penitence of David in regard to the entire matter. The fifty-second Psalm was written in view of the slaughter of the priests by Saul upon the information of Doeg, the Edomite. The bitter evils of a lying tongue are therein graphically set forth, with special regard to the additional falsehoods of Doeg, but surely also with due regard to the falsehoods of the Psalmist himself, less malicious in design, but the source of so much evil. The thirty-fourth Psalm was composed when he changed his conduct before Achish. In it he again brings forward, in a remarkable manner, the importance of keeping the tongue from speaking evil and the lips from uttering deceit; so that when we connect the Psalm with the Psalmist's thanksgiving for his escape upon that occasion, we can hardly regard it otherwise than as his recognizing a most unmerited forbearance on the part of God toward his deception, as his conviction that such deception is by no means necessary to their safety who are under the divine protection, and as his earnest dissuasion to prevent others from imitating a course like that which he pursued.

But it would scarcely be proper to overlook an important reference made in the New Testament, and by our Lord Jesus Christ himself, to this portion of David's history. When David and his men were hungry, they received from the hands of the priests and ate the shew-bread. This bread was made of fine flour, and twelve cakes or loaves of it stood continually upon the golden table in the tabernacle, an offering to God from the children of Israel as a memorial of their continual providential dependence. These loaves were replaced every Sabbath day by fresh ones, and since the whole had been devoted to God, it was unlawful for any one to eat of them except the priests. This was the express commandment. On the plea of necessity, David and his men broke this express law. They were hungry; they could scarcely tarry till other bread could be prepared, and it seemed a violation of the great law of the Sabbath to prepare any. They ate the shew-bread. Our Lord justifies the action. His citation of this case seems the more in point for his argument with the Pharisees, because they charged him with violating the Sabbath, and this act of David's occurred on the Sabbath. It is a matter of interest for us to ask, In what respect does our Lord here justify David? and what is the true bearing upon the perpetual obligation and sanctity of the Sabbath of our Lord's controversy with the Jews? We may get true views of the Sabbath from the Son of Man, the Lord of the Sabbath.

We have no just reason to think that our Lord here would derogate from the full propriety and perpetual obligation of the law of the Sabbath. He himself kept the Sabbath, and spoke of it as an institution which should remain in force after the disappearing of the Jewish dispensation.* And when he tells us that the Sabbath was made for man, whatever else he implies, he teaches that it is not a local, sectional or national institution, not one belonging only to this age or that, but that as the necessity for it and the benefits of it belong to man as a race, so its institution was at the Creation,

* Matt. xxiv. 20.

and its obligations belong to man whenever or wherever he lives. If the Saviour had at all designed to deny the obligation and sanctity of the Sabbath, his language would have been quite different. But his argument is plainly directed to the just interpretation of a law whose obligation is acknowledged. As no lawyer would argue any cause by explaining a law which is no longer of force, but as such a law is dismissed as needing no interpretation, so the very arguing of the case by our Lord is the acknowledgment of the yet binding force of the Sabbath. Indeed his discussions with the Pharisees seldom had reference to the Old Testament laws themselves, but to the false interpretations put upon those laws. He could say of the laws themselves, "I am not come to destroy the law, but to fulfil." The true spirit of any law is the law itself. The false rendering of a law is of no obligation. Our Lord vindicates the law of the Sabbath from the glosses of the Jews, and teaches us that the true spirit of every law is rather to be regarded than the mere letter of it.

It is plain that the letter of the law was violated both by the disciples and by David. The disciples were allowed by the law of Moses to gather and eat as many heads of barley as they pleased while they passed through any man's growing field, but they were not allowed to gather for the purpose of carrying away. This law itself suggested the merciful character of the Lawgiver, since it gave the hungry the opportunity of supporting life, while it stopped short of supplying more than their necessities. The law made a nice distinction between what a man might carry away to increase his own stores—which would be theft—and what he might need for his present distresses, which charity might easily grant him. The law of the Sabbath has the same two aspects. If the disciples had gathered food for other days as they passed through that field, they would have violated both the law of honesty and the law of the Sabbath. If they had entered that field as harvest labourers under the direction of the owner of the grain, their work would have been honest enough, but it would have broken the Sabbath. Gathering grain for their hunger and to eat as they passed along was not dishonest, for the law expressly allowed it; it was no violation of the Sabbath, for while the law of the Sabbath forbids servile work, the design of that prohibition is to be justly considered, and any work that conflicts not with the end of the Sabbath law is not forbidden by that law.

The case of David is remarkably analogous, and our attention may well be called to the wonderful readiness of reply and the close adaptation of every thought and word to its place which ever characterized our blessed Lord. No matter how difficult the topic or how unexpectedly he was called to discuss it, his extemporaneous replies confounded every adversary and delighted every friend at the time, and have been the delight and amazement of keen-witted friends and foes ever since. Well may we say of him, "Never man spake like this man." This case of David is exactly in point. David plainly broke *the letter* of the law. No man but a priest ought to eat the shew-bread. But times and circumstances are to be regarded. So Samuel had previously assured Saul that sacrifice was inferior to obedience—that no ceremonial observance could claim precedence of spiritual duty. It would have been wrong for David to eat the shew-bread had there been other there; his necessities laid aside the ordinary law and justified what had else been sacrilege. It was right to argue that God would be better pleased that the special necessities of David and his men should be satisfied than that the bread be used for the ordinary necessities of the priests.

While it is just that the law of the Sabbath should be thus interpreted as we should explain every law, it is obvious that to set aside a plain precept on the plea of necessity or expediency throws the door open to wide abuses, and of this men who care little for the Sabbath will take all advantage. Suffice it for the present to say that no man can have a clear conscience upon the subject of the Sabbath, or any other moral subject, who does not take pains to study it, so that he may understand it, and that those who are unwilling to submit to the law as God has imposed it will find some kind of subterfuge to stupefy their consciences and allow them peaceably to do as they please. If any man is really disposed to know and do his duty toward God in regard to the law of the Sabbath, he can easily know what that duty is. Let any one keep before his mind the design of the Sabbath as hallowed to the Lord's service, and he can easily decide upon the duties enjoined upon the irrelevant engagements which yet are allowed. The line is clear and distinct which separates doing our own ways and finding our own pleasure and speaking our own words upon the Sabbath, from the duties appropriate to the day. Allowing that it may be right to do some servile works on the Sabbath, yet ordinary labour violates duty; the labours allowed are justified only so far as necessary, and the conscience should be careful to notice when we are disposed to urge this allowed and necessary indulgence too far.

But we must return to the narrative. David received from the hands of the priest the sacred bread and the sword of Goliath, and by the use of the ephod—how we do not understand—he inquired of the Lord for him. It would seem from this as if David's hurried flight to Gath was by divine direction. If so, it would relieve him of the apparent wrong of going into a heathen land, but it would aggravate his unbelief in God's protecting mercy as shown there. Perhaps the fact that he had Goliath's sword with him may have increased the danger to which he exposed himself in going to Goliath's own city. But there was a man at the city of the priests who took sad note of the proceedings. This was Doeg, an Edomite and the chief of Saul's herdsmen. This man was there "detained before the Lord;" which doubtless means that he was not allowed to travel upon the Sabbath. It is not likely that this man understood David's fugitive character at the time, but, knowing his devotion to the interests of Saul, David was afraid of him as soon as he saw him. And not without good reason; for soon after this Saul reproached his servants for their delay in searching for David, and charged them with seeming not to favour his cause; and Doeg related what had occurred at Nob. To the whole transaction he gave a colour which really belonged not to it, but which, before a monarch so jealous as Saul, was fatal to Ahimelech and the entire city. The lying lips of Doeg would make it appear that the priest knew David as a fugitive, and had assisted him through disfavour to the king. The enraged Saul sent for Ahimelech, and charged him with a conspiracy with David against his throne. The astonished high priest answered with dignity and truthfulness, like an innocent man. He had known of no charges against David; he had regarded him as one intimately related to the royal family and esteemed in the army; he had been accustomed to inquire of God for him; and in this case he had been told, and he believed the assurance, that David was going on the king's business. But this just and dignified defence availed nothing before the anger of Saul. He was resolved that no favour shown to David should go unpunished. He therefore gave command to his guards to fall upon the priests of the Lord and put them all to death. The reverence which the Hebrews paid to the ministers of God forbade their obedience, and the guard shrank back with horror from the wicked and cruel command. The king then gave the command to Doeg. It does not appear that this man was even a nominal proselyte to the Jewish religion. He was an Edomite, and felt restrained by no scruples respecting the servants of the God of Israel. Possibly, too, having told his lying story, he is fearful that close inquiry might implicate him in the doom of the high priest; for the question might be asked, If Ahimelech knew David's errand, did not Doeg also know it? And if so, why did he make no effort to stop him? But Doeg felt no scruples. With the aid of men under his command, he massacred in cold blood eighty-five priests, together with the women and children and the very cattle of the place. Abiathar, the son of the high priest, escaped and fled to David, and filled his heart with remorse as he reflected that his falsehood was the first cause of this great calamity. So he said to Abiathar, "I have occasioned the death of all the persons of thy father's house."

Two important results to the progress of affairs followed this cruel massacre:

First. It must have produced a great shock to the authority of Saul all over the land; have filled the minds, especially of pious people, with horror; and, while it awakened the nation to the controversy between the king and David, have spread abroad also the conviction that the words of Samuel for Saul's rejection were soon to be fulfilled. And it is worthy of our notice respecting this wicked man that from first to last his rejection and ruin were the legitimate results of his own sins.

Secondly. The cause of David was promoted by the wicked and ill-advised measure. Not only would the tide of sympathy flow in his favour as for one who had given the king no just ground of persecution, but had been the rather distinguished for his zeal and faithfulness—not only would the tidings now begin to circulate that Samuel had anointed him for the crown—not only would Saul and his cruelties now be put in contrast with the virtues of the son of Jesse—but the entire religious sentiment of the land would turn in his favour, since now the high priest had been forced to join him in his exile, and since there was little reason to believe that religion would again flourish in Israel while Saul maintained his throne.

## CHAPTER VI.

### *THE PERSECUTIONS OF SAUL.*

THE danger of David, when he trusted himself in Gath, was not imaginary, for in the title of Psalm lvi. we are told that the Philistines laid hold upon him. But his feigned madness was successful in deceiving them, for in the title of Psalm xxxiv. we are told that the king drove him away. He returned to Judah and took refuge in a cave at Adullam, which is near Bethlehem. By this time, and especially perhaps after the slaughter of the priests, the malice of Saul and his unfitness to rule became more clearly exhibited to the nation, and they began to form a party in favour of David. It would seem that the relatives of David now became the objects of Saul's rage. So we find David compelled to remove his parents out of danger. Not willing that they should share his privations in the cave, he committed them to the care of the king of Moab, with whom they dwelt in safety. Gradually David gathered about him a band of men, some of whom remained with him during all his reign and were among the renowned men of his army. Some of them came to him now, and some came after this, when he was in Ziklag. Originally a great number of them were lawless men. Some came to avoid their creditors; some to escape punishment for their crimes; some because of the oppressions of Saul's government, and others from sympathy with David, from attachment to right or from restless love of adventure. Some of these had been David's companions in many a fierce battle. Three were David's own nephews—the sons of his eldest sister, Zeruiah—and they became famous in the history afterward—Abishai, Joab and Asahel. It is not certain that the Amasa here named is the same as Amasa who was the leader of Absalom's army, but Benaiah, the son of Jehoiada, was long after this the leader of the armies of Israel in the days of Solomon. It is greatly to the credit of David that he gradually brought under wholesome discipline these various materials, and that under his control they formed, not a mere predatory band, but a valuable foundation of a future army. He checked their lawlessness and forbade any outbreaks that would seem disloyal to Israel. The presence of the prophet Gad and of the priest Abiathar was doubtless of great assistance to him in maintaining a wholesome discipline, while, as we have before intimated, the slaughter of the priests had alienated the minds of many pious men from Saul; and many of these were perhaps present with David. The strong attachment of his soldiers to him reminds us of the enthusiasm which all great commanders are able to inspire in their followers. One instance is given of attachment and valour on their part, and of piety on David's. The war now in progress had so far turned in favour of the Philistines that they occupied the city of Bethlehem, and perhaps because it was the scene of war, as well as for Saul's jealousy, David had removed his aged parents. In the heat of harvest, and perhaps poorly supplied with good water, David thoughtlessly expressed a wish for a good drink from the well at the gate of Bethlehem. He had often drank there when he was a boy, and the enjoyment of it naturally came up before him now that those times of careless and hearty cheerfulness were past. The expression of the wish originated a plan with three of his mighty men to procure the water for him. We can hardly think, from the result, that they asked his consent to the plan. They broke through the guard at the gate, drew up water from the well and brought it to David. But David would not drink of it. Much as he desired it, there was something here of which he highly disapproved. Not their valour, but their foolhardiness. It would have been a noble act for these men thus to break through the guard of the Philistines if any adequate motive had called for the enterprise. But true courage is to be judged, not simply from its daring, but from the proper object that calls it forth. True courage is moral courage, and moral courage is based upon reasonable motives. To rush into a burning house when nothing is to be saved from it, to stand before a coming danger when wisdom bids us stand aside, to hold out an unflinching finger that a venomous snake may strike it, are instances of folly, not of bravery. We want something more than steady nerves. David wished no act like this to be repeated for him. This water, secured at the peril of life, seemed too costly; he could not venture to drink it. No man should peril life but when God calls, for the voice of duty is the voice of God. Rather than drink the precious draught, so rashly, so dearly purchased, David poured it out before the Lord. He thus taught his army, in the most significant manner, that their valour should be wisely directed—that their lives should be put in jeopardy only at the call of duty.

Perhaps it was immediately after that harvest that David learned that the Philistines had come up against Keilah that they might destroy the grain which the Israelites had just gathered. David and his men, though persecuted by Saul, remained faithful to Saul's kingdom. Yet, when he had smitten the Philistines and delivered Keilah, the ungrateful citizens plotted to betray him into the hands of his great enemy. But made aware of their treachery, David left the city and the scheme failed. But David's help in defeating the common foe only gave Saul greater leisure to pursue him. He roused all his energies to seek him, and at one time he nearly laid his hands on him. The Ziphites promised to deliver him into Saul's hands; and while David and his party went on one side of a certain hill, Saul and his men were in full pursuit upon the other. It is likely that Saul's force was larger than that of David, but we may justly judge that an encounter between them was prevented by David's policy. He did not wish to fight against one whom he still regarded as king. His sole effort was to avoid any conflict. He succeeded in doing this until a reported invasion of the Philistines called Saul off in another direction.

In his absence, David drew off his men to a safer position. Near the Dead Sea, upon high and inaccessible rocks, is a fountain called Engedi—*i. e.*, the fountain of wild goats, as though that venturesome and surefooted creature alone could reach it. Here Saul followed him as soon as he was relieved from his anxiety concerning the Philistines, and this time he took with him a force of three thousand men. David continued his eluding policy, and his loyalty and generosity were soon made apparent. Saul fell into his power. He chanced to enter alone the cave where David and his men were hidden, and they had him completely in their hands. Yet the passions of his men were so under the control of their leader that no harm came to Saul. But David himself ventured to cut off the skirt of the king's garment—for what purpose it is hard to say. It would seem trifling and dangerous merely to allow the king to depart with a token that he had been in the power of the enemy, since it would be a plain clue to find David's secret place. But so great was David's loyalty that his heart smote him for venturing an indignity even so trifling as this against the anointed king. Following, therefore, his own generous impulses, he went forth and called after Saul, exhibited the proof that he had indeed been in his power, and urged in a forcible expostulation that he was innocent of the charges made against him or of any harmful designs against Saul. If he had been at all disposed to do violence to the king, or to put forth his hand toward the kingdom, he surely had that day possessed a favourable opportunity for the death of Saul. Scarcely any man could have decided otherwise than that such an act in him was a justifiable self-defence.

The words of David had a strong effect upon Saul. His conscience bore witness to their truth, and though, like all other good influences upon this unhappy man, the effect was transient, and he soon began to pursue David as bitterly as before, yet he now confessed all that could be wished. He was even affected to tears, perhaps in part from his own near escape from death, and acknowledges that David had behaved far better than himself. He could scarcely call him an enemy when he allowed him to go free though he could so easily have taken his life; and he discerns beyond all this the certain truth that the crown shall belong to David. So he exacted from David a solemn oath that when he did reign he should not cut off the family of Saul. This oath David made and kept. We have no account that he took the life of a single descendant of Saul to gain his throne or to make his seat more secure. If the death of Ishbosheth enlarged his dominions, yet he had no share in that crime, and he avenged it upon the murderers. But evidently David had little confidence in the promises of Saul: he still kept in his strong place, and had need of his vigilance as much as ever.

The next incident in David's history is the account concerning Nabal. This man—whose very name signifies a fool—was possessed of great riches, especially in flocks and herds. David's men were needy, and perhaps often even pressed with hunger. Their position of self-defence was the most difficult possible to maintain. If they had been at open war with Saul and the Israelites, they could easily have supported themselves. The forbearance of David is fully equalled by the control he had over his troops to restrain them from acts of outlawry. We get here a glance, however, at their means of support. Large flocks were kept in this frontier portion of the land, but constantly exposed to attacks from the Arabs and other wandering tribes. We need not wonder that the borders of Israel suffered from such predatory incursions. The like was suffered by the North of England from Scottish marauders for many years; and on our own frontiers incursions of the Indians have been frequent and are still feared. David and his men protected the shepherds who had these flocks in charge, and received in return provisions for their support. Hearing that Nabal, whose flocks were large, had sheared his sheep and had appointed a feast of rejoicing for it, David sent some of his men to salute him, to plead the privilege of a festive occasion and to ask of him such a gift as he might be pleased to bestow. The answer of Nabal was exceedingly rough and repulsive. He was, perhaps, attached to the house of Saul, but his own penurious disposition and his churlishness were the real reasons for his rejecting these demands in so rude a manner. All this was the worse because needless. If he had chosen to decline, he might at least have done it without such insulting language. Courtesy is, perhaps, not strictly a virtue, but it is at least near of kin to the virtues. The injunction, Be courteous, is one enforced upon us by apostolic authority. Mere manners can never make a man; it is not seldom that the most refined manners are allied to villainy; yet the true spirit of politeness is one of importance, and the usefulness of many a good man has many a time been marred by the rudeness of his carriage. "A soft answer turneth away wrath, but grievous words stir up anger."

Both parts of the proverb here find their illustration. Nabal had wellnigh paid dearly for his folly and rudeness. David could exercise almost any amount of forbearance toward Saul, but he will bear little with Nabal. Indeed, his anger was excessive. Though indeed this fool had done little against him, compared with the injuries he received from Saul, as if to show that we need to guard against lighter as well as against severer injuries, David rashly swore that he would cut off the house of Nabal. He gave command to his followers to gird themselves for a march, and with four hundred men set off for Nabal's abode.

The catastrophe was prevented by the prudence of Abigail, the wife of Nabal. Learning from one of the herdsmen the application which David made and the repulse of her husband, she made hasty but liberal provision for averting the coming storm. Without acquainting her husband with her design, she rode to meet David. The address she made when she met him is full of wisdom. Well, indeed, might any man, before he engages in any rash deed, ponder the weighty words of Abigail. After all is over, forbearance, forgiveness, mildness and kindness will bear to be remembered and reflected upon, when harshness, revenge, injury and violence breed only remorse. How often do we wish in vain to recall the harsh word, the hasty deed! Even those men who are usually calm and just are liable to the rising of indignation, and need the restraint of wholesome advice at the nice and proper moment. David appreciated the wise counsel of Abigail, and thanked her for it. He returned without coming to Nabal. The result was, that Nabal, when he heard of the imminent danger to which he was exposed, was greatly terrified, and died about ten days afterward. David soon after married Abigail, by whom, perhaps, he received the chief possessions of her former husband; and he also took Ahinoam of Jezreel to be his wife. These, with Michal, detained from him by Saul, made three wives then living.

We do not know how long the calm continued between David and Saul. Our next record is of the renewal of strife. Saul, having received such information of David as led him to suppose he could easily take him, came out with an army similar to that he had before brought. David, however, was upon his guard. He not only knew of his coming, but with his nephew, Abishai, he ventured to go into his camp in the night. We can hardly suppose that, even with a superior force, Saul would set no guards around his camp when he came against a warrior of David's experience; yet it is possible he was less careful because he knew well David's policy of escape and avoidance. Whether they had sentinels or not, the whole camp was providentially asleep when the two came, and they penetrated to the very midst where Saul lay—his spear stuck in the ground at his head, and a vessel of water beside him. It had been an easy thing now for David to put an end to his persecutions, to pave the way to the throne and to revenge all his sufferings. And Abishai not only urged this, but offered to do it effectually himself at a single stroke, and argued that the opportunity was afforded him by the very providence of God. But David does not argue so. And here he teaches us a lesson we may not lay aside. We are far too prone to interpret providence upon Abishai's principles. The favourable opportunity to do what we desire is regarded as an indication of providence that thus we should do. And indeed providential openings are to be regarded and carefully improved. But we are to interpret providential opportunities upon righteous principles. It is plain that the opportunity of stealing a sum of money with little danger of detection is no providential indication that we ought to do it. The opportunity to do evil is a trial of principles, not an indication of providence. David decides upon righteous principles. He judges that it is not his place to avenge himself; especially that, as Saul was a king lawfully anointed, no private injuries could justify him in striking at his life, and that he is bound to leave in the hands of God the termination of Saul's life, and the vacancy of the throne that he was yet to ascend. We have no reason to regard this as a kind of fatalism in David, which, sometimes in silliness and sometimes in absurdness, says, "What is to be will be." For in all the Scriptures no pious man expects the fulfilment of God's purposes except in the use of appropriate means. David knew that the crown and throne of Israel should one day be his, and he now refuses to do that which may make them his, but he does not therefore teach us that no means were necessary to secure this predestined and predicted end. He rather teaches us that no matter how certain or how proper is the end proposed, we are at liberty to use only lawful means to secure it. It was, perhaps, a great temptation to David to free himself from his troubles and to wear a little sooner the coming crown by one decided act; but in his present forbearance he is but carrying out yet farther the lesson he has learned of Abigail. It should be no grief to know, no offence of heart, that he had not shed even Saul's blood causelessly, nor avenged himself for his malicious persecutions. We follow providence when we abide by principle, and every offence against righteous principle, whatever may seem to be the apology for it, is an offence also against the providence of God.

David therefore restrained Abishai, and taking with them the spear and the cruse of water, they left the camp. Choosing the summit of a hill from which he could make himself heard, but which was doubtless difficult of access in case of pursuit, he called to the camp of Saul, and taunted Abner with the little care he had taken of the person of the king. His voice was at once recognized by Saul, and he takes this new opportunity of expostulating with him upon these causeless persecutions. As he has gained new proof that he has no designs against Saul's life, as the wickedness which Saul charges on him, if indulged by him, could have urged him to use his advantage and to slay him, his very forbearance is proof of his innocence. Saul's conscience again decides for him. He sees again how near he has come to death, and that he had played the fool and erred exceedingly. Moreover, he sees in David's conduct a plain proof of the divine guidance and protection, and he feels assured that he should succeed in reaching the throne. He recalled his men therefore from the pursuit, and allowed David to go his way.

It is evident, however, that David had no confidence in Saul's present state of mind, and indeed past experience had taught him that he could rely upon none of his professions. But the next incident we read is in wide contrast with his previous faith. A little while ago he is sure that God will fulfil his purposes without undue interference upon his part; now he gives way to the promptings of unbelief, and says, "I shall one day perish by the hand of Saul." Then he would use no unlawful measures; now he exclaims, "There is nothing better than that I should escape into the land of the Philistines." And this is his language just after his signal deliverance should have increased his faith. Through the unguardedness of our sinful minds we often fail to improve our mercies, and temptations to evil beset us successfully when we are elated by some signal advantage. Why did not David argue for God's protection from his past deliverances?

We believe David was clearly wrong in deciding to throw himself among the Philistines, and this the more from his past experience there; and we need not wonder, therefore, to find this unbelieving step followed by other proofs that he has grieved the Spirit of God and goes farther in the way of backsliders. But now that he goes there, we may be surprised that it is to the same city of his former refuge, and that the king of Gath receives him so favourably. It is possible that he goes there now upon an invitation. By this time the Philistines are fully aware of the breach between him and Saul, and Achish, at least, may be disposed to use David against his king. As he now took with him a body of six hundred men, he found that their support would be too much of a tax upon Achish. He therefore requested that the king would assign him a city to dwell in. This the king did with great liberality. The town of Ziklag, in the southern part of Canaan, originally belonging to the Israelites, but now possessed by the Philistines, was assigned to him, and from this time forward it belonged to the kings of Judah. Here David abode for a year and four months: the original is, *days* and four months, and Josephus says he was there four months. From Ziklag, David went forth upon an expedition against some of the Canaanitish tribes upon the south, destroying them and taking their spoil. Not much is said concerning this warfare, and what is said is not to David's credit. If these nations were friendly to Achish, then we must pronounce the conduct of David at this time a base abuse of the confidence reposed in him by Achish. But we need not aggravate his sin beyond what is plainly told us. It is possible that these tribes were a remnant of the nations with whom Israel was commanded to make war—as we know the Amalekites were—and they may have been not at all the allies of the Philistines. In this case the offence of David would consist in his falsehood, prompted by a desire to stand well with his new friends, and to leave the impression upon the mind of Achish that the breach between Saul and himself was entirely beyond repair. But David here shows us that disingenuous conduct only leads a man into greater difficulties. What he would have done at a later period, had he been called to be actually present in the battle where Saul was slain, we do not know. Crooked policy is never safe or comfortable policy, and it bears explanation as badly as it bears to be practiced. Happily, upon that occasion the providence of God, bearing with this erring servant and treating him far better than he deserved, delivered

David from the embarrassments into which his untruthfulness had led him, and he was neither compelled to be ungrateful to the king who had sheltered him in distress, nor an enemy to his own people.

We will take further occasion to remark upon the great difference we may so often see between religious persons and religious principles. The principles of piety are of infinite excellence; the practice of pious men is often widely inconsistent. The Bible teaches us in no case to apologize for the wrongs it records. Indeed, the candour of the sacred writers in telling us the faults of even religious men is proof that we are not to copy them. But chiefly now let us reflect upon the dangers and difficulties to which we are exposed by long-continued and ensnaring temptation. Before we find too much fault with David, let us sincerely consider whether we could have escaped from the like severe trials with our principles less compromised. David was a man of like passions with ourselves. The weary months he passed in exile, far from the privileges of God's worship, exposed to unusual fatigue and privation, and with companions who seldom sympathized much with his pious feelings, may have found him often depressed in spirit and filled with fears that his enemy would prevail. In these circumstances let us admire him that he so steadily kept his loyalty to Saul, returned good for evil, turned the left cheek to him who smote the right, and maintained his earnest longings for the sanctuary of God's worship. Let us pity and sympathize with him in all his trials; let us rejoice in every instance where we find him sustaining his own proper character; let us learn not so much David's weakness as the weakness of human nature when we find him faulty.

## CHAPTER VII.

### *SAUL AND THE WITCH OF ENDOR.*

THE train of the inspired narrative now leads us to consider the closing scenes in the life of Saul. The war between the Philistines and Israel was at this time renewed with fresh vigour, and heavy necessities pressed upon the unhappy king. He had indulged his pride and unbelief and revenge until God had rejected him and would no more hear his prayers—until he had driven into exile not only David, but many of those brave and, in some cases, pious men who had now joined David, and who became, in a few years afterward, the chief warriors in the resistless armies of Judah. Withal, the troops who remained with Saul had less of the animated and cheerful spirit which is so needful to the success of an army. Saul was deeply discouraged, yet God refused to hear. His neglected duties testified against him; the slighted worship of God in the brighter years of his reign was remembered with anguish, and the blood of the innocent priests cried out against their murderer. Samuel, upon whose kind sympathy he could always reckon, was now numbered with the dead, and Saul begins too late to appreciate the love of the departed prophet. The unhappy king here exhibits no strange aspects of our human nature. Men too frequently find out the value of their friends after they have lost them. It is our too common folly to be wise too late.

Superstition and religion are two very different things. A man may have not a particle of the true spirit of piety, and may set religious obligations at defiance, and yet be bound in the shackles of superstition. Nor is it only the ignorant that are thus entangled and enslaved. The truth seems to be that men of all classes—the wise and the foolish, the learned and the untaught, the strong and the weak—are very nearly on a level when left to the unaided resources of their own minds for support in trials. A profound sense of the weakness of man in his best estate is a wise attainment in human experience. In the consciousness of a strong mind, a person once said, "I do not think there is anything that would drive me mad." The wise reply was, "You might as well say there is no weight which could break your back."* Man is a dependent being. Religion is the wise and just support of our weakness. Superstition is prompted by the same sense of dependence, from which no man can free himself, but it is the blind groping after a miserable support—of a mind that is too ignorant to find the true God or too wicked

* Article in Littell's Living Age, July, 1857

to desire his aid, or, like Saul, rejected of God and given up to the delusions of wickedness. Saul begins now to reap the bitter harvest whose seeds he has been so long planting.

Given up of God, and now fallen into deep trouble, Saul was wretched, and he must find some support in his trials. The next scene of his life is a strange one indeed. The king of Israel seeks advice and counsel from a fortune-teller and a witch.

In all ages and in all lands, not even excepting the nineteenth century and the Christian land in which we live, there have been persons professing acquaintance with the unseen world and the secrets of the dark future. Whatever names we give to those persons—sorcerers, magicians, astrologers, wizards, witches or mediums, augurs, soothsayers, fortune-tellers or necromancers—they are everywhere much alike in the characteristics of their arts. We need not wonder that men have never very well understood the subject, for the foundation of all is mystery, both as to the alleged facts and to the mode of acquiring a knowledge of them; and all is addressed to our ignorance. If a man tells me a wild account of the inhabitants of the planet Jupiter, how they live or what they say, I have no means of knowing how he acquired his information on the one hand, nor on the other of decidedly affirming that not a word of all this is true. So a prediction of a future event is palmed off upon those who have no means *now* of deciding its truth or falsehood. Tricks, darkness, mystery have ever belonged to these things, and are alike necessary to their success and to their power over the minds of man. This single characteristic is as different as possible from the openness and simplicity of truth, which fears no investigation, and which ever aims not to confound, but to instruct the mind.

The Scriptures have ever forbidden the practice of these arts and all consulting of those that profess them, and these direct prohibitions are against the spirit that prompts men to seek for instruction where true teachings never can be found, as well as against the wicked arts of those who profess thus to guide men. Apart from all consideration of the unlawful means by which men seek to learn those secret things which belong to the Lord our God, it is not hard for a wise man to discern that the knowledge of the future is wisely kept back from us, and that it is folly, therefore, for man even to wish to draw the veil aside. God has made man to live in ignorance of the events before him, that he may be guided by the principles of duty; he has left us in helplessness, that we may recognize our dependence upon him. There is scarcely any prospect that can open up before us with infallible certainty without disastrous effects upon our present comforts and our present duties. If we knew that deep trouble was before us in the future, we would suffer deeply now in anticipation. Perhaps more than half our troubles are through the fear of evils which we imagine may come: how much more would we be depressed by certain sufferings before us! Such anticipations would unnerve the arm for duty and unfit the mind for peace. On the other hand, were we sure of future prosperity, our present trials would grow more burdensome and our present duties insipid. It is better for us that we see only one step forward in the journey of life, and must take that step before we see the next. We enjoy our comforts more, we bear our sorrows better, we are better prepared for all our duties, since now we ourselves grow up to our circumstances, as the duties of manhood can neither be foreseen nor understood nor borne by the child, who is fitted to know at the same time that he is called to do them. It is in divine wisdom that the Scriptures even forbid our inquiring into the secrets of futurity: nor need we think it strange that while expressly condemning the acts that may be classed under the general names of sorcery and witchcraft, these writings make no attempt to describe or define what the thing is beyond this: that witchcraft purports to be communication with the unseen world—not through the revelation of God, but by finite agency, that of spirits, human or angelic.

There can be no reasonable question that imposition upon the superstition, the weakness, the ignorance and the credulity of man has ever been the chief element of those arts. Many of the tricks of the ancient magicians are now well understood, and were practised through a knowledge of natural laws above the attainments of men in general. Other things were done by jugglery and sleight of hand, and we know that an expert juggler can do many surprising things that are not supernatural. But we do not deny the possibility that the masters of these arts did at some time receive the aid of evil spirits in deceiving men. We know too little of the spiritual world wholly to deny the possibility of this, and there are some matters of their doings which find their easiest explanation in supposing that this may have been so. And when we know that devils have possessed and tormented the bodies of men, we need not wonder if they have had other dealings with the wicked of the earth. Yet many wise men think that the whole power and success of these persons is to be referred to imposture, without supernatural assistance. They consider the language of the Bible, when it speaks of a woman having a familiar spirit, to refer rather to what she claimed than to what she really had. In either case, the Bible is justified in classing these arts among the most wicked things to be found among men. If it is possible for any one to have intercourse with evil spirits, and to secure from them any information from the unseen world which God himself has hidden from us, it is highly wicked to consult them. If these things are impossible, then it is exceedingly iniquitous to pretend to a thing that is impossible to be true, and wrong if even true. So the immorality of all such things is plain enough, however obscure is the nature of the crime.

It is no alleviation of this sin that those who consult fortune-tellers do it often in jest, for no man should dare to jest in things which God claims as belonging peculiarly to his prerogative. It does not help the matter to say that men are sometimes sincerely persuaded that these things are true. A deluded heart is a very common result of wicked practices, and if men will venture into known evil and dangerous temptations, they have no reason to complain if the divine protection is withdrawn from them—if they are left to believe the lie they have tampered with, and if, after seeking for unlawful knowledge, they are deceived into the belief of a gross falsehood. Without needing to grasp after anything unlawful and of questionable truth, we have all we need for our instruction both for present duty and for future prospects; but if any man is not content with these, but seeks after things which God has kept in his own power, there is no telling how far he may go astray or how firmly he may believe his own delusions. The Scriptures teach us that all our information of the unseen world and of future events must be obtained through divine revelation alone; that God alone can give such teachings; and that for us to apply to any others for secrets of this nature is a profane prying into matters which God chooses to conceal, and it is the idolatrous attributing to other and inferior beings those characteristics which God claims as peculiar to himself. Hence the great wickedness of claiming to possess such powers, and every person shares in that wickedness who, through curiosity or in jest or in seriousness, encourages those who claim to possess them.

It is proper here to remark that in the Bible we have no such ideas presented upon the subject of witchcraft as are now commonly attributed to it. Take the lamentable delusions which prevailed in the world and in the Church but a few hundred years ago, and which led even good men to subject suspected witches to torture and death, and their ideas are in no case favoured by any scriptural teachings. That a witch could transform herself or any one else into the shapes of inferior animals, fly through the air, torture the bodies of others by some invisible malignity, or make a compact with the Evil One,—all these are things of which we read not a single word in the Scriptures. Our conceptions, then, of what the Bible means by witchcraft are not to be shaped by the vulgar ideas of that sin.

While upon this subject a word may be said concerning the modern form of witchcraft, known by the name of Spiritualism. We need not think it strange that such a form of delusion should spring up and spread in an age of light and knowledge like the present, for no amount of scientific knowledge can satisfy the cravings of man's spiritual nature, and human depravity remains in force in the most enlightened communities. We need not think it strange that many infidels have been converted to Spiritualism, and profess, through its teachings, to believe in God and a future world, for superstition and skepticism have been twin sisters in all ages of the world. Nothing is more common than for a depraved mind to reject the most weighty evidences in favour of the Bible, and agree to the most frivolous pretensions in favour of a system of falsehood; and the conversion of such men, after all, is no conversion to purity of character or to devoted usefulness of life. We need not even wonder that men well instructed in the principles of true piety are found among the earnest advocates of such a delusion, for in all ages men have gone out from us who were not of us, and in all the experience of the Church the most bitter opposers have been nursed in her own bosom; and because they would not submit to the truth of the gospel, they have been ready for any delusions of error. Two classes of Spiritualists now exist in this country. One class professes that all the teachings of Spiritualism are consistent with the Bible, and that Spiritualism is but a higher form of Christianity; the other class teaches the barest infidelity, denounces the pulpit and denies the Bible. The whole system is but a modern form of the ancient witchcraft. There is the same seeking of information from departed spirits; the same practices of shunning the light lest the methods of imposture should be detected; the same tendency to unhappy results, in the wrecking of minds and morals, which have ever been found in the spread of such delusions. Witness the reports of our lunatic asylums; witness the tendency to licentiousness which has separated so many households. "*Even so every corrupt tree bringeth forth evil fruit.*" But does it not seem the master-proof of men's depravity and fondness for a lie that such a system can prevail? For if the phenomena are all true, they are useless. Not a single new truth has been put forth, and no confidence can be placed in the teachings of Spiritualism, its own strenuous friends being judges; for the contradictory teachings of the spirits compel them to say that both bad and good communicate with man, and, as we have no means of discriminating between them, so we can acquire no possible knowledge from them. Should any new truth be even communicated, we dare not trust the communication, lest it should prove false. The utter absence of all reasonable evidence that any of these manifestations rise above the rank of imposture or delusion, the utter failure to teach the world any new secret in science or in morals, and the entire inutility of the whole system, even when its claims to truth are admitted, are reasons good and sufficient for regarding the whole matter as among the lamentable delusions which have so often prevailed among men. And if we are to wonder at anything, it is at the lamentable blindness of the human understanding as darkened and defiled by sin, and at the deluding influences of the god of this world, the prince of the power of the air, the spirit that now worketh in the children of disobedience.

We may further remark on this subject before proceeding with the narrative. We charge mystery and darkness and concealment upon all these forms of error, and we regard it as the peculiar characteristic of falsehood that it seeks mystery and concealment. Communications are made in the most uncouth and awkward manner—made in the dark, and no fair investigation ever examines the phenomena. So, sorcery, witchcraft, necromancy, magic in all ages have been without explanation, dim and without definition, reminding us of the terms used by Milton when he attempts to describe the shape of the monster SIN:

> "If shape it might be called, that shape had none
> Distinguishable in number, joint or limb;
> Or substance might be called, that shadow seemed,
> For each seemed either; black it stood as night."

Now, what we designed to remark is this, that mysteries in religion are sometimes mentioned as reasons why men may believe the mysteries of iniquity. But let every man fairly consider that the mysteries of the Bible are in perfect contrast with the mysteries of sin. They differ in nature as light differs from the blackest darkness. There are mysteries in revealed religion, but they are not mysteries of fact. When the Bible records a miracle, the wonder itself is plain; the spectators all see it; there is no room for supposing that delusion was practiced in the thing itself, however wonderful the power that has wrought it. Not a follower of Moses doubted whether the Red Sea opened, whether the manna fell day by day, or whether the pillar of cloud and fire guided his marches. Not a Jew that stood by the grave of Lazarus doubted his death or found any mystery in the fact of resurrection. The mysterious doctrines of the Bible, the Trinity, the incarnation, the decrees of God, the new birth and the resurrection of the body, are not at all mysteries of fact. The facts are plainly taught. They begin to be mysterious only when we ask, How are these things so? So, a man may lift his hand and ask, How does my will move my arm? So a farmer may stand in his field and ask, How does the grain I sowed last fall produce this wheat? There is no mystery in the facts. But mysteries of iniquity are mysteries of fact. The priests in the temples of the Great Mystery of Iniquity profess to change a wafer into the body of Christ, and it is a mystery, without a particle of evidence that such a change has ever occurred. The dealers in magic in every age use their strange rites, practice incoherent mutterings, and prevent the spectators, as much as possible, from seeing what they do, for their mysteries are mysteries of fact. No man under their influence is allowed to witness fairly whether the things alleged to occur do or do not occur. Truth has no mysteries of fact. We may ask, How does the seed grow? and we may get no answer. But the fact that it does grow is plain enough. We may ask, How are the hearts of men renewed by God's holy Spirit? and we are told, The wind bloweth where it pleaseth, and the methods of the Spirit's working are inexplicable, but that he does work is a fact plain enough. We may ask, How are there three persons in one Godhead? and the Bible replies not, but the doctrine, as a doctrine, is plain enough. We may ask, How did the dead body of Lazarus revive? and no answer is returned, but the fact of the miracle is as plain as any other historical fact. The great distinction is, that truth hides not her deeds, though there may be mysteries in the causes and reasons of them, while delusion and falsehood are mysteries in their alleged facts; they love darkness rather than light; everything about them is vague and kept in concealment, and favourable circumstances must be chosen that their votaries may have any chance of succeeding in their efforts to convince others. The mysteries of iniquity and the mysteries of truth are as opposite as light and darkness.

It may be further remarked, upon this general subject, that no man is bound to refer to a supernatural origin every wonder which he is unable otherwise to explain. There may be an explanation, and a very simple one, to the strangest phenomenon, but because I lack the explanation I am not bound to judge that supernatural power produces the wonder. There are many tricks of sleight of hand that to me are as strange as if Satan wrought them, yet I am persuaded they are *tricks*. If a man had never heard a ventriloquist, he might well be startled at the tricks such a performer can play. If the telegraph was a profound secret, we might well attribute to Satanic agency the power of knowing almost instantly the news of a distant city, as we know that the first books printed were ascribed to the devil's agency, for only he could produce so many so soon and so much alike. The chief arguments for impostors are ever addressed to our ignorance; mystery is thrown around them, and all our attempts to gain information are baffled; and time is the surest test of truth. Old and well-established principles that have never shunned investigation, that appear stronger the longer acquaintance we have with them, and that are of unquestioned utility, may be firmly held; while the strange wonders that constantly appear, and after a brief course die and are lost, without adding one particle to human knowledge or happiness, may deceive those who wish to be deceived, but are scarcely worthy of a wise man's wonder, much less of a good man's faith.

We return to the narrative. Saul had formerly made direct efforts to banish from the land those whose aid he now sought. "Thou shalt not suffer a witch to live," was the express direction of the Mosaic law, and acting upon this the king had put away this iniquity from Israel. Yet one of their number, doubtless practicing her art in the most secret manner, lived at the village of Endor in the tribe of Manasseh, and this very near the camp of Saul on the mountains of Gilboa. The king, in disguise and with but two attendants, repaired to her. It is quite likely that the woman knew from the first who her visitor was. Natural shrewdness, habits of keen observation carefully cultivated, and a great facility in reading character are usually found in such persons; and the unusual danger attending her practices in Israel would make this woman fully on the alert. Living near the camp at this time, she knew, it is likely, the distresses of the king, and the unusual stature of Saul among the people would enable her easily to penetrate through any disguise he could put on. That she does not own her recognition of him until surprised into it may have been from policy. She has the caution to secure her safety, so far as her visitor is concerned, by exacting of him a solemn oath before she proceeds with her incantations.

All the writers of the Bible have this remarkable peculiarity, that they seldom make any comments upon the events they record. They state things as they happened, and their readers are left to judge of them upon the principles of truth and rectitude which the Bible gives. So, for example, we have the most dispassionate narratives of the persecutions of Christ and his apostles: there is not a single burst of indignation in the New Testament against the malicious cruelty of their persecutors. So upon this page the narrative is given, but so much is left unexplained that the most various opinions have been formed of the interview of Saul and the woman of Endor. We are unable to decide how far the mere agency of the witch extends, or whether any of the supernatural is to be attributed to her workings. Some are disposed to regard the whole matter as effected by the mere machinery of her art, aided by ventriloquism and by trained confederates.

But let us consider several points separately.

1st. It seems plain that Samuel did actually appear. It is not, indeed, said expressly that Saul saw Samuel. The woman saw him—at least she declared she did—and she so described him that Saul perceived that it was Samuel. This ambiguity of the narrator leads many to deny that the prophet appeared at all, and they make the whole matter a deception on the part of the woman. Nor is it any real objection to this that the words of the apparition foretell the truth of Saul's defeat, nor even that they rebuke Saul so solemnly for his sin. When Saul had so sinned against God; when he had driven from him so many of his most valiant officers and soldiers; when there was so much disaffection in different parts of the kingdom; when the army was beaten almost already by the dejection prevalent in the ranks; and when, evidently upon the eve of a great battle, the very king is driven to hold this counsel with such a woman,—it seemed to require no large wisdom to foretell a great defeat, and even the utter extermination of the brave but desperate family of Saul. Nor need we wonder that Saul's sins were brought before him, for whatever are the earlier deceits of sin, the great adversary is ever ready to reproach the guilty when they are deeply and hopelessly entangled. Yet we adopt the view that Samuel did indeed appear. So Saul evidently believed: this is the simplest meaning of the passage, and the entire address of the prophet is more consonant with his character and with the wretched condition of Saul than any counterfeit which such a woman could so easily bring forward.

But 2d. Supposing that the venerable prophet did indeed appear, it becomes a question of grave importance, Was his rising in answer to any invocation on the part of this woman? This question is usually answered decidedly in the negative. The sorcery of this woman did not cause Samuel to appear.

The grounds of this denial are in part *doctrinal and rational.* We have no reason for supposing, when we have attributed to such a woman the very highest powers, even in league with the Prince of Evil, that she would have power to disquiet and disturb a prophet of God who had already entered upon his rest. But we may base our denial upon the terms of the narrative. It is to be especially noted that nothing is said of her making use of any of the usual arts of muttering or incantation. Samuel appears immediately upon the uttering of Saul's wish to see him,* and the woman seems to be as much surprised as he, and far more alarmed. Her whole language seems to say that this issue of the matter was wholly unexpected to her. She had designed to work as usual, but her imposture is anticipated by this unlooked-for reality.

3d. We suppose that Samuel was permitted to appear—that his coming was by divine agency, and that it had no connection with the arts of this woman beyond the mere fact that it occurred when Saul applied to her. We do not consider this explanation as free from all objection and difficulty, for we regard the whole scene as one of great obscurity. But since Saul so earnestly desires an answer to his inquiries, he is permitted to have the final teachings of the same prophet whose words

* The word *when* in v. 12 is not in the original Hebrew. We are not to suppose that a lapse of time occurs between the request of Saul and the appearance of Samuel.

he had so often disregarded, who had already foretold his rejection, and who now declares the early end of his career and the close of God's long forbearance with him.

The whole tenor of the narrative gives the impression to every unbiassed reader that Samuel did indeed appear, and that the apparition was no counterfeit. If the whole matter seems wonderful and beyond the ordinary experience of man, we have but to remember that we know almost nothing of the spiritual and unseen world, and that things revealed to us are not to be judged by our preconceived ideas, but by the proofs rather that are afforded of their real occurrence. We have no just occasion to doubt the record upon the sacred pages, though, as we have said, there may be different methods of understanding the same narrative.

Perhaps the chief difficulty of this interpretation, which makes the appearance of Samuel real and the effect of divine power, is, that it seems to exhibit God as co-operating with this wretched woman, and as leaving the impression that her art could raise the prophet. But surely the Scriptures are sufficiently explicit in condemning all arts like hers, and thus they afford us principles sufficient to refute any such inferences. And on the other hand, why may we not say that the divine power here invaded Satan's territories, prevented this wretched woman from imposing upon the king, and buoying him up with false comforts at such an hour, and thus rebuked him in this last great sin? We have in the case of Balaam and Balak another instance where vain enchantments were overruled by divine power, and a false prophecy desired by a rebel against God gave place to a true prophecy to the confusion of the sinner. Certainly it is true that God sometimes meets wicked men in their own chosen way, prevents them from finding comforts in the falsehoods they seek after, and shuts them up to all the grief and remorse that justly belong to their own iniquity. And certainly we may be assured that when the guilty soul is rejected of God, has grieved his Spirit, and draws near the end of his wretched life, he shall be permitted to find no true peace. God will not bless him; truth is no relief, and even his refuges of falsehood will be vainly sought to hide him or to comfort him.

## CHAPTER VIII.

### *ZIKLAG SPOILED AND RECOVERED.*

THE Philistines had now made their preparations for a great battle with Saul. The king of Gath placed great confidence in David, and resolved to take him with him to the field. We do not know what David would have done had he been present in the conflict where Saul fell; nor does it even become us to decide what he ought to have done. The truth is, David had here placed himself in a position of great temptation, and, beyond his calculation, he had become entangled in the net of his own falsehoods. No man can foresee how he will come out of temptation when he foolishly ventures in. Happily for us and for David at this time, the Lord deals not with us even as we deserve. He sometimes delivers us from evil when we have the least reason to look for his delivering mercy. This truth we should not abuse to embolden us in evil, yet it may encourage us to believe that he will help us when we seek his aid. So says the wise commentator, Matthew Henry: "God is sometimes found of them that seek him not, but he is always found of them that seek him."

The deliverance of David from the jealousy of his enemies arises just at the needful time. When the other leaders of the Philistines saw these Hebrews in the train of Achish, they were alarmed and offended. They knew them well, for they had felt the power of their arms in many a fatal conflict. They knew not only David, but the mighty men of his band were their old acquaintances. Perhaps it was from a knowledge of their defection from the armies of Saul that they now hoped for an easy victory; and they had no idea of giving them an opportunity of changing sides in the hour of battle, and thus of reconciling themselves to Saul. From considerations of honour, since these men are the friends of Achish, they made no attempt to attack this small band of Hebrews, nor to detain them as prisoners deprived of their weapons. But they persisted in demanding that Achish should send them away. Achish communicated this determination to David with many expressions of regret, and David, though really relieved, yet maintains his arts of dissimulation. But he took his early departure from the camp, and a new set of circumstances at Ziklag completely separated him from the final battle of Saul till the whole matter was decided.

Perhaps in revenge for David's previous invasion, and with a knowledge that he and his men had left the town defenceless, the Amalekites came against Ziklag, burned the place, carried off the spoil and made captives of the women and children. That this was wholly unexpected is very plain from the conduct of David and his men. Every man was deeply grieved, and for some reason the whole tide of anger turned directly against David. We think it is not hard to judge what the reason was which turned the displeasure of the people against him. Ziklag had been left defenceless just because of the unrighteous policy of David. If he had plainly told the king of Gath that his friendly relations would not go the length of any hostilities against Saul, had he let him know just the truth of his feelings upon the subject, it might have offended Achish, but it would have vindicated David. Neither he nor his men marched to the camp of the Philistines with any good design. They should not have gone at all, and the fault of Ziklag's destruction lay largely at David's door. It is possible that the grief of his people made them disposed to judge more harshly of their leader than they otherwise would, and we can make allowance for the distressing circumstances in which they were. The destruction of the city was a light matter compared with the captivity of their children and wives in the hands of a cruel and revengeful foe.

In this hour of distress and perplexity the mind of David acts with both prudence and piety. From this time, indeed, there seems a sudden change in his conduct. We have freely censured where we thought he should be censured; but from this time forth, till the one great sin that darkens the later life of David, we have little reason to speak of him in terms of reproach. May we not suppose that the great calamity at Ziklag was the providential chastisement which aroused the slumbering conscience of the backsliding man of God, and restored his feet to the paths of uprightness: "It is good for me that I have been afflicted. Before I was afflicted I went astray, but now have I kept thy word." Ps. cxix. 71, 67. We have no special record of David's religious exercises in this time of affliction save this important expression, "David encouraged himself in the Lord his God." This teaches us sufficiently the turning of David's mind toward religious reflections and to principles and duties of piety. Although Abiathar had been with him all along of late, we do not read that he asked counsel of God at any time after leaving Keilah. When he fled to the Philistines, when he spoke falsely to Achish, when he put himself in that false position in their camp, he acted without asking counsel of God, and he sinned in each case. But now this trouble has come upon him, and he begins again to ask the Lord's will. He encouraged himself in God. The *natural* tendency of affliction is discouraging. We are cast down, distressed, and if the grief is very heavy we are indisposed to all exertion. This was, perhaps, the first effect upon David. But it lasted not long.

The *gracious* tendency of affliction in all ages is encouraging. We cast our burden upon the Lord, and he sustains us. Tribulation worketh patience, and patience experience, and experience hope, and hope maketh not ashamed. The character of God and his methods of dealing with his people ever bid us put our trust in him. So David felt, and the result justified his reviving faith. God dealt with him better than either his fears or his deservings. His ways are not as our ways, nor his thoughts as our thoughts. The destruction of Ziklag not only led to David's recovery from a lamentable condition of backsliding, but it soon gave David the means of securing at a most important juncture the favour of many in Israel, whose influence was of great use to seat him upon the throne.

With as little delay as possible, David now set out in pursuit of the band which had spoiled Ziklag, and which held their wives in bondage. And it is a matter of proper inquiry just here, Had he any further aid in this pursuit than the aid of the men whose families were thus in captivity? From the record in 1 Chron. xii. 19–21, we would judge that he had important aid. The only objection to understanding the whole passage as referring to this time is that David previously had six hundred men, and that now, with this increase, he had but six hundred wherewith to pursue the foe. This, however, is a very small difficulty, for we can easily see that it would be wise in David, if his band was as much as two or three thousand strong, to choose out the very best for an expedition that would test the endurance of the strongest. From this entire chapter we learn several things that are omitted in the narrative in First Samuel. We learn that David's original band was one of choice strength and courage. We get a further insight, also, into the desperate state of Saul's affairs before that final battle. His soldiers were either disaffected toward him, or so discouraged at the poor prospect of success that they will not risk the coming strife. So many of them, as David left the camp of the Philistines, including several captains of the tribe of Manassah, joined themselves to him—perhaps taking with them a portion of their men. After this battle, it would seem, a large number of the Israelites came to David, of whom we will have more to say afterward.

It is likely, then, that the six hundred men who set out with David to overtake the Amalekites were selected carefully from a much larger band which now he had with him. They began the expedition under unfavourable circumstances. It was at the close of their march from the camp of the Philistines, and just as they expected to enjoy the repose of the city, that they were called to fresh exertions. It took them till the third day's march to reach the city, and these marches homeward had been made perhaps as rapidly as they could go; and now they make a march yet more forced and rapid and long. They were encouraged to this, however, by divine word. David, in the renewed exercise of piety, asked counsel of the Lord, through the priest Abiathar; and his faith was answered not only by the assurance that he would overtake and overthrow the enemy, but that he would surely recover the spoil. With this assurance they pressed on. Yet two hundred of even this chosen band became so weary in the eager pursuit that he was obliged to leave them behind. But David made use of even this circumstance to make the pursuit more earnest and successful. He took the opportunity of lightening the amount of baggage and arms they carried with them, and of making these men guard the articles left. As he desired to take the enemy by surprise and before they had any intimation of the pursuit, the decreasing numbers of his men and the lighter armament would be nothing against his success.

As the band pressed on, they found a young man in the way who had belonged to the very company they were now pursuing. He was an Egyptian, a captive in war, and a slave by the usages of those tribes. But he had fallen sick, and his master did not deem it worth his while to carry him with him upon the march. It may have been from motives of humanity that David and his men stayed long enough to revive the stranger, now nearly dead from sickness and starvation, but it is more likely that it was the wise delay of a commander who knew the value of definite information to the success of his expedition.

The young man gave him the very tidings he wished, and, upon the promise of David of his personal safety and his freedom, he was able to lead the band on their very route. The number of the foe exceeded the present number of David's men, as we learn that a number equal to David's entire force made their escape from them. But neither their number nor the weariness of the attacking party was of any avail. David's men were weary, but they were extraordinary warriors, and they took the foe by surprise. Perhaps, as they drew near the camp, they halted and waited the setting of the sun—partly that they might themselves have a little rest, when now near enough to know that the foe could not escape them, and partly that they might approach close to the very camp in the growing darkness. They began the attack at twilight.* They found the band carousing upon the great abundance of the spoil they had taken. Yet it is possible that they found no easy victory. The conflict continued until the next day, but how much of it was a mere pursuit we cannot decide. The result was not only the recovery of their wives and children, and of the spoil of the city, but also the acquisition of a

* Scott suggests the *morning* twilight.

vast variety of spoil yet further, which the marauding party had gathered in other quarters.

Two matters are to be noted in the distribution of the spoil:

First, it was decided by David, and made a law in Israel from that time forward, that even those soldiers in the army who took no actual part in a battle should yet share in the spoil. There were some men in the camp disposed to withhold from the two hundred men that remained behind at the brook Besor any further share of the spoil than the mere restoration of their families. David, however, decided that as these men were there in the discharge of their duty, as indeed they were doing all they could do, and it was from no cowardice that they were not in the fight, they were justly entitled to a share in the spoils. In arranging the details in such matters there may be many practical difficulties. It would not be just for every man to share alike, and it would not be policy to give no larger encouragement to those who press into severer services and encounter greater dangers. How much ought to be given to a successful commander and how much to a brave private soldier? how much does the camp deserve beyond the quiet garrison? are matters which much wisdom and experience must decide. But the decision of David in this case does not settle where a man's duty lies, nor what proportionate reward should be given for this service or that. He simply settles this, that every part of duty deserves its reward. There was less toil and less glory, and perhaps less real service, done by the two hundred men who remained behind, but they were doing all they could do, and just the service to which their commander had appointed them. The judgment therefore that would rank them with the idle or the inefficient would be wholly unjust. This principle should govern the world and the Church. It may be found in human and in divine administration. Men differ in their conditions, abilities, opportunities and services. Some are in high stations, some in low. Some are active, some are patient. It is not always easy to decide who has the hardest service. Beyond all question, either Paul or John Bunyan would have preferred, if the choice had been left to them, to labour hard in actually preaching the gospel rather than to lie ingloriously for years in a prison. Yet they were serving God by their patience and by doing what his providence allowed, and they were as faithful in the stocks as in the pulpit. And many a man has glorified his God in the only way possible to him by patiently enduring the afflictions of his hand through long months of pining sickness; and many have sojourned in a dry and thirsty land and said, "My soul longeth, yea, even fainteth, for the courts of the Lord's house;" and many have been kept back from earnest duties, as we shall soon see David himself, forbidden by the Lord's own command from his desire to build a temple. In all these cases, and in a thousand others easily imagined, there is acceptance before God "according to that a man hath, and not according to that he hath not." It is not for us to say that the reward of a minor service will equal the reward of a greater, or that the desire to do is equivalent to an actual service. But a man's acceptance depends upon the state of the heart. A man may serve God as truly, if not as largely, in one place as in another. In the service of God many ministers are required, as Paul so felicitously and so beautifully teaches us in his figure of the body—many members in one body, and all members having not the same office. Since God has so many servants, we must expect that some will be engaged in the less weighty duties. So Milton beautifully says that the angels who are waiting for his orders are as truly doing his will as their more active brethren :

> "Thousands at his bidding speed,
> And post o'er land and ocean, without rest—
> They also serve who only stand and wait."

Let us but have our hearts right before God ; let no duty remain undone through lack of our disposition ; let us carefully watch the indications of his providence which tell us where we ought to live and how we ought to labour, and then, doing what our hands find to do with our might, we shall receive his approving smile and our fitting reward, whether our lot be "to abide by the stuff" or to press forward to the fierce and stern conflict.

The second matter in reference to the spoil of the Amalekites is the share that fell to David, and the disposal he made of it. A very large portion of the spoil fell to him; it would almost seem as if he received the entire portion that remained after deducting the booty from Ziklag, which of course his companions claimed as belonging originally to them. But it could scarcely be by any equitable division that David received all this. It was more likely given to him for public purposes, and thus he used it. He kept nothing of it for himself, but sent liberal presents to various quarters. It is likely that he sent part home to the rightful owners, from whom these Amalekites had taken it. As the spoil had, in a good degree, come from the tribe of Judah, and as doubtless there were prisoners enough to tell where it belonged, he laid the owners under a double obligation to him by sending home the rescued captives and the stolen property. As a large part had been taken from unknown owners and from the Philistines, he sent liberal presents to the chief men of the tribe of Judah, and was careful not to forget those who had befriended him and his men in the times of their distress. There was policy, as well as liberality and justice, in all this. David was now approaching a time of his life when he would need all the friends he could gather about him. It may be that already he had heard, before actually sending the presents away from him, of the disastrous battle of Mount Gilboa, but, at all events, he must judge that the indications of Providence pointed out an early fulfilment of the promise of Samuel. The time approached for David to take the kingdom, and it was wise in him to make in Judah as many friends as possible.

But let us turn once again from David to Saul, and now to behold the last scene of his life. The battle between Israel and the Philistines was upon Mount Gilboa. It was possibly a severe strife, for, if we have had evidence that the army of Israel was discouraged and disposed to desert the fallen fortunes of a man forsaken of his God, we yet judge that the leaders were desperate. Unhappy Saul, we may believe, rushed forward into the thickest fight. He seems to have been made a special mark for the arrows of the archers. His brave sons were not behind their father; and theirs was a happier lot, as three of them fell at their posts and upon the field of carnage. With Saul it occurred otherwise. Finding that his wounds were severe, and fearing that they might not result in death, at least until the enemy had laid their hands upon him, Saul resolved to anticipate his death. He called upon his armour-bearer to slay him. This he very properly refused to do. The despairing king then took his own sword and threw himself upon it, and died there upon the ground.

This kind of death was esteemed honourable among the wise men of pagan antiquity, and a sage among modern infidels has not scrupled to apologize for suicide. But Saul learned not this lesson from any legitimate source of instruction. Not a single line upon the pages of the Bible can be found to give countenance to the crime of suicide. No deed deserves to be thought of with more horror than this. For a man to appear by a moment earlier before the bar of God than he is bid to come; to stand there fresh from a crime that in its very nature admits of no repentance; to come there guilty of so great a crime as the shedding of his own blood,—this is a thing for which no array of desperate circumstances can constitute a sufficient apology. Unhappy Saul could not bear to fall into the hands of the Philistines, yet he gave poor proof that he was prepared to fall into the hands of the living God. Death is solemn under any circumstances, but such a death of an unrepentant man is awful indeed to contemplate.

Great was the joy of the Philistines to find the king and his three sons dead on the field of battle. His head and his armour were held as trophies; the tidings spread throughout their cities; the bodies were ignominiously exposed upon the wall of Bethshan, and public thanksgivings were rendered to their god Dagon. The inhabitants of Jabesh-gilead rescued the bones of their honoured king, in gratitude for his former kindness in delivering their city. It is rather surprising that we hear no more of this victory. It seems to have been very decided, and yet for some reason—perhaps through the terror of David's name on his accession to the crown of Judah—the victors seem to have secured very little advantage from it.

On the third day after David's return to Ziklag came a messenger from the camp announcing the disastrous defeat and the death of Saul. The unhappy man who brought these tidings was evidently prompted by a desire to secure a large reward from David for the welcome tidings; and doubtless, knowing the enmity of Saul to David and the chief cause of it in David's prospects for the throne, he thought to make his tidings more welcome and to secure a large reward for himself by claiming that by his hand Saul had died. It is probable that this young man—a mere camp-follower in the army of the Philistines—had been passing over the field immediately after the battle in search of plunder. He was, perhaps, the first man who saw the fallen king of Israel. If he had been content to say this much, and to place in David's hands the crown of Israel and the bracelets of Saul, he might justly have expected a reward far beyond the value of the jewels thus saved from the triumph of the Philistines. But in the hope of securing a large reward to which he was not entitled the young man added the untruth that he himself had slain Saul. But he uttered this falsehood against his own life. David had certain proof in the crown and bracelets of Saul's death; and believing the young man's story that he had slain him, he felt bound, as the elect king of the land, to punish this crime. He commanded one of his young men, therefore, to fall upon the Amalekite and put him to death. The real crime for which he died was a lie. But this, of course, David did not know. Sins apparently trivial often bring the severest punishment upon their perpetrator. Of the results of truth and justice we need not be apprehensive; but when a man seeks his own advantage by means of a falsehood, he may bear himself the responsibility, and has but himself to blame if fearful punishment is substituted by a retributive Providence for the advantage he sought.

## CHAPTER IX.

### *DAVID'S REIGN IN HEBRON.*

IT has almost passed into a proverb in man's experience of deep affliction that "the darkest hour is just before day." So frequently is this so that we may almost learn to rejoice in a heavy weight of affliction which will be succeeded by a corresponding blessing:

> "The clouds we so much dread
> Are big with mercy, and shall break
> In blessings on our head."

At least, if we cannot practice faith, we may exercise patience—

> "Beware of desperate steps: the darkest day,
> Wait till to-morrow, will have passed away."

When David returned to Ziklag and found the city in ruins and his wives carried into captivity, he had reached the darkest hour of his trouble hitherto, and, as we have already suggested, the farthest point of his own wanderings from duty. We have intimated that perhaps this time of deepest affliction was the time also of repentance and of return to God. And now the shadow of persecution and exile passes away, the long night of trial is nearly over, and the morning of prosperity begins to dawn. The promise that he should wear the crown has been long enough addressed to David's faith; long enough against hope he has believed in hope; whatever were his other delinquencies, this faith has, in the main, proved to be awakening, and now its fulfilment approaches. Events preparatory to David's reign now occur rapidly.

But even after the death of Saul, David does not come forth boldly to claim the crown. In regular succession it did not belong to him, but to a surviving son of the former king; yet he had been designated to it by divine authority, to which every man in Israel should have submitted. Accordingly, after the battle of Gilboa, there was a gradual gathering of large forces to David, until perhaps his army was large enough to vindicate by force his title to the throne. Yet true to the principles that have thus far actuated him, David made no movement in this direction, such as would exhibit undue ambition in him or excite the jealousy of the various tribes. We can easily discern through all the history that the tribes felt the influence of sectional interests and of family pride, and a man who would wisely rule over all must not awaken prejudice nor exhibit partiality. David's first step is to ask counsel of God, and he was directed not only to go up now, but told also to go to Hebron, for there his kingdom was first to be established.

At the first, none of the tribes presented themselves at Hebron except his own tribe, the tribe of Judah. It may have been that a few persons from the other tribes were present, but if so, it was in numbers so small that they could not be justly said to represent their respective tribes, and David was anointed king by the tribe of Judah alone. Perhaps this fact gave occasion to subsequent troubles in the united kingdoms, and made it more easy, eighty years after this, to effect a final division of the tribes into two separate nations. The conduct of David was thoroughly conciliatory. He sent his thanks to the inhabitants of Jabesh-gilead for their prompt rescue of the bodies of Saul and his sons from the insults of the Philistines, and merely announced to them that the house of Judah had anointed him king.

It is likely, however, that a separate kingdom was set up in the two tribes through the ambition of the commander-in-chief of Saul's army. Ish-bosheth, the son of Saul, who now became king of the rival kingdom, seems to have been a man of no force of character, and it is likely that no resistance would have been made by him of his own accord to the claims of David. But Abner doubtless thought that the reign of David would be the loss of his authority. The new king would promote to the command of his armies not the general who had pursued him through the wilderness, but some of the faithful men who had been his companions and supporters in trial; and perhaps Abner knew too well the character of Joab to believe that he would allow a rival like himself in experience and ability to secure a high rank in the armies of David. Ishbosheth, the son of Saul, became the nominal king of the ten tribes, while the general in command of his forces was the real ruler of the kingdom. But though aware of the true foundation of the throne in the power of Abner, David made no effort to resist these designs. He was faithful to the solemn oath which he had sworn to Saul that he would not destroy his house (1 Sam. xxiv. 21), and two years seem to have passed away without war between the two kingdoms.* The Philistines seem to have remained quiet, without energy to secure any great advantage from the battle of Gilboa, and Judah and Israel were at peace. And when war did commence, it was not commenced on David's side, and it was carried forward by him with great forbearance. Abner made the invasion, and Joab, the leader of David's army, went out to meet him. They met at Gilboa, and Joab stood upon the defensive in pursuance of David's policy. Abner then proposed a battle between a picked band of men on each side—perhaps to decide the issue of the war. To this Joab agreed, and twelve chosen men from each army advanced to mortal combat. It was a terrible battle, and fatal to the entire number. It

* 2 Sam. ii. 10.

would seem as if they advanced without shields, and each man resolved that his antagonist should die, whatever became of himself. Each strong warrior caught his opponent by the beard, and with each right hand disengaged, struck a sword to his heart, and twenty-four mighty men fell dead upon the spot. This battle therefore decided nothing, for neither party could claim the victory; but a conflict began immediately between the armies, and the army of Abner was sorely beaten. The severe pursuit that followed the defeat was remarkable chiefly for the death of Asahel, the brother of Joab and the nephew of David. Asahel was one of David's mighty men, and specially noted for the swiftness of his running. In the eager pursuit he fell upon the track of Abner, and desirous of winning the honour of taking or of slaying the hostile general, he refused to turn aside, even at the earnest expostulation of Abner. As Abner desired him to take the armour of one of the young men, it is possible that Asahel was lightly armed and prepared rather for rapid motion. But perhaps Abner meant that the disparity was too great in strength and skill between a veteran like himself and this younger warrior. But Asahel, perhaps confident of victory, disregarded his words, and was slain in the most unexpected manner by a backhanded stroke of the experienced captain. We have no reason to lay the fault of this upon Abner, who indeed acted generously toward an enemy eagerly pursuing him; yet the affair furnished a pretext to the unscrupulous Joab to take the life of Abner several years afterward. The pursuit in this battle ended at the expostulation of Abner, and he and his men marched through the entire night away from David's army, while Joab and his men marched in a different direction.

The war thus begun was kept up for several years longer, but no incidents are recorded. We are simply told that the advantages all lay with David, and that the sole strength of Ishbosheth was in the power of Abner. And the son of Saul soon learned what a mere shadow of power belonged to him. He had ventured to charge upon Abner a fault concerning one of the concubines of Saul. We have no just reason to believe that Abner was guilty in the case. He answers the charge with indignation, which may be attributed to his consciousness that the power was in his hands, and that the poor tool of a king should not regard this thing, even if it was true; or it may be referred to his innocence of the crime. As the woman here named appears afterward in the narrative in such a manner as to call forth our sympathies for her sorrows as a mother, and our approbation for the strength of her maternal affection (2 Sam. xxi. 10, 11), it is the verdict of charity that she was not guilty as here charged by the nominal king of Israel. But the charge against Abner betrays the jealousy of Ishbosheth for Abner's power. For any man to aspire to marry a widow or concubine of a deceased king is regarded in the East as a token of seeking for the throne. So Solomon put to death his elder brother, Adonijah, because he sought to marry Abishag, the Shunammite. 1 Kings ii. 13–25. But if Abner had such a design, the king was too weak to resist him, and now he openly and indignantly declares that he will use his power to establish the throne of David. The very threat of Abner betrays his consciousness that all this time the right belonged to David. He knew that the Lord had sworn to put the son of Jesse upon the throne.

And now the commander of the armies of Israel made proposals to David to secure his reign over the united tribes. It would have been better if a result so desirable had been sought for through the influence of pious principles. But what is here sought at the impulse of passion is lost for the time through the influence of a jealous ambition. After some preliminaries were settled, especially the return of David's wife Michal, Abner consulted the elders of Israel and sought their consent to the deposition of Ishbosheth and the reign of David. He then sought for an interview with David, and the terms of the covenant were arranged between them. As the whole matter was defeated, the terms were not carried into effect, and are not mentioned by the historian. It is very likely that, as Ishbosheth was too much in the power of Abner, so David began to feel himself too much in the power of Joab. This man was a nephew of David, and it is likely near about his own age. He was a man of tried valour and a commander of experience and success. From first to last, though he was commander-in-chief of David's armies for not less than forty years, we have no account that Joab ever lost a battle or turned his back on the foe. He seems to have been only too powerful for a subject; and the king, though himself beloved by the people and generally executing his own will, has no power to withstand the will of Joab, nor even to punish him for his crimes. As we find long afterward that David intended to make Amasa the commander-in-chief in the room of Joab, and Joab treacherously slew his rival as the easiest way to retain his command, so it is likely it was here. It is very probable that part of the terms which David made with Israel provided that Abner should receive the post of commander-in-chief of the allied armies. Joab would have been inferior to him, and the increase of force from the ten tribes would have put it out of his power to make any resistance to the king's will. Joab had no disposition to submit to this. We cannot indeed say that it was ungenerous in David thus to requite the services of Joab, and to give such an honour to one who had been an enemy, rather than to one who had stood by him in trying times. For Joab had no right to presume upon his position and to make David feel so much his dependence upon him. When a man merits the honours of the State, and wears his honours meekly and loyally, let them be justly continued with him; but when any man seeks rather his selfish ends than the well-being of the government, he puts too high a value upon his services, let them be what they may. Joab was absent when Abner came to Hebron, and throughout the entire conference, but, returning soon after, was made acquainted with his coming and return. He reproached David for entertaining him, and especially for sending him away in peace. Without the knowledge of the king he sent messengers after Abner, doubtless with the pretence that David desired to see him for some matter that had been overlooked. Abner returned to Hebron, and Joab, under professions of friendship, spoke aside with him, and took the opportunity to assassinate him. The pretext for this dastardly act was revenge for the death of his brother Asahel. But this is no justification for the deed. The death of Asahel occurred in a time of war and during the pursuit from a battle, and Abner had been generous and forbearing toward him. And the excuse for slaying him for his brother's death was taken away by the very place in which Joab chose to kill him, for Hebron, where this deed occurred, was one of the cities of refuge; and it may be remarked, as an instance of retributive justice, that when Joab was finally put to death, for this very crime, after the lapse of nearly forty years, he failed to find a sanctuary even in the tabernacle, but died at the very altar of God. 1 Kings ii. 28–34. They that take the sword shall perish by the sword, and he who disregards the refuge divinely appointed shall seek protection in vain in the late hour of his own distress.

David was deeply distressed and shocked at this base assassination. The tendency of it was not only to break off the present negotiations, but to render it unlikely that the kingdom of Israel would ever be reconciled to the reign of David, when a man of Abner's ability and popularity—especially one that at the very moment was a public ambassador—was thus cruelly murdered almost in the royal presence. But the whole language and conduct of David in reference to this matter set him clear not only in the eyes of his own people, but also before the kingdom of Israel. Perhaps the plea of Joab, that he did this to avenge his brother's death, made it more difficult under the peculiar laws of the East upon this subject to bring him to punishment, especially as Joab held a post of such authority. So David complains that the sons of Zeruiah were too strong for him, and that he was weak though anointed king. But his sense of the crime may be seen not only from the strong terms of the curse he pronounced upon Joab, but even more from the fact that thirty years after this, when David was about to die, he enjoined on Solomon the duty of punishing Joab for this and a similar crime afterward committed.

David made a public funeral for Abner, and served himself as chief mourner on the occasion. He even caused Joab and Abishai, with the rest of the people, to rend their clothes; he composed a song of lamentation for the occasion, and fasted as in deep affliction.

And yet it is likely, after all, that Joab's political views in this case were correct, and that the death of Abner was better for the prosperity of both kingdoms. This does not, indeed, justify the wicked deed of Joab. But this man is no ordinary character upon the sacred pages. Joab was a man of extraordinary abilities—a wise counsellor, a judicious statesman, a mighty warrior, a successful commander, an ardent patriot and a faithful friend. He stood by David from first to last; and except one late error, in consenting that Adonijah should succeed David on the throne, he never stepped aside from loyalty to his uncle. David owed much of the success of his reign to the support of Joab. And yet these excellent qualities in Joab for a public officer, which justify David in giving him the command of his armies for so long a period, and which explain the influence which Joab had in Israel, were in striking contrast with serious defects in Joab's character. If Joab was politic in discerning, he was unscrupulous in executing his plans. He saw now what mischief Abner might work in the united kingdom; he saw after this how unwise it was in David to wish to save the life of Absalom; he knew that Amasa was promoted above him in the army—the rebel chief defeated promoted over the head of his conqueror; and Joab had no scruples, on all these occasions, to carry his own purposes without regard to the feelings of David or to the dictates of justice. In short, Joab was a worldly-minded man, with the wisdom of a statesman, but the selfishness and cruelty of a wicked mind. It is the wretchedness of the world that it has too many such statesmen, and that the success which often attends unscrupulous plans is regarded as vindicating the wisdom of their adoption. Yet David's words came true in the case of Joab, and they will not fail of their fulfilment in every case: "The Lord will reward the doer of evil according to his wickedness." True piety is not always in accordance with worldly wisdom, but it is real wisdom, as the end will plainly show.

The death of Abner put an end to the present design of adding the kingdom of Israel to that of David, but it is likely that it really made that event inevitable. Not only had the people of the ten tribes now, through Abner's influence, acknowledged that the divine will had designated David for the throne, but it appears that they had before this "sought for David to be king over them" (2 Sam. iii. 17), and the ambition and influence of Abner had chiefly prevented the union of the tribes.

The sword of Joab had taken away the chief agent of discord—had taken away one who might have been a mischief-maker after the union was formed, and had stricken down the main support of Ishbosheth's throne. The weakness of the king of Israel was now apparent. If David had pursued a vigorous and offensive policy against the house of Saul, he might now have united the crowns; but a wiser and more righteous and peaceful policy secured a firmer victory sufficiently soon. So manifest now was the weakness of the Israelitish king that the men of his own army began to contrive how they might secure the favour of David. Two of his captains therefore basely assassinated Ishbosheth and brought his head to David, expecting to receive a reward for their wickedness. The event shows how little they understood the character of the righteous king, and how little they had made themselves acquainted with his former history. The mind of David was filled with horror at this cool-blooded deed of wickedness. If on a former occasion he had put to death a foreigner and an enemy who boasted that his sword had slain Saul, he will much rather put to death these murderers. They were officers in the army of Ishbosheth; they rose against one who had done them no wrong, but who was entitled to their obedience; they treacherously slew him in his own house. The due reward—far otherwise than they had looked for—is quickly given them. They were speedily executed, and their hands and feet hung up as warnings for others. Mutilation for offences is often mentiond in Eastern authors, though less in the Bible that in other Oriental writings. It is remarkable that the English law, even yet, sentences a man to have his hand cut off who strikes a blow within the limits of the king's court or in a superior court of justice;* and even the exporting of live sheep was as late as the reign of Elizabeth punished with the loss of the left hand.† The Jewish law forbade that the bodies of persons executed should be exposed, as the Philistines exposed Saul and his sons, to the horror of Israel, one single day being the limit of exposing the body. So the members of those murderers were set up as ghastly examples to deter others from like crimes.

It is not easy to decide why mention is here made of Mephibosheth, the lame son of Jonathan. Perhaps it is to intimate that Ishbosheth was an usurper even while he held the throne of Israel, since the regular succession devolved on this descendant of Saul through his eldest son. But the succession through the eldest son was not the settled policy of the kingdom. Perhaps it suggests that the avenger of Ishbosheth was too young to pursue his murderers. Or, it may be simply to intimate that the transfer of the kingdom to David was not for lack of one of Saul's race. But the

* Blackstone's Com., iv. 125. † Ibid., iv. 154.

whole people now judged it better to submit to the divine indications. David had proved himself every way worthy of the throne; it was every way better that the tribes should be united; and it would have been a great damage to Israel to prefer the rule of a lame child to the sovereignty of a man like David.

## CHAPTER X.

### *THE REST FOUND FOR THE ARK.*

THE death of Ishbosheth prepared the way for David's reception as king by all the tribes. The growing conviction on the part of all the people that this was the divine appointment seems to have had great influence in bringing about the union of the different states of Israel, and especially under this king. In 1 Chron. xii. 23–40 we have an account of the gathering of the tribal armies to David at Hebron. A very small number is mentioned of the tribe of Judah. We may account for this either by supposing that there was a small body of that tribe that had hitherto adhered to the house of Saul, or by considering that the tribe, already governed by David, kept rather aloof from the present solemnities, that they might not seem to be too active in their king's new triumph, and that all might appear the voluntary action of the other tribes. An immense concourse of people came together; great preparations were made for a festival; and for three days a joyous commemoration was had of this happy union of the entire nation. It was worthy of their joy, for it was the beginning of the brightest days of the Israelitish history.

Being now the king of all the land, having attained at length the honours so long before predicted for him by the prophet Samuel, David began to meditate wise and enlarged plans for the prosperity of his kingdom. His first project is the transfer of his capital from Hebron to a more important and stronger position. And now first comes into prominence upon the sacred pages the most famous city of human history. Not excepting the fame of Rome, we may place Jerusalem in the front rank of famous places on the earth. We first read of this city, as is generally thought, under the name of Salem, when, in the days of Abraham, it was governed by Melchizedek. In the conquest of the land by Joshua the city, by the name of Jebus, fell to the lot of the tribe of Benjamin, but, being a border town, lying between that tribe and the tribe of Judah, it either never was taken from the Jebusites,* or it afterward fell again into their hands. David now chose this spot as a suitable site for the chief city of the united kingdom, and subsequent ages have vindicated the wisdom of his choice.

From this time forth till the present day, Jerusalem has been one of the chief spots of the earth. A picture now of the city, as she sits in her decay, would be of deep yet mournful interest. We would

* Judges i. 21.

see the minarets of the false prophet towering where rose the pinnacles of Jehovah's temple; we would see remains of ancient grandeur, deeply impressive to teach us what Jerusalem was, yet deeply painful in the contrast of what the city is; and as we hear the screech of the owl and the cry of the jackal rising above her walls, we might wander among the forlorn magnificence of her domes and convents and churches, as a modern traveller expresses himself, "pitying everything and everybody," causing every street to be to us a "via dolorosa," and preparing us to sit down with her outcast children in their place of weeping to bewail the degradation of their holy city. And yet a vivid panorama of the city of David would be inferior in interest to a correct conception of her graphic history. Could we have the scenes, not of space but of time, pass before us, what various changes, what rejoicings, what lamentations, what festive celebrations, what battles of the warrior, what important sieges, what repeated destructions and restorations would crowd the canvas! This city was the scene of Solomon's magnificence; here came the sovereigns of the world to hear his wisdom; here rose his splendid temple, the only place for many generations appointed for Jehovah's worship among the sons of men; here lived some of the most excellent men of the world's history; and through these streets passed that most amazing sight that ever met the eye of man—as amazing for its condescension and love and humility as for the rays of divine splendour that struggled through the veil. Along these streets passed the form of the Son of God made in the likeness of sinful flesh. Alas! Jerusalem has been as full of woes as of joys, for she has been as full of crimes as of privileges. These favoured streets have "been filled with innocent blood from one end to the other" (2 Kings xxi. 16), shed from the veins of their subjects by her own anointed kings. Here have died by violence so many holy men and apostles of God that scarcely could a prophet perish out of Jerusalem. If the stones of this city have listened to the voice of Him who "spake as never man spake," they have witnessed also his rejection and his cruel death. The priests of Jerusalem refused their Messiah and arraigned him before a Gentile judge. The Jewish populace urged his crucifixion. Along the Dolorous Way passed that meek and suffering form, and the master-crime of the world filled up the cup of Jerusalem's iniquity.

And what a city of war! Jerusalem has again and again been destroyed. More obstinate conflicts have never elsewhere been witnessed than around her massive walls and beneath her craggy precipices. Surely each conqueror might confess, as the Roman destroyer of the city did confess, that God was his help against such fortifications and such determined resistance. Yet Jerusalem has often fallen. The Egyptians, the Assyrians, the Babylonians, the Greeks, the Romans, the Persians, the Saracens, the Crusaders and the Turks have been its masters. No scenes of war have ever better deserved a graphic description, and in no abodes of men have been endured greater miseries of famine and destitution and violence. Suffice it to justify our darkest thoughts that the voice of unfailing truth, speaking of Jerusalem's miseries for Jerusalem's greatest sin, has named it "great tribulation, such as was not since the beginning of the world, nor ever shall be." Matt. xxiv. 21.

The name Jerusalem signifies the "dwelling of peace." This is entirely consistent with the tenor and design of those great doctrines of revealed religion which have had there their centre of origin and influence. And to this significancy of name the prophet Isaiah perhaps refers when he predicts the future prosperity of the city, "Thine eyes shall see Jerusalem a great habitation." Isa. xxxiii. 20. It may be, according to the views of many, that Jerusalem shall be the glorious centre toward which the eyes of the earthly Church shall look. It shall be that the doctrines first taught in the holy city shall triumph in all the earth. And surely the devotional interest associated around the past history of the city is greatly heightened by the transfer of this name to the holy city of God on high. Jerusalem is the mother of us all: beautiful for situation, the joy of all the earth, is Mount Zion. No temple is there; but apostles, prophets, martyrs and the saints of all ages are the worshippers, the Lord God in the midst of her is her king, and the new Jerusalem above is an "abode of peace."

In order to establish his capital in this city, David must first wrest it from the Jebusites. It seemed, indeed, a reproach to the tribes that now for four hundred years so strong a fortress in the very heart of the land should remain in the power of the Canaanites. While carrying the terror of his arms abroad, David should surely not leave this city unharmed. The Jebusites, confident in their strength, sent him a challenge, couched in words quite obscure to us: "that if he did not take away the blind and the lame he could not take their city." Some understand this as exhibiting their confidence in the strength of the place, for even blind and lame men would suffice for its successful defence. But this explanation does not explain sufficiently satisfactorily how the blind and lame should be "hated of David's soul." Others, therefore, understand by the expression that the city was under the special protection of some of the gods of the Jebusites. It was a very common thing with the heathen to put their cities and fortresses under special protection, and sometimes to possess a pledge of this. So the goddess Minerva was the patroness or protectress of cities, and the city of Athens was called by one of her names (Athené), and there the Parthenon—a temple to her—was said to contain a column that had fallen from heaven, and an olive tree, the gift of the goddess to man. So in the city of Troy was a wooden image of this same goddess which was supposed to have come down from heaven. This was called the Palladium, from Pallas—one of the names of Minerva—and it was believed that Troy was impregnable so long as this image remained in the citadel. Hence the word palladium is used to signify a bulwark or safe protection. So the great temple of Diana at Ephesus seems to have contained an image that was believed to have fallen from Jupiter.

The citadel of Jerusalem while in the hands of the Jebusites may have contained such an image. Nor is it any objection that it is here described as blind and lame, for these very infirmities were assigned to the gods of other nations. Fortune was represented as blind. Vulcan was lame. The tutelary divinities of the heathen Jerusalem may have been blind and lame, and as idols they were abhorred by David. It would stimulate his zeal that such a city should be so protected in the heart of a land where the Lord reigned. Yet David knew the strength of the place, and he held out to his troops a prize of valour. Displeased at Joab that he had basely assassinated Abner, he now offered the chief command of his armies to the man who first made good his entrance into the garrison and secured the capture of the city. If this prize was open to any man in the army, it was no very wise offer on the part of the king, for a man may be of unflinching bravery and of a strong arm and yet be totally unfit to be a commander. It is likely the offer was made to his superior officers; and Joab himself, stimulated by various motives, pressed boldly forward and won the city and the coveted honour. This was doubtless contrary to David's desire. Yet it may have been greatly for the better—for the prosperity of his kingdom—for though Joab was an unscrupulous man, yet he was a faithful and energetic warrior, and his high capacity was of great advantage to David not a few times afterward. It is likely that David became quite reconciled to him after this, though he seems ever to have feared him more than a king should fear any subject. But Joab was ever as loyal to David's interests as a man could be who was as self-willed as he.

From this time the prosperity of the united kingdom was apparent. David admired Jerusalem, and built there a palace for himself by the assistance of the neighbouring king of Tyre. From this powerful city the Israelites seem to have received some of their arts, and especially in the reign of Solomon we find the Tyrians affording the assistance of their skill in building the temple. David also carried on successful wars with the Philistines, and the power of the kingdom sensibly increased.

Perhaps it was early the definite design of David

to make Jerusalem the central place of worship for the tribes of Israel. God had long before promised that he would choose a place in the promised land, and there the people were to congregate for his worship (Deut. xii. 5, etc.). Doubtless such an ecclesiastical capital was desirable for the spiritual welfare of the people, and indeed necessary to the forms of worship in the Levitical economy. We are not informed that the divine will had directed David to this city, but we know that this city became, in fact, what David designed to make it. But to carry on his pious purpose, it was needful that the city should become the resting-place of the ark of God and the residence of at least the high priest. Arrangements were therefore made to bring up the ark to Jerusalem.

The wanderings of the ark had brought it to Baale of Judah, elsewhere called in the Scriptures Kirjath-jearim. There it was placed on the return from the land of the Philistines, and we have no positive mention of the ark from that time till this. It seems implied that the ark was at Nob, since the shew-bread was there placed before the Lord, but it is not expressly said that the ark was there. Now, at least, it is at Kirjath-jearim, and in the house of the same man where it had then been left after the judgment on the men of Bethshemesh. But so long a time had now elapsed that it is likely Abinadab was dead, and the ark appears to have been in the custody of his two sons, Uzzah and

Ahio. It seems strange, when there was so great a desire on the part of David and the Israelites to do honour to the ark, that they did not more carefully inquire as to the law upon the subject. They seem to have taken counsel of the Philistines rather than of Moses. When the Philistines let the ark go, they had sent it away upon a new cart. Now David does the same. The ark is placed upon a new cart. Not the same employed before, for that had been used to burn up the kine as sacrifices before the ark. But another cart was now made. This was a great mistake. It might be tolerated in Gentiles to lead the ark home so; but Israelites and their king at their head ought to have known better. The express law upon the subject was, that the ark should be borne upon the shoulders of the Levites, and that no one but a priest was at liberty to put his hand upon it under pain of death. The judgment upon the men of Bethshemesh ought to have called attention to this point. This oversight had a fatal termination. As the oxen shook the ark, Uzzah put forth his hand to steady it, and the Lord smote him, and he died for his error. We are not told that Uzzah was even a Levite. Whether he was or not, it was not his place to touch the ark. He may have sinned ignorantly, but he ought to have known the law. To sin in ignorance of the divine requirement by no means implies innocence, nor secures exemption from the divine displeasure. God judges men indeed according to the light they have. But no man can shut his eyes to the light which God has shed around him, and then claim that he ought to be judged by the same rule as if he had been born blind. God gives us laws, requiring in the most reasonable manner that we should make ourselves acquainted with them, and they who are too negligent to do this may justly be held responsible for guilt that is only the greater for their neglect. Should a man in a land where the gospel is preached yet lose his soul and say truly that he knew not the way of salvation? This plea on the one hand would not prevent his condemnation before God, and on the other hand its just force would be to increase his sin and to aggravate his doom. Uzzah died before the Lord, for he presumed to put forth his hand to steady the ark without inquiring how God had directed that the ark should be treated. It was his place, before assuming such a duty, to know how to discharge it. A man is as truly bound to learn the duties of his station as he is bound to discharge those duties, and no man can be excused for ignorance of religious principles and religious duties in a land where the abounding of religious privileges makes such ignorance not a misfortune, but a crime. He cannot escape who neglects the great salvation. When we see the record of such a case as Uzzah, stricken dead before God for such an act as this, though we have no reason to impute to him any other than upright intentions, we may well say, with the smitten people of Bethshemesh, "Who is able to stand before the holy Lord God?"

And let us learn that there is a presumption in ignorance of which we do well to beware. There are important limitations to the excuse when a man sins ignorantly. He who knew no better in a thousand instances should have known better. Men readily learn according to their full opportunities in all cases where their hearts are truly and deeply interested. Our ignorance, then, in such cases, betrays how far the heart is wrong. It was now seventy years—as some suppose—since the ark had been first placed in the house of Abinadab. His son Uzzah had been long familiar with it. Perhaps through all his life its sacred presence had blessed his father's dwelling; he ought to have known the divine cautions respecting its treatment, and he could scarcely have been ignorant of the judgment which had caused the ark to be carried to his father's house. And surely it is a plain inference from these thoughts that if any man has been familiar in his own father's house from his childhood with the worship of God, and the great book of his law and God's gospel, it is but the proof of sinfulness and the aggravation of his guilt to say that he is ignorant of his duty. If the very presence of the ark should have urged Uzzah to inquire the will of God concerning it, surely the possession of the Bible and the inestimable privilege of being taught of God upon the most important topics, and in reference to our own eternal life, should lead us to diligent exertions to know what God has here revealed. It would certainly seem that all ignorance of scriptural teachings in a land like this is inexcusable, and that all sins through ignorance may justly be regarded as sins of presumption, aggravated rather than extenuated by an ignorance which itself argues indifference to divine instructions and recklessness to the sinner's own immortal interests. It is a sinful thing that so many men have but a small acquaintance with the teachings of the Bible, and that such should perish in their wilful ignorance is a result we may reasonably anticipate.

From these thoughts the transition is easy to remark that sins against well-known and acknowledged duties are of yet more flagrant wickedness. While wilful ignorance aggravates rather than extenuates sin, yet it does not furnish the highest degree of aggravated iniquity. We regard it as no excuse for a physician that he ignorantly administers a poison instead of a medicine, since it was his place to know the drug before he gave it. Yet, though we judge him guilty in such a case, and regard his act the more criminal because his very ignorance was a wrong, it must be confessed at once that his wilful prescription of a poison immensely swells the enormity of his guilt. Even so judge we of the man who wilfully disregards and tramples upon the gospel of Christ, well knowing its truth and his duty respecting it. The crime of Uzzah is light, the sin of neglecting the great salvation is small, if compared with his sin who turns deliberately away from convictions that have pierced his soul, from duties that have burdened his conscience and from mercies that have been somewhat impressed upon his heart. Sin has its various degrees. The wise man would not wish to bear its lightest burden. We ought gladly to receive those assurances of the divine word which teach us that the blood of Jesus Christ cleanseth us from all sin. But unhappy is he who is ignorant of the gospel while yet its teachings are all around him; and most wretched indeed is that man who knows the provisions of the gospel, yet fights against them; knows the truth of the Scriptures, yet opposes their influence; knows the excellency of this salvation, and yet remains a rebel against God and an enemy to the cross of Christ.

The awful death of Uzzah put an immediate stop to the progress of the ark. The music ceased and the immense multitude trembled, perhaps with apprehension that the judgment of Bethshemesh was about to be repeated. The feelings of David on this occasion were not as they should have been. Perhaps we too seldom reflect upon the mingled feelings of our worship before God. In some respects we may feel right; we are inflamed with zeal for God; we desire his glory; we would be filled with joy at the manifestations of his presence.

Yet we may indulge self-complacency in our earnest doings, or murmur against God if things turn not out as we wish. We are here told that David was displeased at the death of Uzzah, at the same time that he was greatly afraid of God. But he was to learn that God will be worshipped in an orderly manner and according to his own directions. Perhaps it was the more important that such a lesson should be just now impressed, because a new era was beginning in Israel. He was transferring the ark to the central city, where the people were to assemble for regular worship, and the nations should learn at the outset the true methods of divine service. But David did not immediately understand the lesson there taught. He was afraid to go on with his designs, and he turned aside and deposited the ark in the house of Obed-edom. We are expressly told that this Obed-edom was a Levite and a porter. It was his place to keep the door of the tabernacle where the ark was deposited. It is likely therefore that the error of the proceedings which had issued in the death of Uzzah was immediately discovered. But they were afraid to go on now, and they deposited the sacred charge in the house of this Levite.

It seemed an awful deposit for any man's private dwelling. When this ark abode in the tabernacle, it rested in the Most Holy Place (Ex. xxvi. 31, etc.; Heb. ix. 3, 4), behind the significant veil, and no mortal eye dare behold it, save the eye of the trembling high priest who came once every year, after offering solemn propitiatory services, and moved his censer in the presence of God (see Lev. xvi. 2, 34; Heb. ix.). It was a solemn thing for the great congregation of Israel to stand around the tabernacle and offer their prayers while the high priest drew aside the veil and appeared before the mercy-seat. And now it seems more solemn unspeakably that this venerated ark should rest beneath the humble roof of a Levite. Yet we never know our God aright until we understand that in him meet the extremes of dignity and condescension. He is greatly to be feared and tenderly to be loved; he allows no presumption, he encourages holy boldness; the proud may tremble before him, but the humble may rejoice. Uzzah died before the Lord, but Obed-edom and his house are blessed with the presence of the ark. While ignorant and presumptuous sinners may well tremble, humility and obedience and faith have nothing to fear, but may hope for good at the hand of the Lord. And though it does seem a solemn thing to have the dwelling-place of the Lord God in the abode of a private family—though we may feel like adopting the language of the Roman centurion, "Lord, I am unworthy that thou shouldst come under my roof"—yet there is a sense in which the ark of God abides in the house of many an Obed-edom; and it is a truth most delightful, in the rich experience of believers, that where the ark abides the blessing of the living God is also there. There is a worship of God in the families of his people that may properly be likened to the abiding of the ark in the house of a humble Levite. God promises specially to the dispensation to which we belong a protection, not visible, but as real as the guiding pillar which led Israel through the pathless desert; and this not for his Church alone, but for each family in Zion. "The Lord will create upon every dwelling-place of Mount Zion, and upon all her assemblies, a cloud and smoke by day and the shining of a flaming fire by night." Isa. iv. 5. In our age we have the veil rent, the throne of grace accessible, and we are encouraged to come boldly there. The ark of God needs now no visible symbol of its presence, but we should bid it welcome to our abodes. Our God is the God of the families of the earth, and he should be worshipped in our families. The altar should be set up, and the offering of prayer and praise should, morning and evening, ascend upon it. How little do those parents feel the proper sense of their responsibilities who neglect the duties of family devotion! How far wrong is he who regards these duties as a responsibility too heavy for him to bear! For the responsibility of his neglect is a far weightier burden, and we are able to bear our duties only as we earnestly endeavour to meet them. But the blessing upon the house of the Levite should remind us that the worship of God in the family is a rich blessing upon the household. We are not told in what respect it was that Obed-edom was blessed, but evidently it was with such favour from God that in the short space of three months it was well known to all around that the ark was a treasure there. And to have God's worship in our dwellings is a rich blessing to all. No parent can engage in the duties of God's service without receiving in himself a rich reward. His own character must be benefited by the humble and serious devotion which thus sanctifies every day. It seems a thing most unlikely indeed, if not quite impossible, that any man can sit down in a serious manner to read daily in his family a portion of God's word, and to offer up his prayers for the divine favour, without becoming himself better acquainted with the truth of God, and without feeling the influence of such exercises to make him a more consistent and holy man. Equally obvious are the influences of such services upon the training of the children in the family. As the most important agencies to mould the character operate almost insensibly, as growth is gradual, so we may expect to teach the young the principles and duties of piety most successfully when we bring those matters most constantly before them. If experience is a proper witness in a case like this, it is easy to know that those who have most carefully maintained the duties of family religion are the most disposed to consider it an inestimable privilege, and the most ready to acknowledge that by it God has blessed their households.

The interval of these months had sufficed to convince David of his folly in being displeased, and to show where the fault had really been; and the tidings that God had blessed the house of Obed-edom reassure him that God is willing to bless. Arrangements are now therefore made to remove the ark to Jerusalem. A place is prepared for it, and a tent pitched for its accommodation. The just rule of God's worship is now acknowledged, and while David says that "the Lord our God made a breach upon us, for that we sought him not after the due order" (1 Chron. xv. 13), he says also, "None ought to carry the ark of God but the Levites." 1 Chron. xv. 2. The Levites, therefore, are commanded to sanctify themselves; a great assembly of the people is called to the solemnity; a choir of singers and performers upon musical instruments express the joy of the people; and solemn sacrifices are offered as the ark passes forth for its resting-place on Mount Zion. The use of instrumental music is nowhere enjoined in the laws of Moses, except the use of trumpets, which were employed to call their assemblies together, and were sounded over their solemn sacrifices. Num. x. 2, 10. But instrumental music was used before the giving of the law as well as after, and the Psalms abound in exhortations to praise God by the use of such. The objection that in the New

Testament no such worship is enjoined is of no force, when we consider that usage and not law sanctioned their use in the ancient Church, and that the New Testament contains no rebuke of a kind of worship which then was unquestionably common usage. The Psalm used specially upon this occasion is not found entire in the Book of Psalms, though similar sentiments occur in several of the Psalms. We may judge, from the usual practice of David, that it is lawful for us to express our devotions before God in psalms or hymns that are written expressly for the occasions that call them forth. There seems no more impropriety for those who are able so to do to compose sacred songs for our occasions than to make our prayers suit the times when they are offered.

In these solemn services David took a deep interest. Indeed, it is likely that upon that glad day was accomplished a long-cherished wish of his heart. In the one hundred and thirty-second Psalm we are told that David had long vowed that he would provide a dwelling-place for the Lord. In Ephratah, in Bethlehem, in his early years, it had been a grief to the young shepherd that so little store had been set by the holy symbol of the Jewish faith. When Samuel first anointed him for the kingdom, his youthful imagination had been formed to royal designs, and prominent among them was the honour of the ark; and in the midst of his afflictions his vow was to give himself no rest till he had found a habitation for the Lord. The ark was at Kirjath-jearim, which name signifies the Forest City. So the Psalm declares, "We found it in the fields of the wood." With all his heart the king of Israel joined in the glad celebration of that eventful day. He girded himself with a linen ephod and danced before the Lord, and joined his voice in the songs of the sons of Levi. And indeed it was a day more worthy of a triumph than the usual celebrations of mighty kings. Many a feast such as David made that day to all the people, many such a procession, with instruments of string music, has been made in honour of cruel conquerors whose fierce ambition has desolated happy homes and devastated flourishing kingdoms. Let David set an example to the kings of the earth; his triumphal day is for the worship of the Lord of hosts established in his capital, and he knows no larger blessing for his people than the maintenance of pure and spiritual worship among them.

Carnal minds think not so; and here we have renewed reason to contrast the new king with the old. Unhappily, too faithful to the principles of her father's house, Michal, the daughter of Saul and the wife of David, looked forth from her window, and in her heart despised her husband for his zeal for the Lord. Better for her, better for her father and better for the kingdom had the same zeal been shown in Israel for fifty years now past.

## CHAPTER XI.

### *DAVID'S DESIRE TO BUILD THE TEMPLE.*

THE throne of David is now firmly established, and there is already a great contrast between the state of the kingdom as he received it and as he now possessed it. Under Saul the feebleness of the State exposed it to constant attacks from the nations around, and at his death all was distraction and discord. Now the entire tribes have been led to acknowledge David; he stands in high favour with all the people; his enemies have learned to fear and respect him; the boundaries of the kingdom have been enlarged; and his fame has gone abroad to distant countries. 1 Chron. xiv. 17. The natural tendency of such a government ever is the prosperity of the people—a prosperity which shows itself in the improvement of property, in a greater care to increase the products of the land, to build more valuable dwellings and public buildings and to promote the moral and religious advancement of the people. In a land where the government is feeble, where the people are oppressed and where hostile invasions are liable to sweep suddenly away the hard-earned fruits of honest labour, there is but little encouragement for that earnest industry which, by the daily care of a busy population, clothes the fields in waving harvests, adorns the smiling landscapes with the cheerful-looking abodes of a thriving husbandry, and enlivens the highways with the voices of the children as they pass to and fro from happy parents to diligent teachers. When the chief employment of a people is to fight the cheerless battles of self-defence against a superior invader, where their chief buildings are the strong walls that defend a half-starved population in their miserable towns, and where their jealous ruler employs his energies chiefly to oppress his most faithful subjects, there is little encouragement for the industry and toil which bless a land and its people. And the ancient description of Israel too well applies till the very times of David: "The highways were unoccupied, the travellers walked through byways, the villages ceased." Judges v. 6, 7.

David was a man of war, but his wars were foreign and successful. The people not only dwelt securely at home, but, as was usual in the ancient wars, the chief burden of sustaining the troops fell upon those whom they attacked. The kingdom of David was enriched, not impoverished, by his warlike policy. The citizens had ample protection for person and property; and this is the chief thing needful to national prosperity. An industrious people, with a fertile land and the blessing of

Providence, will soon possess abundant resources, and rise in comforts and wealth and power, if wrong and oppression are not allowed to crush them. The kingdom of Israel, from this time forward for sixty years, enjoyed its days of palmiest prosperity.

An important element of David's prosperity must be sought for in the attention paid to religious matters by the king and people. This unquestionable truth appears in the history of that people: that they had the largest measure of prosperity when they were most mindful of their duty to their covenant God. We have seen that it was in pursuance of a plan long cherished, and in fulfilment of a vow long before made, that the king had now found a settled habitation for the ark of God. And now that this much is accomplished, the king is desirous of going yet further. The most important enterprises of our lives are not, perhaps, in most cases, the result of plans deliberately and fully weighed at the outset, but we set out with smaller matters and are gradually led on to larger, beyond all we had designed. This is indeed the case with what men accomplish, both of evil and of good. In evil, men think not of going so far, but the mind becomes reconciled to thoughts which at first awaken fear and horror, and before he is aware of his progress many a sinner is hopelessly entangled, and perhaps in the very sins which once his soul loathed. In good, an earnest heart devises more and more liberal things, finds new opportunities opening up beyond what he had contemplated, and easily effects results which, with less experience, he would have thought visionary. Successful enterprise encourages more comprehensive plans and more extended efforts. The evident smile of Providence upon David's rebuilding of the tabernacle suggests that it is his duty and his privilege to promote yet more the honour of religion, and a pious heart prompts him to care at least as much for an abode for the ark as for a dwelling for himself.

Hitherto the Israelites had been an agricultural people, and had paid but little attention to art and science. Of late, however, David had been led to cultivate friendly relations with the neighbouring city of Tyre. This celebrated city of antiquity was already renowned for its arts and commerce, and it was greatly in the interest of that people to cultivate friendly intercourse with the Israelites. Not only is the large commerce of any city best promoted by the maintenance of peace, but a seaport without much adjoining territory would wish to draw supplies from the inland States that lay near it. So we find that both David and Solomon kept up a brisk trade with the kings of Tyre. On the one hand, the Tyrians furnished timber and other building materials and workmen, and the Israelites paid them back in the produce of the country, especially in olive oil and wheat. Such was Solomon's agreement with Hiram. 1 Kings v. 10, 11.

David by the aid of the Syrians had now built for himself a palace of the cedars of Lebanon. But the ark of God dwelt still in the tabernacle. We can scarcely think it was the same built by Moses, which would now be over four hundred years old, but it was probably made according to the same directions given to Moses. Such an arrangement was suited to the wandering condition of the tribes and of the ark, but now it gave way to a more permanent abode. David first mentions this matter to the prophet Nathan, and he, highly pleased with the thought, supposes that it would be according to the divine will, and encourages him to go forward. But we learn in this instance that the inspiration of the ancient prophets was not a continual but an occasional and official influence resting upon them. As the apostles of Christ appear to have put forth miraculous powers only on certain occasions, so here we find Nathan giving utterance to sentiments which he is afterward bidden to recall. Doubtless the prophet thought that the proposition of David was one so plainly for the honour of religion that he might readily encourage him to go forward. Yet he was mistaken in the case. Let us be jealous even of the plans we form to do good, that they may lawfully be made to accord with that written Word which is our sole and perfect rule. In not a few things men decide according to their own ideas of what may please God, and yet he is pleased only when we seek direction from him.

That same night came the word of the Lord to Nathan declaring that David should not be allowed to build the house he proposed for the worship of God. But the refusal is one that gives due credit to the upright and pious nature of the king, and it is not based upon the impropriety of the thing itself which he proposed. It arises from the incongruity that appears between the usual engagements of David as a man of war and the erection of a temple in honour of God. It is one thing to justify the terrible work of war; this we may sometimes do. It is quite another thing to look upon the engagements of war as desirable in themselves, or as tending by any legitimate influence to promote the honour of God or the good of man. Results of the most desirable character have been secured to men by the violence of war, but it is deeply to be regretted that the same results could not be reached by better means. War and fighting come of men's lusts. There is great wrong somewhere whenever they occur—perhaps usually on both sides—and the burden of war is heavy, and the mischiefs of war are great, and the crimes springing from it are numerous, even in cases where we most fully justify its undertaking and most largely rejoice in that which it accomplishes. War is a temporary return to barbarism, though it is often the deep ploughshare that breaks up the land in preparation for a valuable harvest. David's wars were justifiable. He found the tribes in a wretched and feeble condition, on every hand exposed to insult from the nations around, and scarcely enjoying a few years of relief from time to time, purchased rather through their poverty, which presented few inducements to tempt an invader, than through their strength, that held cupidity in check. From this condition of division and weakness and poverty, the tribes of Israel, ruled by the wise and strong hand of David, soon rose to prosperity and strength. No fault is found with David for these patriotic efforts. They were the noble discharge of his duty. And yet his was an undesirable task. He must needs be a man of blood if he would raise his people from the dust. True, indeed, the trade of war was not his chosen avocation in preference to other paths of honour and duty. The stirring trumpet was less his choice than the devotional strains of the soothing harp. In the camp he mourned that he was exiled from the courts of the Lord; and through all the clash of warfare he looked anxiously forward to the time when the ark of God should have a settled abode in the land. Yet with all these vindicating thoughts the engagements of David were not consonant with the service of a holy God; therefore he must not build the temple, the abode of peace. God said to him, " Thou shalt not build an house for my name, because thou hast been a man of war and hast shed blood." 1 Chron. xxviii. 3.

It is an obvious reflection here that the piety of David appears more eminent from these very circumstances. That amidst so many temptations he kept his straightforward course—that he could maintain his devotional spirit while surrounded by so many uncongenial things, excites our admiration. Yet the formation and development of the human character present many curious problems, and in considering these things carefully we must adjust and reconcile circumstances of various tendency. The best characters are seldom formed without the stern mingling in their experience of adverse influences. We might think that the best method of making a scholar is to place a lad at his books from an early age, and let him pass upward through the best schools and under the influence of the most thorough teachers; and so have been furnished some of the most profound scholars of the world, and the advantages of books and schools and wise teachers no man should willingly forego who desires a cultivated mind. And yet some of the most profound thinkers of the world, some men who have exerted wise and beneficent influences, have reached their eminence of fame and strength without these early advantages. In view of this, there are many who undervalue a training in schools, and contend that self-education is the only way in which to make a man. The truth seems rather to be this—that no man ever can be a scholar without self-education. The best schools and the best teachers will waste their advantages where the scholars are dunces or sluggards. Many an energetic man, without such advantages, will push his way upward to knowledge and influence, yet this very man is not the one to despise the advantages he would gladly have used if he had but possessed them; and no one can say how much easier his toils would have been or how much higher his position with these aids. Every man that is ever educated must educate himself, must learn to exercise the powers of his own mind—for this is education—and must master knowledge by his own thinking. Every man that rises in the world must rise by his own exertions, or, if providential circumstances put him forward among men in an elevated and influential position, he must maintain it by the propriety of his own conduct there. No position can be maintained respectably, no claims will be allowed by the gazing world, unless they deserve to be. The true problem for us to solve is to mingle in just proportions, and wisely adapt to our education, the advantages and the disadvantages of study, the prosperous and the adverse influences. We may learn a lesson from the flying of a boy's kite. The wind that drives it from him is needful to make it rise, yet it would not ride in the air without the string which he holds in his hand. The two forces are necessary to success, and when they are nicely balanced the sport is complete. Too much stress upon the kite will break the string; too much force used upon the string will draw down the kite. Wise education, intellectual or moral, is the nice balancing of forces. The scholar must have difficulties to overcome which will call forth his powers; yet if the obstacles are too great for his strength, he will become discouraged. Teach men so plainly that they do not need to think, and you have overshot the mark; yet teachings incomprehensible are an error in the other extreme. The education of no soldier, of no mechanic, of no engineer is complete without a practical experience of the rough and hard work that belongs to their respective occupations. The wise mingling of theory and practice, of study in the house and of conflict in the field, of leading them by the hand and of teaching them to go alone, is needful to their successful training. The deep foundation of David's piety was laid in his father's family and in the seclusion of shepherd-life on the plains of Bethlehem, and the trials of a busy life afterward but seemed to complete a training thus carefully begun. Yet how many, in like circumstances with David, would have failed in his severe trials! If many rise in spite of serious obstacles, many also fail in spite of great advantages; and success is never achieved except by those who earnestly contend for it. Advantages help an earnest man to secure larger success, but he deserves praise who successfully contends with the most adverse circumstances. It is greatly to the credit of David that, in the weariness of exile and in the stern ferocity of a warlike life, he still maintained his religious views and his pious character.

And though it is true that now he was forbidden to build the house for God, it is also true that the denial of his desire affords no evidence of the divine displeasure.

That God was well pleased with the desire of David to build him a temple is plain from the message borne to him by the prophet Nathan, assuring him of the establishment of his throne and family for ever. From the tenor of David's reply we may believe that he understood the promises of God to refer to the establishment of his family through the coming Messiah. It is not easy to determine how far forward some of these ancient believers were allowed to look, and how much they really comprehended of the coming Redeemer. David humbly confesses that his house was not known in Israel, yet God had exalted him and had spoken of his family for a great time to come. From this time forward, doubtless, it was understood that through David the Messiah was to descend.

Several important wars are recorded after this, but we will not tarry to speak much of them. His wars with the various nations around were successfully carried on by the energy and skill of Joab, and the boundaries of the kingdom were enlarged according to the promises made to Abraham (Gen. xv. 18), from the Euphrates to the Mediterranean Sea and from Lebanon to the Arabian Gulf. Some of the victories were splendid indeed, and some were stained with cruelty toward the conquered. All wars are cruel, but some, from the spirit of the age or people where they occur, and some from the spirit of retaliation, are peculiarly marked with severities. We learn from other passages of the Scriptures that some of Joab's severities, at least, were retaliatory for some of the worst outrages committed upon the Israelites. (See Amos i. 3, 13.) The names of the nations thus contended with successfully, and some of them laid under tribute, show the growing power of the kingdom. An insult shortly after this offered to David's ambassadors gave rise to a new war with a people hitherto friendly, and against them and their allies David was still successful. This war may give us a large idea of David's resources. The Ammonites paid an immense amount of money to secure the aid of the Syrians with a large force of chariots. With great skill Joab prevented the union of the allied armies, and beat the larger while his brother attacked and routed the less formidable portion. The Syrians, chagrined at this defeat, assembled another army and made an invasion which David met in person, and the enemy was again overthrown with the loss of his commanding officer and nearly fifty thousand men. This decisive victory forced them to make a peace in which the interests of their allies were disregarded, and the Ammonites were left to bear the weight of a war provoked by their own folly, and made ruinous by their own acts of cruelty.

David now stands before us on the highest point of his earthly greatness. We shall hear of him next a sinner against God and a rebel against his own peace. "Call no man happy until the day of his death," said one of the ancient wise men. But we will only so far anticipate the sad history of his fall as to remind ourselves of our need of watching and prayerfulness lest we enter into temptation. Let us learn our weakness. We are safe only when we trust in God, keep our hearts with diligence, avoid temptation and humbly keep his ways. Even Christians are not safe from sin if they flee not from temptation. God made a covenant with David, yet how soon he falls! Watch and pray. But well may they fear who have entered into no covenant with the Lord. If God's friends may fall into sin, his enemies may fall into perdition.

It is interesting to notice that the immense spoils won by David in his wars were dedicated to the erection of the future temple, and they constituted no inconsiderable portion of the resources which enabled Solomon to erect so magnificent a house. The expenditure of modern wars is so immense that perhaps no war is ever carried on now with pecuniary profit to the conqueror.

## CHAPTER XII.

### *THE LATTER WAYS OF DAVID.*

LET us now stay a little season to make a brief review which will revive our recollection of the earlier scenes of David's history, before we pass on to the latter and more painful portion of his life. In a later book of the history it is said that the Lord was with Jehoshaphat because he walked in the first ways of his father David—referring to one of David's descendants, a good and a great king of Judah, and commending his character. We design now simply to take notice of the contrast that is thus implied between the earlier and the later periods of David's life. We are pained to read this implication against the good king's character, and especially we lament the evil that chiefly caused the change. We have many reasons for loving this sweet Psalmist of Israel. In his language we have addressed our praises to God; with him we have longed for access to the courts of the Lord; with him we have lifted our eyes to the hills of our help. We have clothed the burdened petitions of our hearts in the humble words of his penitence; we have wept in the sympathy of his mourning spirit with our sorrows; we have followed his Shepherd, Jehovah Jesus, in the green pastures beside the quiet waters; we have longed for the guidance and protection of his rod and staff in the shaded valley of the deep-rolling Jordan. We love the sweet singer of Israel; we lament that there should be any sad change in the course of his upright history; and yet we feel bound to investigate the matters of contrast which are suggested between his earlier and his later days.

We have seen the origin of David. We found him first upon the sacred page a shepherd boy; kingly neither in his appearance nor in his stature; held in low esteem by his brethren, and even by his father, yet approved by the Lord, who searcheth the heart, and preferred before his brethren for the anointing oil of the venerable prophet.

These first days of David we have characterized as times of serious reflection and devotion, and they may remind us how the young should improve their early favourable opportunities for pious thought. It is true, indeed, there are no situations and no periods of life when a pious mind may not find some opportunities to enjoy religious privileges and to strengthen pious feelings. The worship of God cannot be shut out from a religious mind by external persecutions; it will not be forgotten amidst the heaviest pressure of other duties, and its support is most needed in the severest temptations. The busiest life will yet afford the earnest believer its stated occasions for serious meditation and prayer. In the midst of a heathen court, burdened with the cares of a mighty empire and embarrassed by the interested intrigues of unscrupulous foes, Daniel neglected not, three times a day, his devotions before God. A mind truly engaged to serve God will find its time to do so. Yet favourable opportunities are of great value to form devotional habits and to give enjoyment in devotional duties. It is very plain that the earlier opportunities of life are generally less disturbed by care, and that the occupations of some men afford times and advantages peculiarly favourable for serious thought. Thus favourably situated was David during his life as a shepherd. Alone for days, and sometimes for sleepless nights, on the plains of Bethlehem, his flocks feeding or reposing around him, his harp by his side and perhaps the inspired roll of Israel's covenant—the record of God's loving kindness—in his hand, David had abundant time and occasion for serious devotion—for meditation upon the works and word of God. These were the days of David's early and advancing piety—of happy enjoyment, of glowing love, of simple dependence, of modest humility. These were his duties when he learned to strike so sweetly the chords of his soothing harp; these were times of delight to his soul as he meditated in the night-watches. In those early avocations he learned that child-like dependence upon God which first strengthened the shepherd's arm against the lion and the bear to rescue the lambs of his flock, and next sent the stripling forth with sling and stone against the proud giant of Gath who dared to defy the armies of the living God.

We have also followed David in his first ways beyond the shepherd's lowly place. We have seen him a rising military leader in the camp of Israel, the object of the people's pride and affection, of the king's malice and jealousy. We have found him still prudent, meek and faithful; and the record still is, "David behaved himself wisely in all his ways, and the Lord was with him." We see the evidences of grace in his affectionate attachment to his friend Jonathan. We have here a model of pious friendship; and let those who would study the self-sacrificing principles of a true attachment observe the friendship of those two young noblemen of Israel's ancient times. The display of disinterested feeling seems greater on the part of the son of Saul, but the son of Jesse exhibits an amiability of temper, a strength of character, a nobleness of purpose and a settled piety well justifying the love of Jonathan. To the credit of David, he never forgot his attachment to his early friend. He mourned in pathetic strains his premature death, and maintained through life the only surviving child of Jonathan.

We have walked on yet farther in these first

ways of David. We have followed him amidst the persecutions of Saul, and have seen him pursued from place to place, "as a partridge upon the mountains." We have had occasion to censure him for sins, alas! too common in the age to which he belonged; yet we have had reason also to rejoice that in the trials so severe he maintained so much of the spirit of piety. The better, indeed, we understand the entire circumstances, the better will we appreciate the general uprightness of his conduct, notwithstanding his delinquencies. This was a period of severe affliction. Let the aggravations of Saul's station, conduct and character, be considered in contrast with the station occupied by the son of Jesse and the line of conduct he pursued. Saul had every reason to be grateful to one who had so signally delivered his kingdom, but his heart became bitter through that very triumph and the rejoicing of a grateful people on account of it. The next day after Goliath's death he aimed a javelin with his royal hand at Israel's champion; he proposed to David an alliance by marriage, but designed a snare for his destruction. He endeavoured to stir up his son and his servants against the husband of his daughter; again he aimed a dart at his life; at a midnight hour he sent to apprehend him in his bed; when he escaped he sent messengers after him, and in his impatient rage so far forgot his royal dignity as to proceed in person after the fugitive; in his anger he slew eighty-five of the

Lord's priests and massacred a whole city because one man had innocently, and out of regard to the king's own honour, furnished food and arms to the flying David. He went forth with his armies to encamp through several campaigns, in the mountains and in the wilderness, against a faithful servant, an affectionate son-in-law. But during all this time we have seen in David an admirable spirit of loyalty, of piety and of forbearance toward Saul. When he avoided the javelin of the king; when he escaped from his bed; when his wife was given to another husband; when he was forced into a mournful exile from the altars of God, and even compelled to act the madman among the Philistines; when he was burdened by the injustice of all these things; when his soul was burning as it must have burned with indignation for the ruthless massacre of the consecrated priests,—still the pious David remembered to whom vengeance belonged. When Saul was in his power in the cave, though his followers urged him to kill him, yet his eye spared him; when he visited him in his camp at midnight, and stood over the couch of his sleeping enemy, still he would not strike him. He was ready at any moment for a reconciliation with Saul—ready to lift his hand for a contest with Israel's enemies. With a forgiving spirit that is above all praise he not only slew the man who boasted of slaying the king, but he wept over the grave of Saul and joined his name with the brave and pious

Jonathan. But the bare mention of circumstances as we have noticed them does not bring the whole case before us. We are to remember that Saul for his unworthiness and wickedness deserved to die; that all this time he was a king actually rejected of God; that David was the favourite of the people, and that long before this the prophet Samuel by divine direction had anointed him for the throne; and then let us better appreciate the piety of David's first ways, and his complete loyalty to his rejected sovereign. It has been alleged by some that when the prophet Elisha predicted to Hazael that he would one day wear the crown of Syria, he suggested to him a temptation that cost the life of his lord. But the wickedness of Hazael's heart, even if this was so, stands in strong contrast with the piety of David. David, too, had the promise of a crown; God himself had chosen him, and God's prophet had poured upon him the holy oil of anointing; but notwithstanding the promise and the anointing, notwithstanding his deep personal and unprovoked injuries and provocations, notwithstanding the worthlessness of Saul and his actual rejection—when Saul was in his power, when he could so plausibly plead that he had smitten him in self-defence—still he would not kill him, he would not put forth his hand against the Lord's anointed; and he refused to touch the crown that was to be his until the Lord God himself, who had promised it to him, should, by his own providence, by his own means and in his own time, place it upon his brow.

These are a part of the first ways of David as we have heretofore traced them. They exhibit in him amiable, excellent and pious traits of character. Here we see humility and dignity; forbearance and forgiveness amidst unprovoked injuries and insults; good returned for evil; patriotism in exile; devotion when afar from the sanctuary; patience and submission to the slow movings of Divine Providence; and, at the foundation of all, a firm, intelligent, steadfast faith in God. By faith in God's promises David knew that his crown and life were safe.

But after the brief review of David's earlier days, we have come again to that portion of his history which forms the turning-point between these and the latter time of his life. The inspired historian has hinted to us that the first period of his life is commendable before the latter; and now we turn the leaf of history that divides the record of the first from the last days of David the king, and how is the page blotted with the stains of crime and bedewed and blistered with the tears of penitential remorse! We see David here the king of God's Israel; the tribes are all united around one throne; the flourishing capital stands in the heart of the nation; he is mighty in the power of his arms and strong in the affections of his people; his enemies are cut off; his name is enrolled among the great ones of the earth, and he dwells in a palace of cedars. From the height of his honours he descends to the most lamentable depths of shame. Shall we need to dwell upon the particulars—as full of grief and sorrow as they are of shame and disgrace? Well known is the history of his departure from the paths of rectitude; and it is easy to discern how aggravated was his iniquity in every deliberative, progressive step. We may take up, and with more poignant sorrow, the language of his lamentation on Gilboa: "How are the mighty fallen!" What a lesson of human depravity—how instructive in the deceitful, ensnaring, advancing nature of sin—does the case of David afford! Truly, "lust, when it is conceived, bringeth forth sin; and sin, when it is finished, bringeth forth death." We need not go over the events as they are here recorded, for there are things of which it is a shame to speak, and the reproof of them even is difficult. But with emotions of grief and shame, and for deep and serious profit, it is well worth our while to trace the steps of his transgression, to mark the slighter beginnings, the insidious advances, the increasing power and the awful results of sin. David fell, as our first mother fell before him, by looking upon transgression. He shows here none of the piety of his days of shepherd-life or the times of his persecution by Saul. Mark the steps of sin. First, lust; then, adultery; then, a plot of deliberate dissimulation; and this failing to impose upon the man he had injured, he pursues still his scheme of wickedness, even to the death of a brave and faithful servant. One would think that there were circumstances here to repress and restrain the wickedness of David. This man, Uriah, was a Hittite. He was a converted heathen who had sought refuge from the pollutions of the Gentile world in the privileges and purity of God's chosen people; he is numbered among the mighty men of David's army (2 Sam. xxiii. 39); his pious feelings were plainly shown when called by the king to Jerusalem; and they did not cease to control him even when he was made drunk by the king's deceitful courtesy. Perhaps the conduct of Uriah did pierce the guilty conscience of David, but depravity was master in that heart now, and every obstacle to his desires seemed but to provoke him to more heinous sin. He made Uriah the bearer of a treacherous letter against his own life; he made the unscrupulous Joab, who well understood the sin of David, and was ready to draw from it his own advantages, the agent of his murderous plan; he was satisfied only when this sagacious accomplice announced, with fiendish triumph at seeing David now brought down to his own level, that this brave, faithful and pious officer had been left to perish by the hand of the enemy; he impiously dared to ascribe his death, through the casualties of war, to the providence of God; and hardly had the earth drunk up Uriah's blood and cried to God for vengeance, before he took as his wife the guilty woman whose husband he had murdered. And how sad indeed is the contrast between the first and the last ways of David, when we must add that, with all this guilt, he kept silent for weeks and months! God was displeased, but David was not penitent.

Let no reproach be cast upon the word of God that it contains a record like this. If such conduct was here approved, then, indeed, would reproach, deep and indelible, be justly laid here. But no human language can aggravate more the exceeding guilt of David than the forcible and pathetic words of divine dictation in the parable of Nathan, the prophet. It calls up before the guilty king his own case, that he may unconsciously pass judgment upon himself. It reminds him that beyond his deserving, the goodness of God had exalted him from a lowly estate to the most eminent honours of earth, that he had given him everything he could reasonably desire, and that in the path of duty and holiness he was willing to grant him yet larger blessings. Yet he had indulged this guilty passion, and had followed it out to those shocking consequences, at the expense of honour, of kingly duty, of gratitude and of conscience. Here is the simple record:

"But the thing that David had done had displeased the Lord. And the Lord sent Nathan unto David. And he came unto him and said unto him: There were two men in one city; the one rich and the other poor. The rich man had exceeding many flocks and herds, but the poor man had nothing save *one little ewe lamb*, which he had bought and nourished up; and it grew up together with him and with his children; it did eat of his own meat and drink of his own cup, and lay in his bosom and was unto him as a daughter. And there came a traveller unto the rich man, and he spared to take of his own flock and of his own herd to dress for the wayfaring man that was come unto him; but took the poor man's lamb and dressed it for the man that was come to him." 2 Sam. xi. 27; xii. 1, 4.

Well might David pronounce this judgment upon such wickedness, even his own—*He had* NO PITY.

In this flagitious conduct of David we discern the workings of sense, not of faith; we see not the new man, but he carnal nature; not grace, but sin triumphant. Yet we are not to suppose that all this was without consciousness of guilt, without strugglings of conscience, without feelings of remorse. He concealed his feelings during this season of dreadful impenitence, but when afterward brought to the confession of them, he acknowledges his constant unhappiness; that he was restless and feverish in his guilt, and that day and night the heavy hand of God seemed pressing him to the dust. See Psalms xxxii., xxxix. These inward struggles, so distressing, yet so resolutely repressed, do but aggravate his sin. If ever a man walked in any path of evil with his eyes wide open, knowing whither his steps tended, so did David walk when he forsook his first ways to walk in the broad road of deliberate and flagrant transgression.

We have thus entered upon the contrast suggested by the inspired writer at a later period, between the first ways of David and this great sin of a later time. But this contrast would not be full should we fail to anticipate to some degree the following history, and show in his subsequent life some of the consequences of his guilt.

God freely forgives the penitent. "Whoso confesseth and forsaketh his sins shall find mercy," is the substance of the gracious promises from the beginning of the Church of God. Yet it is not uncommon for men to misunderstand the bearing of God's forgiveness upon their present character and their subsequent experience. It becomes us, therefore, to ponder the true teachings of God's holy Word, and to compare them with their explanation in the actual dealings of his grace and his providence, that we may learn the real influence of forgiveness under the covenant of redemption. We are told in express terms that the repenting sinner is forgiven and reconciled to God; that his sins are remembered no more against him; that "there is therefore now no condemnation to them that are in Christ Jesus;" and that the eternal life of the penitent is sure. Yet it is of supreme importance that a sin-forgiving God should be still seen abhorring iniquity; and we learn from abundant teachings, both in the Bible and out of it, that the pardon of sin yet leaves upon the sinner many evil results of sin, and does not interfere with the ordinary operations of God's providential laws. In no just sense does grace make void the law. We do not regard these results, under the covenant of grace, as penal judgments, yet we see they come even upon a forgiven offender. If they come now as a condemnatory sentence, this would be in conflict with the granted pardon. But they come as natural results of a violated law, which, for reasons of infinite wisdom, the justification of the sinner does not interfere to prevent. See the teachings of the Scripture on this interesting topic. We are told of the wicked king Manasseh that the Lord heard his prayer, and answered his penitence by forgiveness, and restored him to his kingdom; and Manasseh is doubtless now a trophy of redeeming grace before the throne of the Lamb. Yet many mischiefs remained in his kingdom notwithstanding his forgiveness; and long after his death we find in the inspired record this solemn teaching: "He filled Jerusalem with innocent blood, which the Lord would not pardon." 2 Kings xxiv. 4. This is an impressive warning that the awful consequences of sin are not stayed by the transgressor's sorrow. And the same lesson is taught us on every hand by the providence of God. The drunkard can by repentance improve the future, but no reformation can repair the past mischiefs of life. The murderer cannot by any repentance bring back to life the victim of his violence. These may personally become interested in the blessings of salvation, but the terms of the covenant of redemption refer chiefly to spiritual advantage, and reach not so far as to remove those natural consequences of their sins in this life

See how these principles are illustrated in the case of David. Immediately upon his candid and humble confession of his iniquity the reproving prophet assured him, "The Lord also hath put away thy sin." The pardon was free upon the repentance. But how much remained behind of serious evil to David's heart and David's house! That pardon had no efficacy to wipe away the reproach he had brought upon religion; it could not recall his sin; it gave not purity to Bathsheba nor life to Uriah. And we may well consider the long catalogue of sorrows which this sin brought upon him in his after history, to vindicate the divine abhorrence of sin, and to forbid that man should ever venture upon transgression because pardoning grace abounds. The death of the child that was born to him; the incestuous violation of his daughter Tamar by her brother Amnon; the murder of that son by another son for it; the treason and incest and death of Absalom; the rebellion of Sheba; the terrible pestilence that destroyed no less than seventy thousand of his people; the treason and subsequent death of Adonijah,—all these evils sprang up in his house and in his kingdom, and all these saddened and embittered the latter days of David as a man and as a monarch, as a husband and as a father.

And corresponding with these sore chastisements upon his lamentable sin, we think we can discern an evident difference between the earlier and the later Psalms of the royal singer. We may regard the Psalms as recording his religious experience, and as therefore exhibiting his feelings at the time when each was penned. We think in his elder days there are fewer protestations of sincerity, a growing acquaintance with the corruptions of his heart, and deeper and more humble confessions of indwelling sin. We contrast especially the Psalm penned when he was delivered from the hand of all his enemies and from the hand of Saul,* and the Psalms which record his repentance for this later sin. The earlier Psalm says: "I have kept the ways of the Lord, and have not wickedly departed from my God, for all his judgments were before me; and I did not put away his statutes from me: I was also upright before him, and I kept myself from mine iniquity. Therefore hath the Lord

* 2 Sam. vii. 1 may justly be thought to fix the date of Psalm xviii. Its record (2 Sam. xxii.) is no disproof of this. "All his enemies," occurs in both places.

recompensed me according to my righteousness; according to the cleanness of my hands in his eyesight." Ps. xviii. 21–24. But hear his later complaints: "When I kept silence my bones waxed old through my roaring all the day long: for day and night thy hand was heavy upon me; my moisture was turned into the drought of summer." Ps. xxxii. 3, 4. "O Lord, rebuke me not in thy wrath, neither chasten me in thy hot displeasure. There is no soundness in my flesh because of thine anger. I am troubled; I am bowed down greatly; I go mourning all the day long." Ps. xxxviii. 1, 3, 6. "Wash me thoroughly from mine iniquity and cleanse me from my sin, for I acknowledge my transgression and my sin is ever before me." Ps. li. 2, 3. And hear the pitiable complaint of the heartbroken old man: "Cast me not off in the time of old age. O God, be not far from me. Now also, when I am old and gray-headed, O God, forsake me not." Ps. lxxi. 9, 12, 18.

But the thoughts that have now engaged our attention may conclude with some further practical reflections:

1st. We may learn from the subject thus presented that it is impossible for us to foresee our temptations in life, or to know their influence upon us.

Every age, each sex, every condition in life has its peculiar temptations. The temptations of childhood differ from the temptations of youth and manhood, and these from the temptations of age. Poverty and riches, station and subordination, prosperity and affliction, have their respective trials, and a change from one to the other presents new scenes, new companions, new tests of principle. In the plain paths of poverty you may walk safely, but on the giddy heights of wealth your pride may have a fall. In the humble valley of private life you may be contented, useful and safe; but upon the elevated places of official dignity you may find occasions of murmuring and sin. The grand truth to be impressed upon our minds, to awaken our constant watchfulness, to deepen our constant humility, to call forth our ardent prayers, is the truth of our deep depravity. "The heart is deceitful above all things and desperately wicked." "He that trusteth to his own heart is a fool." However sadly we may judge, he is not a wise man who judges harshly of David. However sad we may feel at the tidings of human guilt every day brought to our ears, let us neither be astonished nor censorious. Learn from these things that deep depravity of nature that we also share. You or I might do things like these unsustained by divine grace and under plausible and deceitful temptations. This is the concurrent testimony of those who best know their own hearts—who have most closely watched its tendencies and its depravity. Watch and pray lest ye enter into temptation. Watch against the beginnings of evil, for no one can tell how long it may increase. Pray earnestly for guiding and restraining grace. But for God's restraining mercy your sins might now be greater in number and more aggravated in character than they are. Lean constantly upon God. Learn your weakness, and keep yourself humble by reflecting that in the changes of life before you there may be many distressing temptations which now you do not dream of. Every morning we go forth to unknown duties and unexpected events; and every morning should bear witness to one earnest prayer, in His language who knew so well what our petitions should ask: "*Lead us not into temptation.*"

2d. The peculiar form of our present meditations suggests this inquiry: Are there not some of us who do not live so near to God as once we did!

It may be true with many of us that our first ways have been our best ways. This is so with every unconverted man. The tendency of sin is to grow worse, to get stronger power over the soul, and to harden the heart to this increase. Some of you are not so easily impressed by solemn truth as once you were; your desires for good are feebler, and your salvation is less likely the longer you live unreconciled to God. But perhaps the lamentation may suit professedly pious men. Such cannot indeed truly say, if they are truly converted, that they have not improved upon their days of impenitence. But some mourn for the earlier days of their religious experience. They say, "We are farther from God now than we have been; farther from him in sweet enjoyment, in lively affection, in zealous obedience. We mourn with Job, "Oh that I were as in months past!" xxix. 2. True, indeed, many a Christian can soberly decide that his later days are days of clearer knowledge, of more intelligent faith and firmer and more decided principle. Yet many look back and with just reason deplore the difference between the present and the past. Because many "have left their first love" we see feeble evidences of zeal and affection and faith. We hear lamentations of coldness and desertion. The hymn of the melancholy poet is a favourite known by rote by almost every Christian—

"Oh for a closer walk with God."

Is it not evidence against our piety that it suits us so often to sing,

"Where is the blessedness I knew
When first I saw the Lord?"

Let it not be said, as explaining these things, that it is natural for Christians to decline from their first love. Such a charge is libellous to the gospel. In strength of principle, in zeal and knowledge, in love and communion, in obedience and faith, we ought ever to advance. Our faith should grow brighter and brighter. Our history should fulfil the petitions so often appropriately offered for those that are advancing in life—"May the last days be the best days!" Grace ought to grow stronger and stronger, and nature weaker and weaker. "I know thy works and charity and service and faith, and thy patience and thy works, and *the last to be more than the first*," said the Lord to the Church at Thyatira. Rev. ii. 19. Christian brethren! our motives to zeal and love and obedience are every day stronger than ever, and it is sinful to decline from the faith. If you judge that you are declining, beware lest a day of temptation draw near; lest your life be embittered like David's; lest you bring reproach upon religion. Awake, thou that sleepest. Our salvation is nearer than when we believed. Let us take up the resolution which the prophet predicts for Zion: "I will go and return to my first husband, for then it was better for me than it is now."

And may the Lord allure his people and speak comfortably to them, and give them a song of hope and cause them to sing as in the days of youth.

Finally: "If the righteous scarcely be saved, where shall the ungodly and the sinner appear?" If good men suffer and decline thus; if their remaining corruptions sometimes overwhelm them in evil, what may be the just apprehensions of unconverted men? Impenitent sinner! your first ways were better than the present. I do not know how far you may go, neither can you foretell. You have done already things you never intended to do, and you may do more and worse. You are progressing in apostasy from God. Your habits of sin are perhaps slowly and imperceptibly but surely becoming inveterate. You are adding sin to sin, and every day you have increasing reason to fear that iniquity will be your ruin. You may flatter yourself that this can never be, but many a flatterer has fallen beyond his fears. You may say with Hazael, "Is thy servant a dog?" but you had better pray, "Keep back thy servant from presumptuous sins." Neglect not these warnings of God's holy word upon the presumptuous confidence that they do not suit your case. But now—ere you go forward to the unknown temptations of your future days; before you are deeply and hopelessly entangled in the snares of sin; before God withdraws his mercy—even now, repent and believe. Acknowledge your sinfulness, flee to the pardoning blood of Jesus, rely upon the restraining, reclaiming and supporting grace of God, and go forth to encounter the trials, the temptations, the duties of life in his fear. We are safe in duty, we are safe in temptation, only when we rely upon his grace and obey his commands. He promises his aid to those that trust in him. As your days are, so shall your strength be. God is faithful to make a way to escape from the temptation. So believing and so living, your last ways shall be your best ways, your last days your best days, and a final entrance shall be abundantly ministered to you into the everlasting kingdom of our Lord and Saviour Jesus Christ.

## CHAPTER XIII.

### *THE SIN AND PENITENCE OF DAVID.*

THE fifty-first Psalm is the most remarkable of the PENITENTIAL PSALMS (vi., xxxii., xxxviii., li., lxxvii., cii., cxxx., cxliii.). Penitent hearts have pondered its words, penitent lips have repeated them, and any man who truly sympathizes with its teachings is ready to recognize every demand of God's law, and thankful for every merciful provision of the gospel. To place together the history and the Psalm is to interpret these humble confessions of sin by the occasion that called them forth, and we understand the penitence in the history of the transgression.

We have here a lamentable period of the life of David, but one eminently profitable. In all ages since, David's great transgression has filled the hearts of the friends and the foes of piety with various emotions of reproach and grief; and we can easily judge that the sensation produced throughout the kingdom of David was very great when facts like these became known; especially among the true-hearted lovers of God it was like the panic in a frightened army when a standard-bearer falls, or when in the height of successful battle the white plume of a beloved leader is trampled in the dust. The parties concerned were too prominent and too well known, the guilt of the chief actor was too inexcusable and too gross, the evils too nearly concerned the well-being of society, to allow these events to occur without excitement. Even wicked men, who might do such deeds, start back from them as done by others, and especially as done by those who have been esteemed for their virtues. This serious offence was the first public cause of reproach against David. Hitherto his public career had been wise and exemplary; the kingdom had been only prosperous under him; his people were warmly attached to him; and his character for uprightness was well established. Such a fall from such an elevation was shocking and widely seen; the surprising conduct of no man in the nation would awaken more public attention. He was the king; he sat upon the throne because he feared God, after Saul had been rejected for rebellion; he was the sweet singer of Israel; he was beloved by the righteous; he was even respected by the wicked. The other parties were not insignificant. Uriah was one of the mighty men in the army—a heathen by birth, but a servant of the true God by conversion and upon principle; an honourable and upright man; and his dwelling in Jerusalem, so near the palace of the king, justifies us in supposing that he held a social position of great respectability. Bathsheba, too, the lamb that lay in this poor man's bosom, was allied to well-known families in Israel. She was the daughter of Eliam, one of David's mighty men, and the granddaughter of Ahithophel, one of David's chief counsellors—a man held in the highest reputation for ability and wisdom; and this injury to his family perhaps alienated him from the throne, and made him a chief conspirator with Absalom to avenge his wrong against the king. 2 Sam. xi. 3; xxiii. 34.

These statements bring the case sufficiently before us, and enable us to understand that this enormous iniquity awakened public attention in Israel. Such a secret easily spreads. Every man heard of it, thought upon it, commented upon it. It was the theme of public and private conversation, and it influenced each person in keeping with his own character. We may speak of these things because evidently God, in his holy providence and upon the pages of his holy word, has taken no pains to conceal this sin of his servant. On the contrary, he has taken effectual measures to publish it. David did this thing in secret, but God brought it out before Israel and before the sun. We may be amazed and troubled at so sad a fall to such a man; our views may not be sufficiently clear to enable us in all points to vindicate the providence of God; we may judge that far more evil than good would result from such a case; yet we can scarcely think that for nothing God has made this matter so prominent in the Bible and in the history of the Church. But even when these strange ways of Providence seem too deep for us, there are weighty considerations to reconcile us to such dispensations, painful as they are. Take together the history and the Psalm, and we may see God's glory and man's good even in these dark scenes. Few pages of all ancient records can we less afford to lose than those which pertain to David's darkest sin. Many a man's Bible opens at the fifty-first Psalm more readily than anywhere else; many a believer knows its words by heart and thoroughly wishes he felt its spirit more; many a humbled soul would less easily part with this Psalm than with all the uninspired utterances of penitent feeling put together. Taking this whole matter, indeed, as teaching us of man's sin and of the principles of the divine rule, especially for the pardon of the guilty, it may be very well questioned whether any event in the history of our race, between the fall in Eden and the cross on Calvary, is more worthy of our thoughts than this. The sin of David has been the occasion of preaching the gospel to thousands in his own and in succeeding ages, and the same results that the gospel usually produces have sprung forth, in a remarkable degree, from this great crime.

We have seen among the wonderful creations of human skill some of those remarkable pictures where the background is almost pure blackness, and from the dark starts forth a single figure, which concentrates all the light of the painting upon itself—whose bold relief is owing to the gloom around it, and whose striking beauty is all the more admired from its contrast with everything else in the picture. Such a moral picture have we here. We palliate nothing of David's iniquity. We would not spoil the figure in relief by lighter shading around or behind it. Let the greatness of his wrong be urged; its baseness in itself; its dangers to society; its reproach upon religion and upon God; its tendency to harden the hearts of sinful men; and we have nothing to say in reply. We confess judgment just here. It is also beyond the bitterest reproach of any accuser. But we say that here the gospel is preached; here light is thrown upon the great system for human salvation; here most impressively the principles of the gospel are taught, and here the results of preaching the gospel may be discerned.

What is the gospel but God's methods of mercy for the salvation of sinners? These methods of mercy have we here.

What is the preaching of the gospel but making known these merciful provisions of God's pardoning grace? Now the sin of David is no more famous than his pardon. The Psalm is as widely known as the history. The very notoriety of these scenes, in his times and ever since, has more largely taught these principles. It is no private preaching.

It is public, widespread preaching, whose voice is heard wherever the Bible goes.

The first doctrine we may mention as involved in these teachings of David's sin is the deep depravity of the heart of man.

The simple narrative teaches this if it teaches anything, and the Psalmist's words of self-abasement bring it plainly before us. Shapen in iniquity and conceived in sin, he pleads for thorough washing and entire cleansing. Strictly speaking, the doctrine of man's depravity forms no part of the gospel, as the science of medicine treats of diseases, while it is in no just sense the cause of diseases, but is designed for their relief. Yet it is indissolubly connected with all our preaching. It is the dark background of the world's history from which springs forth SALVATION, the chief and only beautiful figure that angels can discern as they gaze from afar off upon the canvas of time. Man might have all his sin if he had no Saviour. The man who denies the gospel of Jesus Christ in this world, where sin undeniably abounds, has done an act of infinitely greater madness than if he should leave the world full of plague and fever and contagion, and strike from existence every physician, every soothing or healing potion, every tender sympathy around the couch of the suffering. The gospel finds sin in existence—undeniable, dreadful; it teaches of sin, yet its office is remedial.

This world is full of sin, and David's history

and David's penitential Psalm most fully teach man's deep iniquity. And if David was a religious man, if his professions and his character were usually far otherwise, the argument is but the stronger to show that sin thoroughly defiles the nature of man. Here we learn that even the grace of God, though influencing the soul for many years of life, does not so free it from liability to sin that we need not fear temptation. "I have seen an end of all perfection," well may the devout mind exclaim as he hears these confessions. Who should not fear sin when David falls under its power, after having served God from his youth until now? The first lesson of the gospel—the last, also—a lesson that every man needs to drive him to Christ; a lesson, which, because it is so true, we are so prone to forget, and which therefore we must repeatedly learn, and even by bitter experience—is plainly taught us here: "There is none righteous, no, not one; there is none that understandeth, there is none that seeketh after God." In view of such iniquity in such a man, let "every mouth be stopped, and all the world become guilty before God."

The second doctrine taught us here is the very gospel itself. Let us turn aside and see this great sight—more wonderful than the waters of the deluge or the burning of Sodom—God's mercy extended to sinful man! If here we saw David sinking under the judgments which these sins deserve, we could easily justify the righteousness of God. Doubtless many may be disposed to think that God would have been more fully vindicated in rejecting David as Saul had been rejected, and in carrying out the pure sentence of the law against him. But in this certainly there would have been no gospel. We may speak again of the righteousness of God as vindicated; now we simply notice this chief characteristic of the gospel in the prophet's words: "The Lord also hath put away thy sin."

A third doctrine here taught is that salvation is purely of grace. The nature of the case and the terms used imply this, and it is seen also in the Psalmist's pleadings for God's mercy and according to his loving-kindness. And we may the more carefully note this point because a later inspired writer calls our attention to it in connection with this very case. In the thirty-second Psalm David writes in view of this great iniquity, and Paul says he declares the blessedness of the man who is pardoned by grace and without works. Rom. iv. 6–9.

A fourth lesson in these important teachings is one which the scriptural writers delight to present. The gospel proclaims not only pardon, and by grace, but pardon to the chief of sinners. David was a very great offender, yet he is freely forgiven. Here is one of the most important facts in the history of salvation. How would many a troubled soul sink into despair but for such gracious lines as these!—"The blood of Jesus Christ, his Son, cleanseth us from all sin." "He is able to save unto the uttermost all that come unto God through him." God's finger wrote the same precious truths on David's well-known history. The more we magnify his sin, the more must we magnify forgiving grace. Paul thought himself the chief of sinners and a pattern of God's grace for others. So many have thought. It is the language of true penitence:

"I the chief of sinners am,
But Jesus died for me."

Yet we may calmly judge that few men could use this language more appropriately than could David. John Bunyan has written out a book of his religious experience with this title: "Grace Abounding to the Chief of Sinners." But this is no new doctrine in the Church of God. It is as old as the history of grace itself, and we shall but know more of its wonders when grace has turned to glory. Special trophies of mercy have encouraged penitence in all ages, yet scarcely ever, if ever, did grace pardon a greater sinner than this royal transgressor. If a book like Bunyan's had been handed down in the Church, to be signed by all who have reason to wear the title—the chief of sinners—and to thank God for his grace abounding to such, one name, attracting every eye, would be written there with a bold, large hand—I, DAVID, KING IN JERUSALEM!

So this penitent felt. The New Testament words are different; the meaning is the same. Paul's phrases are, "Grace abounding," and "the riches of his grace." David's words are, "Thy loving-kindness," and "the multitude of thy tender mercies."

A fifth lesson of the gospel in David's words reveals the Spirit's agency in the entire work of salvation. We may expect to find less of the Spirit's work in that age of the Church than now, under "the ministration of the Spirit." Yet the true doctrine is clearly set forth. David prayed for God's Spirit in the hour of his guilt; he greatly feared to be forsaken of the Spirit; he needed the Spirit's grace for further usefulness. "Take not thy Holy Spirit, from me" is his fervent prayer; "Uphold me by thy free Spirit" is his earnest language; "Then shall I teach transgressors thy ways, and sinners shall be converted unto thee" is his humble confidence when clothed with the Spirit's power.

Sixth. One other lesson of the gospel is here taught, and one of prime importance in the teachings of salvation. Paul says he was not ashamed of the gospel of Christ, for therein is THE RIGHTEOUSNESS OF GOD revealed. Whatever else Paul means here—*and he does mean more*—he means pre-eminently that God is righteous when he saves the sinner. This would indeed be a marred and unhappy gospel, if, while it saves the degraded sinner, it dishonoured the exalted Creator. No such teachings can we find in the word or works of God from the beginning until now. God's free grace throws no reproach upon God's righteous law. David takes the shame to himself: "That thou mightest be justified when thou speakest, and be clear when thou judgest." And in view of forgiven sin, he says, "My tongue shall sing aloud of THY RIGHTEOUSNESS."

There is no matter of greater importance in the gospel. The Bible only suggests, and the Bible only solves, this mightiest problem of human thought, How can God be just and yet justify the ungodly? Even in the Scriptures the solution of this question was not clear and explicit until after the great sacrifice of Calvary. So Paul expressly teaches that God has set forth his Son "to be a propitiation, . . . . to declare his righteousness in the forgiveness of sins," for the past and for ever after. We may wonder that the divine character should be so long subject to misapprehension, while God *did* pardon sin, but did *not* vindicate the grounds of the pardon. We may wonder at the ancient faith that rested upon the divine promises, and yet so imperfectly comprehended the rectitude of a sin-forgiving God. Yet in all ages there have been proofs of God's regard for his law in every case of pardoning mercy. The remission of sins was ever by the shedding of blood, as typical of the coming Redeemer. When David pleads for pardon, he both recognizes the sacrifices of the altar and yet acknowledges the insufficiency of his whole burnt-offerings. The significancy and the insufficiency of his offerings alike pointed forward to Him who should vindicate the divine rectitude in the pardon of the guilty.

But that righteousness was even then shown in this, that every sinner pardoned was also a sinner renewed. The grace of God ever gives new life to the soul of man; and the penitent David pleads, "Create in me a clean heart, O God." Renewal and forgiveness are never separated, and only the evidences of renewal can be tokens of forgiveness.

And no man can follow the subsequent history of this great transgressor without discerning the displeasure of a holy God against the iniquities he forgives. Here is matter of pious instruction worthy of the serious thoughts of men beyond our present limits. Great as is the efficacy of renewing and restoring grace, the sanctification of the heart is a longer and more painful process. And the words of the indignant David, when he heard the parable of Nathan, pronounce upon himself the measure of evil that must come upon him from his own house to vindicate the divine abhorrence of his sin:

"He shall restore him fourfold." Therefore, first, the child of Bathsheba shall die. Therefore, *next*, the sin of Amnon and the shame of Tamar and the revenge of Absalom renew the royal crimes in the royal house. Therefore, *again*, Absalom's rebellion and dishonour and death bring out the same offences before all Israel and before the sun. Therefore, *lastly*, even the peaceful Solomon but sits quietly upon his throne when Adonijah dies. Follow the forgiven sinner through all these scenes. Think of his anguish by the couch of that suffering babe; see him pass weeping and bareheaded up the ascent of Olivet; drop the tear of sympathy with the bitter weeping of a pious father over the untimely death of an impenitent son; see the reappearing of the royal iniquities beneath the shadow of that palace which he had first defiled. Surely sin is no light thing in the sight of God when such results come upon even a forgiven sinner. How instructive are the latter scenes of David's life! The decline rather than the advance of the kingdom; the loss of confidence in him; the elements of discord among the people; the troubles in his house; the bitter memories of his iniquity—giving grief to the monarch, to the husband, to the father, to the believer—unequivocally prove that God has no pleasure in unrighteousness, and illustrate the remarkable words to Moses: "Forgiving iniquity and transgression in sin, BUT BY NO MEANS CLEARING THE GUILTY."

Thus the sin of David preaches the gospel of Christ. The chief principles of the gospel God here makes known. Sin is here; here also are pardon and grace; and the rich encouragements to the chief of sinners, and the power of his Spirit to renew the soul, and the guards held forth to remind us that God abhors the sin he pardons, are precious lessons here. Dark as these scenes are in the Psalmist's life, they are as instructive as they are sad. Here is the gospel according to David. Here are the same essential principles afterward more clearly exhibited in the New Testament; and the graceful, beautiful figure springing forth in such bold relief from this gloomy back ground is, "THE GRACE OF GOD THAT BRINGETH SALVATION."

But we have intimated that the results of the gospel may be seen here. These results in every age have been twofold—a savour of life unto life, or of death unto death.

1st. Doubtless the entire case of David has resulted in hardening many a heart. Many have grown bold in sin; many have wholly rejected religion; many have scoffed at the grace that so freely forgave such an offender. Reason as we may, explain as we can the divine administration, we see these results. Nor can we decide whether the sin of the man or the grace of God has afforded the most ground for cavilling.

We may be able never in this life fully to understand why God allows such offences to come. Though we might show that they afford no real ground for cavilling at God or religion, let it now suffice to suggest that these things TRY THE SPIRITS

OF MEN. When the kingdom of David was agitated in every private circle by the astounding tidings of David's sin—when men met together to talk of it, when no man could meet his neighbour without showing in his face the influence the news had exerted upon him---it would be easy to determine the religious character of every man from the effect produced upon him. Grief filled the heart of every lover of piety; tears easily started to his eyes; his look was downcast; his words were mild; his tone was humble. But every ungodly man was triumphant. It could be seen at a glance in his whole demeanour; his scoff at religion and religious professors was bolder than ever, and he departed farther than before from right and from God. So yet the falls of Christians search the characters of men, and try them that dwell upon the earth. Doubtless we all have heard the scoff expressed at the sins of those who profess to fear God. We have heard persons, professedly religious, utter the bitter sarcasm at the falls of their brethren, and speak derisively where they should have mourned. Let who may utter such scoffs, their spirit is thoroughly irreligious, and the man who has the heart to speak them or to sympathize with them should be startled at the revelation of his own character. No patriot in the presence of his country's foes ever sneered at her calamities or at the treason of her trusted sons. No fond brother ever scoffed at a brother's fall or a sister's shame; and every true lover of God, in view of sin around him—especially of sin in men of whom better things were expected—feels grief rather than scorn, and mourns rather than reviles. These things, as much as any truth or any duty, try men's principles, nor can they at all be vindicated who, by reason of these things, increase in evil.

Rather, as cases involving like principles reappear in each passing age of the world; as Providence brings the matter to our own experience; as we see the sudden, reproachful fall, every now and then, of some man who had long borne an enviable reputation in the house of God; as now and then a minister of religion becomes a minister of sin; as passing through our streets our eyes are pained with the sight of men now unblushing in guilt, now bloated by dissipation, now ribald and profane, now bitter in their hostility to the cause and the people of God, who once sat reverently in the sanctuary, once read tearfully the sacred page, once humbly bowed in prayer, once partook with deep emotion of the table of the Lord;—in view of these things—the scandal of piety and the grief of the pious—we would like to ask the hardened scoffer, and him also who now but begins to scoff, we would like to ask every man, whether there is not a better and more profitable view of these things. Woe indeed to him by whom an offence comes! But woe to him who takes needless or undue offence! Woe especially to him who makes the sin of a fellow-creature an occasion for departing from his Creator! The end of these things is death. No man can harden himself against God, BY ANY MEANS or FOR ANY REASON, and prosper. The man who takes offence at this gospel, FOR ANY REASON, must perish. Every man needs the full blessings of this gospel for his own salvation. He therefore who looks at any teachings in the Bible, at any providences in the world, at any deficiencies in the Church, so as to harden his own heart or to become more careless of piety, reaches these results to his own perdition. Account for it as we may, these offences ever attend the preaching of the gospel—even attend the march of Providence. But he is a lost man who allows himself, for such or any reasons, to neglect his own duty or to slight the grace of God.

But, 2d. Men may look at scenes like these in David's life and be led by salutary thoughts to honour God, to advance religion and to bless their own souls.

A truly pious man, in view of such things, may well fear for himself, and be led to the deep anxiety of a careful self-examination. If David falls, "let him who thinketh he standeth take heed!" Distrust of self, distrust of man and dependence only upon God we learn here. In all succeeding time the people of God have learned from these records the deceitfulness of sin, the danger of temptation, and the folly of supposing that any eminence in the Church, any services rendered to Zion, any experience of grace or any promises of God's unchanging favour, will allow us to relax our vigilance or to decline from the path of duty.

A truly pious man more firmly abides by his principles when others forsake them, and endeavours to adorn them more when others bring reproach upon them.

And we often need the encouraging aspects of David's case when the forgiveness of such a sinner makes us bold to approach the throne of grace, and when the petitions of David teach us how to pray. Some surprising sin has perhaps brought reproach upon piety and filled our souls with grief, or a long season of backsliding begins to yield its bitter fruits, or we have hidden iniquity in our hearts and the Lord will not hear us. Our deepest griefs are not always when the world reproaches. We may have a well-ordered Church, doctrines and order according to the Scriptures, an educated and laborious ministry, the name and the word and the day and the house of God held in reverence, growing wealth and influence and labours and numbers, and yet reasons for lamentation and humility—for saying, "The ways of Zion mourn;" for gathering the people, sanctifying the congregation and setting the ministers of God to weep between the porch and the altar. Judg. ii. 16, 17. Let us learn from David the perpetual folly of concealing our guilt; let us copy his ingenuous confession—"I have sinned against the Lord;" let us adopt his suitable petitions, his needful pleas for grace, his appropriate vows of duty; let us hope in the Lord, whose mercy endures for ever. Our legitimate reasonings upon this entire case should promote our piety. We have no apologies to make for sin. We may fear and shun it more than ever; we may be grieved when reproach is cast upon religion; but in our gloomiest thoughts for ourselves or others, when iniquity grows strong and the heart grows hard and human hope would fail, the beautiful covenant-bow is painted on this darkest cloud—an everlasting covenant, even the sure mercies of David, God proclaims to us; and the blood of Jesus Christ, David's Redeemer and ours, cleanseth from all sin.

And if a thoughtful man, hitherto unconverted and impenitent, reads this entire history of David, reads this wonderful Psalm, the commentary of God's grace upon it, let just and wise reflections bless his needy soul.

Let him fear sin more than ever. David had many restraining influences. He had tasted God's renewing grace; he had received many promises; he had long formed his habits to virtue. Yet he grossly sinned. Surely, then, an unconverted sinner, with less restraints, unrenewed by grace, without a supporting Providence, with habits giving strength to sin, has reason to fear lest the current of depravity may carry him away.

And such a man may well be afraid of the wrath of God. In view of the distressing calamities in the family of David, we may well adopt the style of the apostle's argument: If judgment begins at the house of God, what may sinful men expect? If God deals so with penitent and pardoned friends, what may they look for who are impenitent and unpardoned foes? If the righteous scarcely be saved, where shall the ungodly and the sinner appear? In view of the penitent David's troubles, every impenitent transgressor may fear the wrath of God.

Yet let every man who desires to secure his own salvation learn from David that God freely pardons sin. What awakens cavillings in other minds may awaken hope and thankfulness in his. This is just what he needs, the riches of divine grace. The more he knows of his sins, the more is he convinced that grace alone can suit him; and tidings of pardon are welcome. Grace to the chief of sinners is glad news to burdened minds. Let my sinful soul approach where David found mercy. Not less than Paul is David a pattern of God's tender mercy. Let the humbled sinner follow his footsteps. Let him take David's prayer in this fifty-first Psalm, and in the presence of his God let him solemnly kneel before his open Bible and make these pleadings his own. Here is a proof of God's mercy and willingness to be gracious; here are words rightly framed; here we may fill our mouth with arguments and order our case before him: and by this Psalm has God's Spirit led many a soul to himself now for three thousand years. And the Psalmist, in so many words, expressly recognizes that God's mercy to him would teach his ways to transgressors and turn sinners to God.

And should any man be still disposed to cavil at the display of God's free grace, let him distinctly understand that he but injures his own soul. Through just such a door of mercy must every sinner pass if he would not be condemned before a righteous God. Let every man beware that he ventures not to sin because David fell or because grace abounded for his free forgiveness. Take especial notice that David was a PENITENT sinner. If in this particular thing we are not like him, all other possible points of similarity are dreadful. We may sin as he did, deliberately, grossly, wilfully; we may sin far less, and if we repent not, sin will prove our ruin. But though our sins seem greater far, more deeply aggravated, longer continued and against clearer light, he can forgive to the uttermost, and we may draw near to God. The only safe thing for an imitation in David is his penitence; but the open door of acceptance for such a one as he, offers a welcome to the guilty of every age.

With what urgency is the gospel preached to us! In history and by precept, by examples living and dead, by every variety of case for six thousand years, our duties and our dangers, God's wrath and his mercy, are set before us. And the great concern of salvation is a matter of importance as infinite to be settled in the personal experience of each one of us, as in the experience of any who have spent their brief period of earthly life and preceded us to eternity. This is a matter that can never grow unimportant. If never a soul before had received profit from these experiences of David, or if thousands have been benefited, let each one who reads these pages fear to sin, and rejoice in God's mercy. Each one must join the crowds who have hardened their hearts against truth and grace, and found the gospel a savour of death unto death, or must join the bands of those who have seen their own sinfulness more fully in the sin of others—who have rejoiced to hear of pardon and to accept of it, as they tread the narrow way to life. Let none be negligent or perverse. We have nothing to gain by quarrelling with God's forbearance and forgiveness to a sinful soul; since, if ever saved, we too must be saved by mercy. Rather forsake every sin; bow before Him who waits to be gracious. Confess truly and humbly, "I have sinned against the Lord;" and hope too for that precious answer, "The Lord also hath put away thy sin."

## CHAPTER XLV.

### *THOUGHTS ON THE FAULT FOUND WITH CHRISTIANS.*

"THOU hast given great occasion to the enemies of the Lord to blaspheme," are the words of pointed, plain and just rebuke which Nathan the prophet addressed to David, king of Israel, in reference to a remarkable, and, we may properly say, a shameful and wicked transaction of his life. Taking the character of David as a whole, we esteem him one of the best men the world ever saw, but, as if to show us the weakness and frailty of our human nature, he was left at one time to himself, the restraints of God's grace were removed, and David stooped to deeds of impurity and falsehood, of injustice and violence, of which any heathen might be ashamed. No apology is made in the Scriptures for David's flagrant wickedness in the matter of Uriah's wife; and we are thus taught that it is never our place to defend or extenuate or disguise with light words the faults of those who may stand high in the Church of God. We are nowhere taught in the Scriptures that pious men are without faults; and the entire administration of the covenant of grace goes upon the principle that God's people need restraint and instruction and chastisement as long as they live. And so dark are the scriptural views of man's depravity that, however much we may be grieved, we can scarcely be surprised at any exhibitions of iniquity in any man at any time; yet would we use means of reproof and remedy toward their defections of whom we had expected better things, not less readily and not less earnestly than toward the sins of others. "We can do nothing against the truth, but for the truth." We would have no sanctions, no excuses for evil; we would recognize a greater delinquency of sin where just expectations have been formed of nobler conduct. The gross iniquity of David in the matter of Uriah—like a defiling stain upon robes of linen pure and white—is only the more manifest and the more gross from of its contrast with the general tenor of his life; he mourned over it as a man thoroughly given up to iniquity would not have mourned; and religion suffered reproach for his conduct as it could not suffer from all the crimes of Sodom or of the Canaanites. Men that profess to be religious are justly identified with the cause of religion, so that their entire conduct and opinions must conform to the principles of piety, or religion itself will suffer reproach and the name of God himself be blasphemed. We are not only aware that the world expects that such as profess piety should exemplify its principles, but we recognize the justice of their expectation, and we aver that God designs to teach the world through the holy example of pious men. We make no objection to the watchfulness of the world over the character and conduct of religious people; we desire to be animated by it to more circumspection. Yet there is one matter which we could wish was better understood. We think the plain tendency of the world around is to find undue fault with the failings of religious men, to throw undue blame upon religion itself, and to draw false, unreasonable and mischievous conclusions, which injure the objectors themselves and do no good to any one. We have no wish to shrink from our just responsibilities; we would by unreasonable cavillings be placed more and more upon our guard, and be led to adorn more truly the doctrine of God our Saviour; but we desire also that those who remain in the world and watch our conduct should do justice to us and to the gospel and to their own souls. Men ought to see that to prove us wrong does not prove themselves right; that our defections from the principles of the gospel do not invalidate the principles of the gospel; and that their discernment of the faults and inconsistencies of Christians, as compared with the principles of the gospel, can but have the just effect to fasten upon them more firmly the duties which they are as truly bound as we to perform.

In considering the matter of reproach cast upon religion for the faults of religious men, we are not willing to "confess judgment" for all the delinquencies laid at our doors. We ask reflecting men in the world, who make no professions of piety, to consider calmly whether there is not undue fault found with religious persons—whether there is not a disposition to exaggerate their inconsistencies; whether, indeed, there is not quite a different standard erected according to which no man would wish himself to be estimated? We are sometimes disposed to think such is the censorious spirit of the world that no Christian can please the world, let him adopt what course of conduct he may. "If I yet pleased men," says the great apostle of the Gentiles, "I should not be the servant of Christ." And higher authority than that of Paul teaches us that fault-finding men were not put to silence by the only perfect and holy example of human life and character that the world has ever seen. According to the illustration of our Lord Jesus Christ, the world is like a gang of children playing in the streets. One child proposes one play, and another a different one. Each child has its own notions and refuses to play at all unless all the rest come to his terms. John the Baptist was an austere preacher, having little sympathy and intercourse with men, and they esteemed him a fanatic. The Son of man mingled freely with all orders of men, accepted invitations to their feasts and had free conversation with everybody, and they complained that he kept inferior company and was too fond of good living. If such a Teacher could not be blameless in the eyes of censorious men, the disciple may not expect to be above the Master. If a religious man is of a silent and reserved temperament, he is reproached as unsociable and his piety stigmatized as gloomy. If he is frank and cheerful and fond of company, then he lacks the seriousness which piety should give. Between these extremes it is hard to secure the proper mean in reality, and especially is it hard to do it, so as to secure the respect of the world. If we live and move among men without active endeavours to recommend religion to them, they justly think that we are inconsistent in so important a profession; yet if we seriously urge the claims of piety, there is danger of reproach for being over-zealous. Industry is in danger of reproach as worldly-mindedness; Christian weakness, as guilty timidity amidst surrounding sin; bold and firm reproofs of sin, as officious meddling; prudent economy, as avarice; and the fear of worldly contamination, as the affectations of an unworthy hypocrisy. The most thoughtful minds must candidly acknowledge that there are practical difficulties in the way of every serious man who would attain the just medium in the formation of his own character and the regulation of his own conduct. We may not now tarry even to suggest hints to assist those that would secure this. We only say that such is the temper of the world toward religious professors that the most careful and exemplary cannot rise above reproach. Even truth will not seem truth when exposed to a false light, and the holiest character will seem distorted when seen through the medium of warping prejudice.

These remarks should ward off the force of many undeserved reproaches cast upon religious persons. But with regard to reproaches which have a better foundation, we may discern the same disposition to find undue fault on the part of the world, because men seldom stop to make a distinction between one class and another of religious people. We all know that large and sweeping denunciation is seldom just; that in every society some men rise far above their fellows, and some bring reproach upon their associates, and that in justice we should distinguish between the good and the evil. The world knows that many members of the Christian Church are worthy of but little confidence, but they so deal out their censures against them as to extend the reproach to all their brethren. No body of men can ever be held responsible for the individual delinquencies of their associates, especially delinquencies foreign to the principles which unite them together; if just pains were taken to let the blame fall where the blame belongs, no complaint could be made; but the tendency to indiscriminate reproach is manifest, but thoroughly unjust.

The severity of judgment exhibited by men of

the world toward religious persons seems the more unjust because it is not the result of any proper principles which they have adopted, and indeed it is quite apart from the usual methods by which they judge other people. There is a species of charity exercised toward even the vilest of men which is in wide contrast with the censures cast on religious men. Nothing is more common than apologies for the delinquencies of men; and with them, if so be they do not belong to the Church of God, one apparent virtue atones for many a fault. For example: a man may be a miserable drunkard, abusing his family, abusing every trust committed to him as a husband and a father, but the world apologizes, "He is a good-hearted fellow when he is sober." He may abuse his body, ruin his constitution and bring himself to the verge of the grave, but "he means well and harms nobody but himself." These current judgments are but a specimen of the world's tolerance toward all creeds but truth, and toward all kinds of conduct except that which seems to reflect upon a prevalent laxity of principle. Now we neither judge it right to speak thus leniently of the iniquities of men, nor desire that such indulgence should be extended to the faults of religious persons. We only mark the contrast as exhibiting a tendency to make the most of the faults of religious people. The faults of Christians are eagerly noted and tardily forgotten; no just allowances are made for the frailties of an imperfect nature, and no remembrance had of the brighter virtues by whose side those delinquencies seem only the darker. A single stumble—and this too in a man who makes no pretensions to perfection of views or conduct—will often be remembered against him—will shake the confidence he has heretofore enjoyed; and no time elapsing, no carefulness of future conduct, can obliterate the memory of it. Now, no man wishes to be judged in this way, and few men in a world like this can abide so severe a scrutiny. That the world should closely observe him, that his errors should be marked and his sins rebuked, are matters of which no one has just reason to complain. Every man ought to take it patiently when buffeted for his faults, and humbly submit when censure is founded on things that deserve it. Yet there are often very important matters wholly passed over by a censorious world. When the man himself mourns over his faults and endeavours to correct them, when over against them is set a life of virtue and a long array of useful actions, and when he keeps in memory his past failings so that he may more carefully avoid them in future, surely justice and candour might admit and admire his excellences, and might esteem the man rather by the tenor of his life than by errors which, at the very worst, cannot be called his governing principles. But the tendency among men is to apologize for irreligious people, to dwell upon their good qualities, to pass lightly over their evidences of depravity, and to attribute even their evil to anything rather than to a bad heart; while there is as plain a tendency to attribute the wrongs of religious men to the worst motive, and to regard them as proof of the most evident hypocrisy.

This greater severity in judging religious men is indicated by the fact that they profess higher and holier principles than other men. Men easily lose sight of the fact that, so far as these are true and holy principles, every man is as truly bound as is a Christian to fear and love God and to keep his laws; and the mere fact that a man professes to recognize his duty, and acknowledges himself bound to its discharge, is no just reason for looking more leniently upon those who neither do their duty nor profess to do it. But when we seriously ask, What is the true amount of the Christian profession? it may confidently be said that there are many who do not, after all, fall so much short of that which they profess. Religious men do not pretend to say that their piety secures them from errors, from temptations, from human infirmities; nor do they claim that because they are Christians they are henceforth perfect. Their professed principles imply far otherwise than this. No man more than a true Christian acknowledges himself a sinner, feels and owns the power of temptation and understands his liability to fall; and such a man discovers more closely his own failings, and grieves more deeply over them, than any one else does for him. So far as the Christian profession is made in the face of the world, it amounts about to this: the Christian acknowledges what his duties are under the law of God, and bewails his past delinquencies, and expresses now his desire and professes his endeavour to meet his obligations. The most worthy men of those that make this Christian profession are generally most aware of their own deficiencies, and least disposed either to boast of their excellences, or even to defend themselves when the world alleges they are not wholly consistent. Yet since they do not profess to reach a perfect standard, since even the most illustrious characters of the Scriptures are imperfect, with one single and exalted exception, they have a right to claim in all candour that their motives should not be misrepresented nor their errors so exaggerated.

But a candid decision upon these matters cannot be expected from a world that is filled with prejudice against religion. It never has been so, and we judge it never will. An unreasonable world will keenly discern the most trivial faults, will continue to judge harshly of them, and will especially attribute to religion itself the delinquencies of unworthy persons who profess to be religious.

But from these thoughts we pass on to say, further, that the judgment of the world in this case is illogical and false. Especially we affirm that the faults of religious persons, at the very worst, are no arguments against the truth of Christianity. Let us make the supposition that the faults of religious persons are in no wise exaggerated by the world, and that they are even worse than have ever been charged upon them, and we may yet affirm, in such a case, that the faults of professing Christians form no just argument against the divine origin of the Christian system. The Bible may be from God, though those who receive it as from him are not what they should be. Indeed, its very elevation above them may afford us convincing proof that they do not receive it as divine, except because just evidences prove that it is so, and that surely such teachings have a higher source than sinful man.

Before we can blame Christianity for the inconsistencies of Christian people, it will be needful to show that it is the natural tendency of the Christian system to originate and promote their faults, or that it connives, in some degree at least, at such delinquencies, or that, through some fault in the working of the system itself, it is incompetent to the task of reforming men's lives. Cavillings upon this subject seldom proceed, indeed, from men of serious reflection; and especially few men will ever undertake to say that either of these things can be affirmed.

Can any one intelligently attempt to prove that the Bible is defective as a system of morals to govern men? We will not allege that men must be satisfied with the arrangements of the truths in the Bible as most according to man's ideas of a perfect system, for it is not for man to decide in what way a system of divine truth may be best revealed. But we do affirm that, as to substance, the Bible is a perfect and complete directory—such as man needs for his guidance, restraint and support in every duty in life.

Let any man take up his Bible and point out the matter or the degree wherein it is defective for human guidance.

It is not defective *in its principles.* For, to go no farther than this, we may affirm that nothing can be more just or more conducive to good morals than the firm foundation of biblical morality. A God of infinite excellence sees and knows all we are and all we do, will hold us accountable for everything, and requires that all we do should accord with his own glorious character.

It is not defective *in its precepts.* For, in all its varied teachings, no man can point out a doctrine of immoral or of dangerous tendency; and in the infinitely various aspects of human life there are no instances where a man, guided by this volume, would lack just principles for his guidance. There is no defect by reason of either redundant precepts or omitted teachings which man's need requires.

Nor can any one say that the morality of the Bible is defective *in the motives* by which it influences men to right. It urges duty and right, honour and pleasure, good and evil, loss and gain, interest and gratitude, love and fear—in short, every influence that can address reasonable and thinking beings. No man certainly can find fault with the punishments denounced in the Bible as not being sufficiently severe; nor can any one reasonably suggest a larger or more attractive reward of virtue than it promises. Everything that can deter from the ways of evil or attract to the path of right is here spread plainly before the minds of men.

Nor is Christianity deficient in the *opportunities it affords* by which men may learn their duties, and gain strength and find occasion for discharging these. It opens the pages of this remarkable volume for man's instruction; it sets apart one entire day in seven, by divine authority, for religious duties; it establishes a holy brotherhood in the Church, where the hands of pious men may be strengthened by association with each other for religious ends; it leads each man to the duty of prayer for divine assistance, and it promises the enlightening, renewing and sanctifying power of the Holy Spirit to sustain and prepare for every duty.

We aver that there is not one single thing in the entire system of Christianity that has the slightest legitimate tendency to weaken the bonds of moral obligation, or to extenuate or apologize for either the neglect or the transgression of duty; and that for these reasons Christianity is not chargeable with the faults of her disciples committed in defiance of her principles. Every man can see the impropriety of charging, for example, upon the science of astronomy the crude opinions held by honest men for many ages in reference to the heavens, or the absurd ideas now maintained in the Hindoo or Mohammedan cosmogony; or of charging upon the science of therapeutics the absurd nostrums of quack practitioners, or even the errors which have been held by careful and sincere physicians. Errors, either theoretical or practical, in reference to any science, do not prove the science false, and are not really to be charged to the science itself. The true science of astronomy is just what the heavens teach, not what men have understood them to teach. All the errors belong to men, not to the divine arrangement of the heavens. True medical science is a just conformity to the teachings of disease and to wise methods of relief, nor can we say that the science is false because men, wilfully or ignorantly, believe or practice irregular and hurtful methods. So we judge of everything. No man gives up his truth because other men have false views upon the same subject. Christianity is not to be understood by what its disciples profess or practice, but by the revelations which are given of it in the inspired word of God. When religious people exhibit the true spirit of their profession, the credit is due to their principles, but when they depart from these, Christianity is still to be judged by what it really is.

It may, however, be still urged by objectors that the sacred Scriptures, as a divine revelation, have measurably failed in their great object; that men have not been made holy by their influence at all, in proportion to the expectations we would form of an inspired volume; and that fault is found not so much with the teachings of Christianity as with its apparent inefficiency in reforming men, and even in sanctifying the lives of its own disciples. It must be confessed that this is a most important view of the matter, and one that cannot properly be discussed within the brief limits to which we are here confined. Yet a few suggestions may weaken perhaps the force of the objections.

The inefficiency of any system is not to be decided by what men may really expect, but by what they should justly expect. If any man will look into the Bible, he will find that it makes no pretensions to form upon earth a pure and spotless Church. It proceeds all the way through upon the principle that many men will conform themselves but partially to its teachings, asserts that many will reject them altogether, and warns its readers both against unbelief and formality. It declares that the wheat and tares must grow together till God himself shall separate them, exhibits plainly the failings and faults of the best of men, and indeed gives us views so dark of man's entire depravity as may keep us from being surprised at any outbreak of human sinfulness. So, that while unblemished purity of Christian character is no more than God's law of right demands, yet the exhibition of such a character is far more than God's word leads us to anticipate. And as we are here taught that Christian sanctification is promoted by the truth, it is natural to judge that the purity of any man's life and character will be in due proportion to his growth in the knowledge of the Bible and to the carefulness with which he brings its truth to bear upon his conscience. We are not warranted by the teachings of the Bible nor by the observations of experience to presume that persons professedly religious will always be faithful to learn all they should from these divine teachings, nor to put in practice these salutary teachings when they have been made acquainted with them.

And these further thoughts may be expressed in reference to the alleged want of power in Christianity to effect what we might reasonably expect of it:

1st. The religion of the Bible never proposes to make any man a servant and follower of God against his own consent. Every man who receives or rejects the gospel of Christ does so in the exercise of his own will. While God governs men efficiently for his own will, it is yet so as to leave them entirely voluntary. Unless we wish to find fault with this, and to say that religion ought to be a matter of compulsion, it seems a necessary inference that the faults of voluntary agents should be laid at their own doors, and that Christianity, as it in nowise teaches or favours the sins of men, should be held in nowise accountable for them.

2d. Even the most prejudiced opposer of Christianity cannot deny that it has reclaimed many men even from the widest departures from truth and the lowest degradation; that it has formed many most excellent characters in the world; that it has elevated the tone of morals and the standard of comfort in every land where it has been introduced; that the human race is now enjoying the largest measure of liberty, intelligence and civilization just in those lands where the Bible is most freely circulated; and that no community ever has received its teachings without improvement in virtue and happiness.

3d. Nor can any man deny that the neglect of the Bible always attends upon vice, and that the more any man is really acquainted with it and cherishes a true love for it, the holier is the influence exerted upon his character and doings. Men never become infidels by a serious study of the evidences of Christianity; nor profane by carefully reading the Bible; nor licentious by punctuality at church; nor drunkards by loving the place of prayer. The steps to these vices turn all away from the sanctuary of God, and men enter into temptation by looking off from the Bible. Making all due allowance for men who have sinister motives for professing to be religious, did any man in the wide world ever believe that a Christian was sincerely attached to his Bible and lose confidence in him for that reason? It is not the man who really and continually brings himself under the influence of the Bible that is prone to bring reproach upon piety. Such men may fall, we do not doubt, for they are yet sinful men, but the tendency of their religion is most assuredly all the other way. If it was while carefully attending to the teachings of the Bible, and in the very act of following out injunctions, that these men were found sinners, then the blame might justly be laid at the door of Christianity. If even it could be said that every professor of piety was intelligent, diligent, humble, earnest and prayerful as he ought to be, we might think these faults flowed from their faith. But a just and candid examination of the matter will compel any upright mind to decide that religious people bring reproach upon Christianity only in those cases where they act in neglect of her teachings or in defiance of her authority. Unless, then, we assert that they should in some way be compelled to do right, we ought to lay the blame of wrong upon them individually.

4th. We may further remark that Christianity more than any religious system, and the Church of God more than any other association upon earth, are liable to be reproached for the deficiencies and faults of men that come under their influence; and that, instead of wondering that so many depart from the faith, it is rather a matter of wonder that the departures are not wider and more frequent. Unless we look for a moral miracle in every case of alleged conversion, such as neither the Bible nor our experience warrants us in expecting, we should anticipate many backslidings and apostasies from religion. The very charity and mercy of the gospel sometimes become a snare. It was a matter of reproach against the Lord Jesus Christ that he frequented the society of publicans and sinners. He justified his practice in this respect—that they above all others needed his care, and were disposed to avail themselves of it. And the apt illustration which he gives forces us to recognize the validity of his plea. It is that of a physican, whose duty, of course, lies not with the well but with the sick, and whose presence in the most filthy and contagious and even disreputable abodes is justified by the objects that have called him there. The same plea precisely has Christianity. Her beneficent influences are always exercised toward sinners; every man whom she blesses was first a lover of iniquity; and some, before they come under her influence, have formed habits of sin deeply inveterate and even deeply degrading. Of course, reproach upon the Church is most likely to flow from those whose previous habits have the strongest power over them. And yet we can easily decide that reproach is often cast upon the Church for receiving to her communion certain persons who have afterward proved unworthy, when in reality all the dealings of the Church with such persons are characterized by the strictest disinterestedness and purity—are prompted by the largest benevolence, and, justly understood, reflect the highest honour upon her aim and proceedings. It is not at all a surprising thing that unworthy persons find their way into the membership of the Church. It is rather wonderful that the proportion is not larger than smaller; and the only just reproach to which the officers of the Church are subject is when they have failed to exercise due care in admitting persons, or when they are indisposed with fidelity to administer discipline—to rebuke or exclude from the privileges of the Church an unworthy person. And the censure they may receive here is not without its important extenuating circumstances.

We may illustrate this matter by a simple example. Let us suppose that a man of a dissipated and profligate character is brought under the sound of the gospel; his sins are exposed; his conscience is awakened; he begins to pray, to form resolutions of repentance, and to associate himself with the people of God. They are perhaps surprised, but certainly they are glad to see these new things. They feel disposed to overlook the past, to feel leniently toward his errors, and to judge charitably of his professed amendment. They are disposed to take him by the hand, to sympathize with him and to encourage him in every possible way.

Knowing, indeed, that they have something to lose if he should prove himself unworthy, they are carried away by the benevolent consideration that he has everything to gain if his professed change of character should prove real, and they hope that the fellowship and sympathy and counsel of Christians, and his new engagements of piety, will be of good service in fortifying him against temptation and in strengthening his hands to do right. Possibly the rulers of the Church sometimes hope in such cases upon too little grounds; but surely this is an amiable and charitable side to err upon. What marvel is it if those too sanguine hopes, even when most carefully indulged, should sometimes be disappointed? We cannot search the heart, nor accurately unravel the web of human deceit or hypocrisy. Who can justly wonder if, among those received to the membership of the Church, some have never experienced a change of heart? Or, even if renewed, who can justly expect that the dominion of vices so long having the mastery should at once be thoroughly broken? And it is obvious that the Church is liable to be deceived in many who have been under the influence of vices unsuspected and undiscovered, till some retributive providence brings them forth to the shame of the transgressor and the sad reproach of religion. But put these defections of church members in their very worst form, and multiply them as you may, so long as Christianity gains no advantage from them, gives no approval to them, is betrayed into her connection with them only by her efforts to do good, and has no apologies to offer for their shame and sin, these things are really no stain upon her principles, and afford no argument against her truth and her divine original. Christianity is more liable to these reproaches than any other system that professes to do good to men, because she stoops lower, is ever ready to help the most vile and wretched, and entertains hopes where others give up in despair. But Christianity is no more justly chargeable with the failure of her efforts to do good—as if this failure was the legitimate result of her principles—than is the physician who undertakes the treatment of desperate disease responsible for the power of the disease, since his efforts are all directed to ameliorate and control it. The reproach against the Church of Christ for the inconsistency of religious professors would be less if the Church would refuse her countenance and sympathy to all that have severe struggles with temptation, and if she would receive none but persons of mature age, of good reputation and of well-established principles. But this would be to give up the most precious design of the Church. She ought to help the weak, to strengthen the wavering, to counsel the tempted, and to stand by those that are in danger, even if she does sometimes soil her garments by venturing into the abodes of sinfulness. Her reproach is really her honour when it springs from such a source. If a physician, through a morbid fear of losing his patients, never went near a sick bed, it would be no more excessive caution than for Christianity to stand back from sinners lest haply some of them should give occasion to her enemies to blaspheme.

We urge, then, that all existing and even all possible defects of professing Christians are no just argument against the truth of Christianity. These things flow not from her principles; and as she does not propose to make even Christians perfectly holy in this life, nor to compel any man to do right, they do not spring from any failure of what Christianity is designed to effect.

But let us pass to another important remark on this subject. As these defections and inconsistencies in religious people are no just ground of reproach against religion itself, so they are no proper excuse in any man for his neglect of the claims of religion upon himself personally; but rather when any man has magnified to the utmost the deficiencies of religious persons, he has but constructed the more powerful argument to urge his own duty and to constrain him to accept and adorn the gospel.

It is an obvious principle that no man can detect the inconsistencies of Christians unless he is acquainted with the laws they ought to obey. For inconsistency has reference to a law, and hypocrisy has reference to a profession. If I say six times five are forty, a man must know the multiplication table or he cannot correct the error. If any man does not know my law, he cannot discern my inconsistencies; if he does not know what my profession demands, he cannot discover my hypocrisy, no matter how far I depart from it. Thus it is only so far as a man is acquainted with the requirements of Christianity that he can find fault with inconsistent Christians; and when he does find fault, his very censure implies that the law is better than the conduct; that Christianity is better than Christians; in other words, slightly to change Paul's language, if he sees us do what he allows not, he consents unto the law that IT is good. All these censures go upon the tacit acknowledgment that if Christians would only come up to their own standard, no fault could be found with them. The principles of Christianity are faultless, even in the eyes of these cavillers. Well, now we may fairly retort upon these men, Why do you not come up to this law yourselves? You can no more be right than I in asserting that five times six are forty. You are no nearer right than I in neglecting the duties which religion lays upon you. God is your Creator as well as mine; his law binds you as well as me; you should believe his gospel as well as I; duty and gratitude and interest are equally laid upon you. You complain that I and others in the Church of God are inconsistent and do not set you a right example. But why do you not come into the Church and set us a right example? You are naturally as much bound to set me a right example as I am to set you; you are as much bound to labour for the salvation of my soul as I am for yours; the calls of the Redeemer are made as plainly in your ears as they are in mine; you can get as many blessings from the gospel as I can; and seeing that you are acquainted with the duties of Christian life, there is no just reason why you should stand aloof. You talk about hypocrites in the Church as if such a character might not be found nearer home. First cast the beam out of thine own eye. If you are able to discover a mote in another's eye, if you can discern even the trivial faults of Christians, how is it that you overlook so large a sin as the utter refusal to submit to the gospel of Christ yourself?

We do not say these things because finding fault with others or comparing our sins with theirs ever benefits our own souls. If men out of the Church have sins, this does not justify the inconsistencies of religious persons, and the faults of Christians do not justify the sins of others. But when men urge that, with such principles, we ought to be better than we are, how can they avoid the conclusion that for them to embrace our principles would make them also better? "Thou therefore that judgest another condemneth also thyself," for you are lacking in the very things which you charge as faults upon them. You do not make the rule which God has prescribed your guide in duty, and at the judgment-seat of Christ it will not be asked, "How many inconsistencies could you discern in the character of another?" But the inquiry will be, "How fully were you acquainted with your own duty, and how nearly did you approach the full discharge of it?" If every living Christian was a disgrace to the Church of Christ, and you knew it, that knowledge would only make it more important for you to vindicate in the eyes of all men the true principles of Christianity, and to exemplify them by your own godly life. So, then, the more reason any man has to find fault with religious people, the more obligation he is under to embrace the gospel himself and to rescue its fair fame from the reproaches cast upon it. Nor can any one possibly construct an excuse from the wickedness of the world or of the Church that will be wise enough and strong enough to justify his own palpable neglect of duty. For indeed the stronger the excuse is, the more thoroughly does it render himself inexcusable.

But we may conclude these reflections with a few additional practical thoughts:

1st. It is important for professing Christians to feel that they cannot too carefully avoid the very appearance of evil. Our duty binds us to live a holy and upright life, and much depends upon the conduct of religious people as recommending religion. Other men may indeed judge harshly, or draw wrong inferences from correct judgments; we may not justify his sin who stumbles over the errors of others to his own destruction; yet it is true that the cause of piety is identified with the characters of those who profess it, and much mischief flows from their ill conduct. Let every upright man avoid the disposition to vindicate in himself or his brethren faults which really ought not to be vindicated; let him bear with meekness the reproaches which he is conscious are deserved. But let him, in view of the exaggerated and even unjust censures which the world loves to put forth, be more watchful and careful to give no just occasion to reproach. Let each man, more earnestly than ever, study the principles and spirit of the word of God, be more devoted to the service of his Lord, be more entirely dependent upon divine grace, and endeavour more in his own sphere to adorn the doctrine of God his Saviour in all things.

2d. It is neither a happy nor a useful disposition in any man to be prone to find fault with others or to magnify their deficiencies. We are not indeed to approve of wrong, nor even to be indifferent while truth suffers reproach and men depart from the path of duty. But if indifference is wrong, censoriousness is not right; especially every man should be careful how he censures while his own neglects of duty are palpable before God and man. "With what judgment ye judge, ye shall be judged; and with what measure ye mete, it shall be measured to you again."

3d. As every man is to give an account of himself to God, we close this discussion by urging that each reader should turn his thoughts in upon himself. We all enjoy many privileges in common. We have the teachings of the same divine word, the calls of the same gospel, and duties substantially alike. A like concern should fill each heart. This Bible is as holy for one as another; there is the same God over all rich in mercy; the same law with its holy and inflexible claims; the same immortality, reasonableness and sinfulness of soul; the same mercy-seat; the same invitations of the gospel; the same duty of faith in the Lord Jesus Christ; the same glorious and everlasting heaven inviting, and the same solemn warnings of an awful and an eternal hell. It is a matter of deep importance that other men should do their duty—especially that religious persons should live consistently.

But for every man the most important pressing matter is a personal one. Let it so dwell upon our thoughts. This gospel is true, it is worthy of our thoughts, and our duty and our interest call us to embrace it. Other men may be wrong; this is a great pity. If we can do anything to set them right, we ought to do it. But let each man's thoughts and prayers and earnest efforts be called forth to set himself right. No possible apology, drawn from the example of others, can atone for your neglect of your own duty. "If thou be wise, thou shalt be wise for thyself; and if thou scornest, thou alone shalt bear it."

NOTE.—Those who would read more upon the subject of these pages are invited to consider five posthumous discourses of Dr. Andrew Thompson, of Edinburgh, in which some of the thoughts here given are forcibly presented, and many others of deep importance.

# CHAPTER XV.

## THE TREASON OF ABSALOM.

THERE was one phrase of Nathan's rebuke to David which doubtless sank deep in his heart, and which rose again from time to time, with the gaze and the tone of the prophet, before the mind of the transgressor, as he learned by repeated experience the meaning it conveyed. In the multitude of words we hear, many things are necessarily forgotten, but every now and then we hear expressions that become a part of our life and are never long out of our memory. Sometimes these are trifling words, ministering only to frivolity; sometimes they are polluting, and impress images upon the mind from which every wise man would gladly turn away his gaze; sometimes they are instructive, and the words of the wise, in a brief expression, control our life for many years and shape our destinies for an eternal existence; sometimes they are the terms of warning and reproof, that especially recur to us as they find their fulfilment in our bitter experience. How often then did David remember the words of Nathan!—"I will raise up evil against thee out of thine own house." As trouble after trouble rose in answer to these words, the memory recalled them more forcibly, the conscience vindicated their justice and the understanding fathomed better their solemn meaning. And if it is our place to acknowledge that the future experience of David flowed naturally from his crime; if we reason that the wisdom of God, as well as his justice, here shows to the world a dreadful warning against sins so great, it is safe also to sympathize with David, considered as a penitent, and we may judge that from this time forth we can enter more fully into the sorrows that rise before us. For whatever public aspects belong to the occurrences hereafter to engage our thoughts, there is a domestic interest in them that affects our hearts. For David *as a king* we may feel but little sympathy. The monarch is lifted above his subjects and is separated from them; much more may a foreign people care little for a distant monarch of a distant age. But here David comes before us as a father; and the relations of the household are as tender now as ever, and we can feel for one who suffers as we may understand. The sorrows of the parent elicit an attention. It is in the very nature of man to sympathize with suffering, and we are prone to lay aside—even sometimes too much—all thought of the cause of a man's sufferings, to feel with him. It is not right so to sympathize with a criminal as to forget or even palliate his crime, or to free him from the just sentence of the law for his sin, yet there is a measure of sympathy even where the sufferer deserves his pains.

We say no more of the grief of David as Death's dark shadow is first cast upon the halls of his palace through his great sin, and as shame and violence break in afterward with ruthless step, for these are but the little cloud that shall gather over that palace in a dense and wide tempest of sorrow.

It is a truth often felt that in this world of grief and disappointment—should we not add, in this world of sin?—our most poignant sorrows spring out of our most precious blessings, and where we have looked for our largest comforts we have found our severest trials. How needful the caution of our sacred poet:

> "Lean not on earth: 'twill pierce thee to the heart.
> A broken reed at best, but oft a spear,
> On whose sharp point Peace bleeds and Hope expires."

We read the chapter of David's sorrows, and we find none comparable to those which he suffered from the hand of Absalom. Yet of all the sons of David up to this time no one seems to have been superior to Absalom. We say nothing now of Solomon, the only other son whom the sacred writers bring before us with any degree of prominence, for he was but a babe at this period of the history; and born after David's forgiveness, he at least bore no part in the calamities brought upon his father. But not a few reasons are suggested in the narrative itself for a peculiar pride and fondness in David toward Absalom; and we can see that these were reasons tending to form the character of the young man rather for evil than for good—rather for pride, ambition and vanity than for virtuous aspirations. The mother of Absalom was the royal bride in the family of David, and this son alone could boast that his descent was kingly from both parents. We do not forget David's first marriage with the daughter of Saul, but Michal bore no children. Moreover, Absalom was a man of great personal beauty. "In all Israel there was none to be so much praised as Absalom for his beauty; from the sole of his foot even to the crown of his head there was no blemish in him." 2 Sam. xiv. 25. Add now to this that the mother of Absalom was perhaps the only Gentile wife of David, and that her only son was perhaps often, as we know he was once, a welcome guest at the heathen court of his grandfather, and we easily see the elements of trouble early sown in the character of this prince. How great is the mistake of parents who foster in their children exalted ideas of their superior birth, who flatter their vanity upon the beauty of their persons or their attire, and especially who suppose that any union of external advantages and polished address can make amends for the neglect of the hidden virtues of the heart, and for disregard of that piety toward God which lies at the foundation of all the rest! Whatever may be the reason for it, we have too much reason to fear that David's sons did not walk in the footsteps of their father. David himself mourns that, though his desire was so, his house was not with God as he wished. 2 Sam. xxiii. 5. The only pious child of David—so far as we know—was Solomon, and it is instructive to remember that he was born after these troubles began. In parental duty, as elsewhere, perhaps David could say, "Before I was afflicted I went astray; but now have I kept thy word." Perhaps we have the key to Absalom's training in what is said of Adonijah, who was a younger brother of Absalom. His father had not displeased him at any time in saying, "Why hast thou done so?" If thus he trained Absalom, we can scarcely wonder at his character, his conduct and his end as they are set before us in these pages.

The children of Maacah, the daughter of Talmai, king of Geshur, were two—Absalom and Tamar. Absalom had four children. One daughter showed his affection for his afflicted sister by bearing her name; and three sons, but these sons, at least, seem to have died early, for we read of a pillar erected by Absalom to keep his name in remembrance because he had no sons. We do not rank very high the capacity of this prince, but his personal manners, to which every man owes much of his influence, were polished and highly pleasing. The language of the scriptural writers is so simple that we scarcely realize the rank in living society which as held by the men thus named. We hardly think of Absalom as a prince in the realm of Judah, as entertaining lofty ideas of his importance and as ambitious of distinction and even of the throne.

We can scarcely wonder at the indignation aroused in the breast of Absalom by the wicked conduct of his half-brother, Amnon; and though we may wonder that he so long delayed his revenge, we are less amazed that he did not suffer the outrage to go unpunished. The delay, however, seems to reveal that Absalom was not a quick-tempered and hasty man. His revenge was of that cool and deliberate kind that never forgets an injury, that can use dissimulation to cover over the real feelings of his heart, and that smiles upon the victim it is only desirous to entrap. When the hour comes, he is ready to go any length to secure his end, but till he is ready every overt act is kept back. It is possible that in the first burst of anger a hasty word escaped of his design against Amnon, for it turns out in the end that when the deed was done, his cousin, Jonadab, the same wicked man who had advised the incest of Amnon, knew also before that Absalom had resolved to slay the insulter. This long-cherished purpose was accomplished amidst the reconciliation and friendship. David himself, with all the king's sons, was invited to a feast. The great expense of such entertainments, especially when the king was present, induced David to decline the pressing invitation; but Amnon was among the company, and to the great dismay of the guests he was slain in the midst of the feast. A panic was immediately created. Perhaps it was thought that the ambitious Absalom designed to put out of his way every rival for the throne, and a swift messenger brought tidings to David that all the king's sons were slain.

The refuge of Absalom was with his maternal grandfather, the king of Geshur. He remained there three years, greatly to the grief of David, who tenderly loved him, but who would not recall him in token of displeasure for his offence. But Joab, who seems to have been attached to Absalom, perceiving that the father's heart was tender toward his son, devised a method of securing the return of Absalom. He sent a cunning woman to David as if to present a petition for the benefit of her own distressed family. The king appears in a very favourable light as listening to her request, and promising her the wished-for relief. But no sooner did she make the attempt to apply the parable than the king understood the object she had in view; and so well did he understand the mind of Joab that he traced his hand in all this thing. He allowed the return of Absalom, but refused to allow him to come near the palace. This kind of life—dwelling in Jerusalem, yet not allowed to see the king—was irksome to the young man. Even his friend Joab refused to meet him when requested to do so. But when Absalom used stringent means to secure a visit, he consented to plead with the king in his behalf, and the young man was restored to his father's favour and to his place at court.

It is not unlikely that his three years' sojourn in the royal court of his grandfather had filled the mind of Absalom with vain and ambitious thoughts. His mother's kindred may have urged that none of David's sons were so fit as he to sit upon the throne; and doubtless during his discontented sojourn in Jerusalem, when he was not allowed to see his royal father, he found company suited to the state of his mind, and in this society he gradually became prepared to entertain treasonable designs against his father's throne. When men, by constraint or willingly, are thrown much among one particular class of people, and have their thoughts run in certain channels, it is almost of necessity that they get partial views of society, and put too high an estimate upon the things that most interest themselves. So long as Absalom was denied the favour of his father, his most likely companions would be those who felt that the king had injured them, and who were therefore disaffected toward his government. Every monarch must of necessity have such around him, for wisdom and justice often give offence as great as the opposite vices, since few men are willing to acknowledge the justice of decisions or appointments that are contrary to their interests. But unhappily, in addition to the occasion taken for offence for unjust reasons, David had given just grounds for disaffection to some of his subjects. With these discontented persons Absalom was likely to be familiar, and the affairs of the kingdom would take the complexion of their thoughts. As they were disaffected; as the more they consulted upon the subject, the more they felt so; as their sense of injury was aggravated by dwelling upon it,—so they magnified the discontents of the nation, and easily persuaded themselves that the tribes of Israel were restive under the yoke of David, and that they would be ready at once to overturn the throne, if only an able and popular leader was ready, around whom they might rally, and whom they might salute as king.

Perhaps these men had reasons to judge that a rebellion could easily be raised up in the land. In point of fact, we find afterward the conspiracy became very strong with Absalom, and there was some difficulty in quelling it, even after the death of its leader. It may be that the wars of David, though of many valuable results, were felt to be oppressive upon the kingdom. By them the boundaries of the kingdom had been enlarged; a large spoil had been brought into Judah; the precious metals had been brought into circulation more than ever before; and the style of living had advanced as the nation became more wealthy. But we can easily judge that both during the reign of David and that of Solomon the burden of taxation was severely felt, in addition to the levies of men and the loss of so many in battle. For, with all the success of David, he seems not to have relied upon his spoils for maintaining the government. He laid aside the immense treasures of gold and silver and brass as so much in readiness for the splendid temple which his successor was to build. It would add to the discontents of the people that these sums were laid aside for an enterprise they could scarcely appreciate, while yet they were made to feel the burdens of the government.

But perhaps personal discontent had much to do with their rising troubles. The chief man among the conspirators with Absalom seems to have been Ahithophel, the Shilonite. We have mentioned this man before as the grandfather of Bathsheba, and in this perhaps we find the causes of his disaffection. It becomes us to notice how, in the retributive operations of Providence, the sin of David comes back repeatedly upon him. His sin was not only a moral offence of the gravest kind, but it was also highly impolitic. Here we see evidence that he has given dangerous offence to one of the principal men of his court. Ahithophel is represented as the wisest man of his time. His penetrating mind and his long experience rendered his counsels almost infallible for their wisdom. In the strong language of the inspired writer, the counsel of Ahithophel, which he counselled in those days, was as if a man had inquired at the oracle of God; so was all the counsel of Ahithophel, both with David and with Absalom. That he was a wicked man at the same time that he was wise is sufficiently proved by his tragical end; and it furnishes us with an instance of that which we often see in the world around us—that pride of intellect is an enemy dangerous to the spiritual interests of man.

Yet, while we may believe that there were discontents in Israel of which these men would take advantage, it is not likely they were widely spread; the more sanguine minds among the discontented would naturally aggravate them, but the subsequent counsels of Ahithophel sufficiently show that he was well aware how desperate was their undertaking to overthrow the throne of such a man as David. There was a dark side to his government, as there ever will be to every government upon earth. David had done things which no ruler should do; he had given private individuals great offence; but the opposition had looked only at their grievances, and had forgotten that, upon the whole, the nation at large had good reason to be satisfied with David. He was a wise, a good, a righteous king; over his faults he himself deeply mourned, and in his virtues his people ought to have rejoiced. He had found the kingdom weak and divided, he brought it to union and strength; he had found the people prone to idolatry and forgetful of their covenant with God, and he had restored the tabernacle and the ark to their rank, and had established the due order of Jehovah's worship; he had found their enemies triumphant against his people, and occupying a large portion of the land which God's promise had given to Abraham, and he had made the nation a first-rate military power, raised his fame among all the lands around, and enlarged the boundaries of Israel to the extent of God's ancient covenant. It was a desperate undertaking, such as discontent and ambition would alone attempt; and we see the cunning of Ahithophel in the first preparations that are made for it.

These preparations were made in the efforts of Absalom to ingratiate himself with the people, and without suspicion to alienate them from his father. He affected a style of splendour such as had never before been seen in Israel. The use of chariots had been forbidden in their wars—perhaps in part to repress the spirit of extravagance, and in part because, in a mountainous land like Judea, wars are best conducted by foot soldiers. In one of David's wars he had overthrown an army well supplied with chariots, and he had reserved a few of those taken upon the overthrow of Hadadezer, rather for state occasions than for warfare. Perhaps Absalom had seen splendour like this in the court of his grandfather, and he now began in Israel to imitate the style of foreign powers. In addition to this magnificence of aristocracy, he assumed the condescending manners which among the common people would gain him friends and admirers. Here we have an ancient and graphic picture of a demagogue; the union of intense pride of self and of station with fawning sycophancy and studied courtesy; the union of ambitious schemes for personal advancement with the most clamorous and busy pretensions for seeking the good of the dear people; the careful stirring up of discontent with the existing rule, and the ready willingness to give up the pleasures of private life to devote himself to the public good. Such is the demagogue in any land or belonging to any party—corrupt wherever he is found, as ready for one side as the other if his interests so point, and with all his pleasant smiles and fair words unworthy of the confidence of any one. Absalom was diligent in his undertaking. He rose early and displayed his fine person and elegant manners where men were wont to gather together. Especially as the people from the surrounding country entered the city, he sought their acquaintance, inquired their business and sympathized with the success of their various plans. The petty grievances of this or that man might have found a ready listener in him, and the promise of redress is a very easy thing to make when offices of power and trust are sought rather than held. The principles of human nature are the same in all ages; political wire-working is much the same thing under any kind of government, and the complaisance of a noble prince like Absalom easily won him popularity in Israel. Perhaps the part of Ahithophel was to prevent or to watch all suspicions in the mind of David; his position as a wise counsellor gave him both influence and opportunity for this, and their plans were ripe for execution before the king knew what was going on. At the precise juncture when he was ready, Absalom asked the king's leave to go to Hebron, and, that he might the more easily secure this, pretended religious zeal. He knew well that his father's heart was alive to the service of God, and that he would be little likely to refuse his son any favour when he thought his request proceeded from religious convictions, or that his granting it would give piety any more power over his heart. Yet Absalom is but adding an odious hypocrisy to the ingratitude and treason he meditates. He took with him a body of two hundred men who had not been made acquainted with his designs; but he scattered the conspirators through the kingdom, who were all at one time to raise the standard of revolt, and to give the movement an appearance as much as possible of a popular and general rising. His first aim was to secure Hebron, which in all likelihood was, next to Jerusalem itself, the chief city and fortress of the kingdom. It will be remembered that Hebron had been the capital of David in the earlier years of his reign, and this may have been among the reasons for making it the centre of the new operations. Besides, having been a royal city even from the times of the ancient Canaanites, and a city of refuge in Israel, Hebron was judiciously chosen for his purposes.

The panic was great in Jerusalem when it was announced that Absalom had seized Hebron and raised the standard of rebellion, and especially as tidings came in that he had been simultaneously proclaimed in different parts of the kingdom. Indeed, the apparent fact that he was the eldest living son of a king now growing old may have made well-disposed citizens averse to taking any hasty steps in opposition to him; and in the activity of his friends the fears of David were highly excited. We see extraordinary evidence of Absalom's apparent success in the movements of David. He immediately resolved to abandon Jerusalem—his capital, his palace and the strongest fortress in the kingdom; and this evidently not because he feared for the fortifications, but because he mistrusted the faithfulness of the population. In Jerusalem, Absalom had been practicing his arts, and he had won the hearts of so many that David feared to trust his own people. Accordingly we find when the king went forth from the city he did not entrust his protection to native Israelites. It is one of the proofs of the prosperity of religion in the times of David and Solomon that we find so many foreigners in the land, and that some of them at least appear to have been drawn to the kingdom by religious considerations. The vital spirit of true piety in all ages is evangelistic; and though the

Jewish Church was, for special reasons, separated from the nations around, the Gentiles needed the gospel from their hands then as much as they need it now from ours. In obedience to the spirit of true piety, the door of the Jewish Church had been left open for the admission of proselytes, and so long as the sins and wants of men outside of Judea continued, and so long as the vital spirit of piety remained in the Church, it was a necessary consequence that any revival of true piety in Israel would bring in proselytes from the nations around. Such a revival would operate just as revivals do now. They prepare the minds of men, inside of the Church and outside, for religious thoughtfulness; and no people can begin seriously to consider these great matters without the uprising of piety. When there is religion enough in a Church to attract the attention of the world and make men feel their sinfulness and need, there will also be a spirit of readiness to seek the good of others on the part of the Church.

So was it in Israel in the days of David and Solomon. The Church was not then free from all cause of blame, but they were the best days of Israelitish history. No wonder that many from among the heathen around then longed to leave their polluting idolatries and to take shelter under the protection of the God of Jacob; and if then the Church had not the missionary spirit that now belongs to her, yet there was not a pious heart in

Israel that would not welcome the poor stranger to share in their inheritance and to worship at the altar of their God. We have had previous occasion to remark that some of the mighty men of David's army—Uriah among the number—were converted heathen; and it would seem that some of the chosen troops of David's army were composed of these foreigners, who formed separate regiments, and were relied upon for their valour, their discipline and their faithfulness in times of deepest peril. David's chosen guards were the Cherethites, the Pelethites and the Gittites; and in this hour of trial, when he leaves Jerusalem, he distrusts his native subjects and will not rely upon native troops. Some commentators have found it hard to believe that these celebrated guards were foreigners, but the chief ground of their objection—namely, that David would not commit himself to the care of uncircumcised men—is removed by understanding that they were proselytes to the Jewish faith, and thus naturalized in Israel. It is not unlikely that David first formed these guards while Saul was yet alive; that they had supported him now for many years; that they were the veterans of the army; and indeed, in an age and region where standing armies were almost unknown, that they were the only organized and disciplined forces in the land. If we look at the homes of these troops, we find one regiment of Gittites, and the brief declaration that they followed him from Gath, the place of his former refuge. We find another of Cherethites, the name of a tribe of Gentiles whom David had attacked and spoiled, and from whose captive children, it is possible, he had formed this band.

While relying, however, upon these veterans, the king also received some proofs of warm attachment to him on the part of the people of Jerusalem. Indeed, notwithstanding his fears, a large part of the population went forth with him, bitterly bewailing the calamity that had come upon the kingdom and their venerable monarch. One man is mentioned especially as showing an attachment which the king scarcely expected. This was Ittai, the Gittite, a man who for some reason had fled from his native country and become an exile at the court of David. That he was a man of some distinction appears from the fact that he had with him a body of men whom he joined to the king's forces, and that David gave him a high rank in his army. That he had not been long in the country is plain from David's own words; yet he seems to have learned the language of an Israelite and to have been sincerely attached to the afflicted king.

It was doubtless a great support to the feelings of David in this time of deep trouble that upon his side were the priests of the Lord. As he passed out of the city he found that preparation had been made, according to the due order of the sanctuary, to carry forth also the ark of God. The priests, Zadok and Abiathar, with the Levites in their proper places, according to the ancient regulations, set down the ark that the people might all pass by it, after which it was to bring up the rear. This act of the priests displayed not only attachment to David and zeal for good order in the state, but just regard for the interests of religion. For the spread of piety had little to hope for in the success of an usurper who was to wear his crown in defiance of his duty to his father and of the will of God; and Absalom has as yet given no tokens that religion would flourish under his rule. Piety does not bestow political foresight, nor do the ministers of religion always discern what is for the good of the state; yet it is of great importance, especially in times of revolution, that the side of truth and righteousness should have the support of all good men.

## CHAPTER XVI.

### *THE PROGRESS OF THE REBELLION.*

AT the close of our last chapter we left the king, surrounded by a weeping multitude, passing out of the city of Jerusalem, in full flight from the rebel armies. This is an hour of deep affliction for David, and we may well sympathize with him as he went up the ascent of Mount Olivet, with his head covered and his feet bare in token of his mourning, and the people around giving every token of grief. There is one remarkable spot upon the Mount of Olives, where it rises abruptly to the east from the ravine of the Brook Kedron, from which the eye can command a complete and advantageous view of the city. A thousand years after this the greater Son of David stood here and gazed upon the beautiful city spread out before him, and wept over her sins, her hardness of heart, her rejection of mercy and her coming desolations. From this same spot, it may be, did David now look down in grief and anguish. He saw the city he had established, the palace he had built and the people he had loved, and from all now he must go forth a throneless exile. He had been homeless and an exile before, but that was in the days of his youth and vigour, when he was inured to hardship; and this was in his old age, and after he had long forgotten the privations and fatigues of such a life. And everything combined to point with bitterness the sting that now entered the soul of David. His own people, for whom he had done so much, whose prosperity he had promoted, whose boundaries he had enlarged, and whom his victories had set free from the fear of their enemies, had now proved faithless. Yet more; his own son was the author of his present troubles. This son was tenderly loved, he had been delicately reared, he had been dealt with leniently, and now he has raised his ungrateful hand against his father. But chiefly did David look back at the real origin of these calamities. Before his mind arose the form of Nathan, and the words again rang in his ears, "I will raise up evil out of thine own house." Before his mind rose up his sin, and he knew that but for this he would not now be an exile. This was the chief bitterness of his present trial. In his former exile David was supported by the consciousness of right. The sin belonged to Saul then. It is far otherwise now. True, Absalom is not to be justified, but David lacks the support of a humble and righteous man.

But we see here a return to the earlier piety of David. His expressions at this time are such as to give proof that he has profited by the chastisements which God's hand has laid upon him. And here, let us notice, is a matter carefully to be considered as we look upon the troubled experiences of life. The difference between godly and ungodly men in this world is not so much a difference of affliction as in the effect produced upon them by affliction. David suffered afflictions when righteous and when innocent, and he bears both with a pious mind. Trouble itself is no test of character; it may come to the evil and the good; it may come for reasons we cannot discern, as the earlier troubles of David, or for reasons we can understand, like these later troubles; but the manner in which we endure afflictions is a test of character. To those who are properly exercised by them they yield the peaceable fruits of righteousness.

Let us look at the mind of the king as he goes forth from Jerusalem and passes weeping up the side of Olivet. Here are proofs of a meekness and humility, of a patience and resignation, of a penitence and faith, that well become the stricken man of God. He bade the priests carry back the ark of God, and to remain themselves in the city. It was doubtless to secure some advantages to David's cause that Zadok and Abiathar had made this movement. If the weight of the priesthood were thrown on his side in the coming struggle, if the ark itself was on his side, they perhaps hoped that the pious part of the nation would join the same party, or at least be averse to operating against

David. And doubtless the king well knew what were the advantages he might hope to secure from the presence of the ark. Yet, either because he deemed it unlawful to take it forth in his wanderings, or more likely as one who felt the frown of his God upon him—because, humbled for his sins, he felt unworthy and indisposed to press his advantages to the utmost—he bade the priests carry back the ark into the city, and to abide there themselves with it. We may regard this as an act of faith on the part of David. It seems to express his confidence that he should yet return to his capital and his palace, and that then he should again enjoy the privileges of the ark. But it is not a presumptuous confidence. Resignation to the orderings of God's holy will is more plainly expressed. He knew he was now suffering the rebuke of God, and fears and hopes mingle together in his words. Faith trusts that he shall return, but it also judges that the Lord is righteous, and bows in resignation in contemplating another result as possible. By a subsequent arrangement, as we shall see, the presence of the priests in Jerusalem was made to subserve David's interests.

As David passed up the side of the mountain, he learned for the first time that the trusted Ahithophel was among the conspirators. The wise counsels of this man seem to have been feared beyond any other power yet on the side of Absalom. When David heard of his defection, he uttered simply this ejaculatory prayer: "O Lord, I pray thee, turn the counsel of Ahithophel into foolishness!" How wise this man's counsel was, and how fully this brief prayer was answered, we will take further occasion to notice. We may simply now remark in passing that David's example teaches us how little excuse any man can have for neglecting prayer. Here we may see that prayer is a spirit rather than a form. Let us have the form when our circumstances will admit of it. If we can enter our closet, if we can be alone with God, if we can bow down on our knees before him,—these are favourable circumstances to enable us to collect our thoughts, to make us more serious, and to enable us to plead our cause with humility and fervency; and we should use all such advantages when we can. But David teaches that when occasion calls for it we may pray in a crowd, we may lift up the heart to God, we may offer but a single sentence, and the prayer be accepted and answered.

Just at this moment another distinguished friend of David came to meet him and to join his march. This was Hushai the Archite, one of David's counsellors. David immediately formed the plan of defeating Ahithophel's counsels by counterplotting. Having great confidence in Hushai, he urged that he should go into the city and profess to be the friend of Absalom, that he might give him counsels, apparently sincere, but designed in reality to further the cause of David. No just theory of morals can decide that plans of this nature are upright, but, as war itself is but organized and premeditated crime and wrong, we need scarcely wonder if it is carried on by means that involve both falsehood and insincerity.

The next man who is named as meeting the king, a little farther on his way, was Ziba, the steward of Mephibosheth, the son of Jonathan. Taking the whole narrative concerning these men, both now and afterward, we may judge that David acted hastily, perhaps harshly and unjustly, toward the son of his early friend. We can scarcely wonder, indeed, at what he says here. Ziba met him with refreshments and food, such as to show clearly his attachment to David, and in the very act of this he utters a plausible but malicious slander against Mephibosheth. If we remember that Jonathan was Saul's eldest son, and Mephibosheth his only child, we may see that the regular descent of Israel's crown would have been to this man. At a time, then, when his own son was a traitor in arms against him, David could easily believe the story that the heir of Saul hoped to secure some advantage from these troubles in the land. But it appeared afterward that this was a pure fiction on the part of Ziba. Indeed, this is such a world of slander that we can scarcely believe any tale we hear of a neighbour, even when there are circumstances that render it plausible; and if David now feels that Mephibosheth has been ungrateful for his past kindness, many a time since has the slanderer or talebearer disturbed the warmth of feeling in friendly hearts; and the few necessary words of explanation are not given because the causes of alienation are never known, perhaps never suspected, by the slandered party. The son of Jonathan easily vindicated himself when an opportunity was afforded him. He had really sympathized with David; he had designed to show this sympathy by coming to him; but he was a cripple, and Ziba had treacherously kept from him the means of coming. The gratitude and faithfulness of this son appears not only from his signs of mourning so long as David was in trouble, but also by the meekness with which he acquiesces in the division of his estate with the unfaithful Ziba. It is harder to reconcile David's decision in the case with either wisdom or justice. If his previous judgment of Mephibosheth was hasty, it ought to have been reversed when he knew the truth. Ziba had rendered David service in a time of need, and there was good reason for rendering him some reward. But Ziba had spoken basely of his master, and that was reason why his reward should be found elsewhere than by giving him half of Mephibosheth's estate. But by these thoughts we anticipate the narrative.

The same kind of anticipation is needful in our mention of Shimei the son of Gera. This man is an example of a time-server. Governed by no settled principles, but by the aspect of the times, he here came forth to reproach David and to cast curses upon him; and yet afterward, when the kingdom was again in the hand of David, he was among the first to show his zeal for the very man he here curses. Perhaps we may look upon the curses of Shimei as an example of the feeling which may have dwelt in many minds in reference to David. For the words of Shimei we may regard not as expressing his own real sentiments, since he so easily undoes all he is now doing, but as expressing his sense of the prevailing sentiment. Such time-serving politicians sometimes overreach themselves as this man now did; yet are they generally very careful to watch the way things are going before they commit themselves. It is remarkable that the reproaches of Shimei have no apparent reference to David's great sin, but simply to his reigning in the stead of Saul.

Though we may despise the man in view of all the facts, we may regard it as rather a bold thing for Shimei thus to curse David. Nor did he do this without danger. It would have cost him his head, but for David's own forbearance; and even after the restoration he was not out of danger. Indeed, the final result was the death of Shimei for this crime, as we shall need to notice hereafter. But now David is forbearing. It is not hard to see why. Forbearance and forgiveness are virtues so nearly allied to penitence that they always dwell together in the same heart. Never was such a sight seen on earth as a revengeful penitent; but whenever a man feels the need of the divine mercy toward his own sins, he is little disposed to think harshly of the offences that others commit against him. It is divine philosophy that teaches, "If ye forgive not men their trespasses, neither will your heavenly Father forgive your trespasses." Beware of harsh judgments, of pride, of revenge, of censoriousness, lest to indulge such tempers proves your own impenitence. David was now a penitent. He recognized the hand of God in these troubles; he acknowledged that he deeply deserved them all; he did not venture to rebel in the least; and he is willing to regard Shimei as rather an instrument in the hand of God to afflict him. Feeling keenly under the afflictions laid upon him by his own sin, he is little disposed to resist those offered by this stranger. So, when the kingdom was restored to him, he is willing still to overlook Shimei's offences, because he would not mar the festivities of a joyful day.

In truth, however, there were two aspects of this crime of Shimei, and by considering these we may reconcile David's forbearance with the fact that he afterward called the attention of Solomon to this case, and bade him deal with Shimei in his wisdom. David was a man, but he was also a monarch. It might be right to do one thing at the prompting of his private feelings, and yet another would be more just and more wise to promote the public interests. So far as the offence of Shimei was against David personally, he was just in that humble frame of mind that would prompt him to overlook it. But forgiveness does not imply that the offence is not considered grave; forgiveness implies a sense of injury, since there is no room for pardon where no offence is given. The crime of Shimei was directly against the majesty of the Jewish throne; he was himself, it is likely, a dangerous man, and the king's feelings should not have overborne the public interests. It is likely that his so dealing with Shimei was found to be a public wrong, and it was in this view of the case that he called Solomon's attention to it. But his words on this occasion will in due time be considered.

David's journey was to the other side of Jordan. Upon that part of the kingdom his reign had been especially beneficial; he had enlarged the boundaries of Judea in that direction, and he looked for the firmest support from that part of the people. These were, perhaps, the wisest measures he could have adopted; and as he passed on, his mind gradually gained greater confidence in God, so that he was but little disturbed even when he heard the possible plans of Absalom and used means to evade his power. The alarms that reached his camp, the danger of his being taken in the night, and his confidence in God are graphically set forth in the third Psalm, which was written at this time.

But we will leave the king for the present, and return to Jerusalem, where Absalom enters with the triumph of a king. It shows the dependence placed upon Ahithophel that he is so expressly named as accompanying Absalom. On the other hand, the grief of David at the loss of such a counsellor is plainly set forth in the fifty-fifth Psalm. If we may regard this Ahithophel as one held in reputation for his piety, as David seems there to teach (v. 13, 14), then his was a fall through hypocrisy, and a fall without recovery, even to his destruction. Absalom was surprised to see Hushai the Archite in Jerusalem, and making overtures for his friendship. But while so many have forsaken David, he seems to entertain no suspicion of deception.

The reputation of Ahithophel was so great that we closely examine his counsel to know wherein lay its wisdom. We are shocked at the wicked conduct to which he advises Absalom. Yet, respecting it, we may notice these things: 1st. Here David's past sin is brought to remembrance and paid in kind. As he has sown he reaps. 2d. Here Nathan's words receive their fulfilment. This is just as the prophet declared to him. 3d. Here we see how the counsels of God secure his ends, while yet the voluntary agency of man is not interfered with. We can scarcely think that either Absalom or Ahithophel thought of Nathan's words, which they here fulfilled, as long afterward the

Jews ignorantly fulfilled the divine counsels in the death of Christ.

But wherein consists the wisdom of Ahithophel's counsel in this case? The wickedness of the matter is plain enough, but its wisdom is as plain if we simply call to mind what wisdom is. True wisdom in its final results must be righteous, but so far as wicked counsels can be wise we may say this counsel was. If wisdom is the choice of suitable measures to secure a certain end, then Ahithophel's counsel was wise. No conduct more suitable to the purposes of this shrewd man could Absalom exhibit. Ahithophel had engaged now in a desperate undertaking, and he was resolved to succeed or perish. Like a general who, on entering the field, flings away his scabbard; like a sea captain who nails his colors to the mast; as Cortes, with his band of five hundred men,* landing on the shores of powerful and unknown nations, and resolving to make deadly hostilities against them, had the art to persuade his companions to destroy their shipping, and thus to shut themselves up to the desperate alternative of conquering or of dying upon that foreign soil; so now Ahithophel would cut off for himself and for Absalom and for Israel all hope of any reconciliation to David. He well knew the warm attachment of David to Absalom; he knew that he would be willing to make almost any sacrifice rather than fight against his son; perhaps he feared

* Robertson's America, 211.

also for the fickleness of Absalom himself, and for the fear or affection of the people for the dethroned monarch; and having full persuasion that all his own hopes lay in the uncompromised success of the rebellion, he had no thought of reconciliation, knowing that he had for ever forfeited the respect of David. Ahithophel, therefore, wishes to insult David as grievously as possible; not a word of treaty is heard between him and Absalom; the people are to understand that the die is cast, and that an impassable gulf yawns between the contending rivals. We see thus that the counsel of Ahithophel was fully adapted to suit the case to which he applied it.

Following out this desperate policy, Ahithophel next counsels the most energetic measures to secure the death of David as speedily as possible. Here again his wisdom seems not to fail him. He counsels prompt action. The experience of all ages has shown that nowhere is prompt and ready enterprise more needful to success than in just such schemes as this of Absalom. To defend a land from treason or invasion, it may be wise in a commander to be slow and cautious, for the double purpose of annoying the enemy by delay and by want of provisions, and of giving time to the loyal people of the land to recover from hasty alarms. It was highly important for the success of Absalom's plans that the people of the land should have little time to recover from their panic, that their sober second thoughts should not get the mastery in their minds, and that David and Joab should have as little time as possible to gather troops. A slight success on the part of the rebels at the outset would be a great advantage, just as the people were in many places hesitating which side they should choose. The counsel of Ahithophel was wise, and this is proved by the effect produced in David's camp when the spies brought intelligence of it. He would have taken twelve thousand men, and that very night strike for David's life, well knowing that if he was dead the strife must turn in favour of Absalom.

One of the difficult problems of man's philosophy is here brought before us. David's prayer was that the counsel of Ahithophel be turned to foolishness, and the inspired writer tells us that the "Lord had appointed to defeat the good counsel of Ahithophel, to the intent that the Lord might bring evil upon Absalom." Now, the question has been asked a thousand times, How are the counsels of God—so wise, so certain of accomplishment consistent with the free agency of man? But here, as elsewhere, there are certain great principles we know well—certain facts we can observe, and yet in the understanding of their relations to each other there are limits which we cannot pass. We know that it is of great importance that man should be a voluntary agent; we know that accountable action must be voluntary action; we know by experience that we ourselves are free, and no argument can really convince us that other men are not also free. But we know also that the importance is infinitely greater—indeed the necessity is imperative—that God should be free, able to carry out his plans, incapable of being thwarted, and yet fully able to do all he desires without interfering with the free nature he has given to man. We see the facts plainly. Absalom and his elders weighed the two counsels of Ahithophel and of Hushai the Archite, yet the result is that they freely choose folly. There is no wisdom nor counsel against the Lord. Our only safety is in being upon the side of the Lord and of right. When we fight against him he can make our own counsels conspire for our defeat. Righteous men will not be disposed to complain of the government which always favours them and causes all things to work for their good, and the wicked have no right to complain if God overrules their wickedness to secure their own destruction.

We need not vindicate the righteousness of Hushai in this matter, but we may admire the skill and wisdom of a man who could so readily frame a plan to defeat the counsel of Ahithophel. His plan did not lack its plausible features. He artfully joined with the temper of those about him to counsel the utter destruction of David, but he awakened their fears as to the ready success of the proposed scheme to effect it. Was it likely that a veteran warrior like David would expose himself to easy attack at such a juncture? Was it likely that a mighty man like Joab, who had never lost a battle, could be easily surprised or overcome? Could the rising cause of Absalom wisely venture the risk of defeat in the first attack, and thus of disheartening his troops and encouraging the royal forces? By suggestions like these, which had no force to his own mind, Hushai succeeded in convincing the counsellors about Absalom that they had better not attempt the bold plan of Ahithophel.

Hushai has given his counsel, but he does not know that it will be followed. His next attempt is to send tidings to David of the two counsels. For this end, following the king's advice, he employed the two sons of the priests—one of whom is afterward named as a swift runner—to carry the tidings to the king, and his advice to secure himself in case the other counsel should be adopted. It would seem that Absalom's guards had secured the city to prevent the escape of any one with tidings. But Hushai's wisdom had prepared for this. The young men were already beyond the sentinels, and a young woman, as little likely to be suspected, was employed to take the word to them. The watchfulness of Absalom's friends may be judged from the fact that even this movement was noticed, and that night pursuit was made of the spies—so closely behind them that they were nearly taken. They found a safe hiding-place in a well that was so artfully covered as to remain unsuspected, and after the pursuers departed they reached the camp of David in safety. Of course the nature of their tidings was unknown to the men of Absalom, or Hushai would have been put in peril.

No sooner is Ahithophel aware that his counsel has been overruled than he forecasts at once the disastrous issue of the rebellion. It may have been in part through mortification that Hushai should be preferred to him, but it is quite as likely it was because he discovered that this course would be fatal to Absalom that he now despairs. He went home, put his house in order and hung himself. Died Ahithophel as a fool dieth. In his life he had been famous for wisdom, and he set his affairs in order in his last moments to show that his intellect was sound; yet the folly of his death can find no vindication at any tribunal of righteous judgment. Be not surprised that a wise man should do so foolish a thing. Remember that his was only worldly wisdom. He had not learned the rudiments in that sacred school whose first lesson is, "The fear of the Lord is the beginning of wisdom." Among heathen and infidel philosophers suicide has been commended, and this of Ahithophel would be justified on their principles. But Christianity knows no circumstances that can vindicate the madness of any man who dares to murder himself and to rush, both unbidden and unprepared, into the presence of God. Of all awful crimes that we can consider, none is more flagrant than for a man to take his own life. Of all the wretched forms of dying which men have ever known, no wise man would wish to follow in the lead of Ahithophel and Judas. And there is another crime included in this, which may be committed by men who die a natural death —the greatest crime of all, the crime of destroying the never-dying soul. To commit this crime it does not need that a man should follow the exact footsteps of Ahithophel. We shudder at the sin and folly of suicide. Shall any of us commit the more common crime of destroying our own souls? It may not be by the deliberate rejection of the gospel of Christ. It may not be with the uttered defiance of God upon our lips. It may be with many serious thoughts of our duties to God—with many purposes formed of repentance. It may be by a simple neglect of the great salvation until the calls of mercy cease to sound and we have entered eternity unprepared. But, however it occurs, the man who is lost from the sound of the gospel is a self-murderer for eternity.

The arrangements for a great battle are succinctly given. The forces of Absalom are entrusted to his cousin Amasa, but another cousin, the indomitable Joab, was commander-in-chief for David. Under Joab, commanding each a third of the army, were Abishai his brother, and the foreign general, Ittai the Gittite. Absalom went forth in person, but David's men would not allow him to go into the battle. David was still tender in his love for his erring son; especially, perhaps, he could not endure the thought of his death—not only a rebel against his father, but a rebel against his God. He gave commandment, therefore, to the officers and to all the army that, whatever might be the issue of the conflict, Absalom might be spared. But here again we see Joab decide upon his own responsibility what ought to be done, and carry it out without reference to the wishes of the king. And Joab was right as well as politic in this resolve for the death of Absalom. Perhaps he was indignant that Absalom had proved treacherous to himself, for by his mediation he had been brought home and reconciled to David, and thus ungratefully had he requited it. But, apart from personal feeling, Joab knew that the death of Absalom was absolutely necessary for the peace of the kingdom, for troubles were now abroad which could hardly be settled even when Absalom was gone, and which indeed resulted in evil fifty years later. He felt also that the death of Absalom was richly deserved for his crimes; that it would save the lives of many better men than he; and in all likelihood he felt that his own safety and the safety of his companions-in-arms depended upon the destruction of the rebel. For if Absalom now lived, if he became again reconciled to David, if perhaps he should one day become David's successor, Joab knew him too well to think that he would ever forgive the victorious arms that had overthrown him in the wood of Ephraim. Joab entered the battle, therefore, fully resolved upon Absalom's death.

The unhappy prince fell ingloriously. He was riding through the wood where the battle occurred when he was roughly torn from his mule by an unexpected enemy. The hair of Absalom was remarkably luxuriant, and it was his pride. As his mule passed under an oak tree this hair caught upon a projecting limb, his mule passed from under him and he was inextricably entangled. We can hardly decide where this happened. It would almost seem as if, with desperate valour, he had pressed beyond his own troops within the lines of the opposing army. If this accident occurred in the sight of his own troops, they would have rendered assistance or formed a guard around him. It seems, however, rather to have occurred in a scattered pursuit, where the armies were fighting in a forest, for Joab blew a trumpet to recall his troops as soon as Absalom was dead. This death was by the hands of Joab himself, for no inferior person would venture so to disobey the king.

Thus died the unhappy Absalom. He had erected a pillar to keep his name in memory among the people, but all knowledge of him would long since have passed away from among men but for the record of his sins and his untimely fate in these sacred pages. Perhaps there is no man that wishes to be totally forgotten when he has passed away from life. We would have our names sculptured on the beautiful marble in the silent city of the dead, whose multiplying population know not the visits of their sorrowing friends; we would wish to be kindly thought of by loving hearts after we are gone. But how much easier and more profitable is that sanctified ambition that desires to have our names written not on marble, nor even in human hearts, but in the Lamb's Book of Life. Of what avail would be the highest honours of earth, or the widest fame after death, to the man who is unprepared to meet his God? There is a sense in which we all shall be soon forgotten. Our places will soon be emptied and soon filled again. Other men will dwell in our pleasant homes, and rove over these fields, and we will scarcely be missed, as we ourselves think only now and then of those we have formerly loved. But there is a sense in which we shall never be forgotten, and shall ourselves never forget. Our names are written, our deeds are recorded, our memory is to survive. Shall we lose in the dying engagements of to-day the infinite importance of an immortal life? Trembling on the brink of eternity, will we never think long enough to prepare for it? Shall we grasp after earth's honours? and it may be, like Absalom, suddenly lose all to be hurried to an unwelcome death!

## CHAPTER XVII.

### *GRIEF FOR THE DEATH OF ABSALOM.*

THE affecting account of the king's lament over Absalom presents to us a scene of the deepest interest and instruction. A momentous battle has just been fought, the fate of a great empire just decided. The serious and parricidal rebellion that had driven the royal David from his capital, insulted him in his most sacred rights, carried away by its seductions ten thousand of his people, and threatened an entire revolution in the government, has just been quelled and its leader slain. The crown that had so nearly been thrown off rests again upon the monarch's brow; the armies of David are returning from victory flushed with success, and anxious to salute the king's ears with their eager congratulations. But did any faithful army ever meet such a response at the end of the strife. The man for whom they have fought, the exile for whom they have prepared a return to his royal city, the restored king whose throne they have now re-established, and for whom their shouts of exultation are raised, has no sympathy with their rejoicings, and gives no evidence that he regards himself as a victor. If his army had been routed, his bravest friends slain and his crown torn ruthlessly away, we could understand all this. But after the victory how strange is David's behaviour! He is overwhelmed with grief, he retires from public view, and he laments with bitter tears the success of his own army and the defeat of an ungrateful, insulting and implacable foe.

It is scarcely a sufficient explanation of this scene to say that the weeping victor was a father and the defeated rebel a son; for we may read upon many a dark page of the world's history that such ties of blood are of slight avail when the interests or the passions of the parties are brought into collision; that the stern questions of ambition and revenge have many a time crushed out of existence all the tender and gentle feelings of social life; that as here we have seen the child rising up in the most wicked and unprovoked rebellion against an indulgent father, so the father has delivered the son to death, and all the most tender ties of kindred have been trampled in the dust. Had David not only suppressed with a strong hand his son's rebellion, but proclaimed also public rejoicings over the victory and set forth the name of Absalom as accursed henceforth in Israel, he would but have carried out the usual feelings of kings at the end of such a strife. Indeed, that he should do something like this seemed almost demanded for the future safety of the throne against like rebellions.

Thus the people expected him to act; and dismay and amazement, like a defeat before their foes, filled the army of Israel, and sent each man silent and dispirited to his tent, that their king should weep in their hour of triumph.

But what is customary among the kings of the earth, or what are the promptings of man's corrupt and cruel nature in cases like this, where towering ambition and gross iniquity and base ingratitude have not a due reward, may be very different from the promptings of correct feelings and a pious judgment. We may find reasons to call forth our deep sympathy and perhaps our wise acquiescence in the strange conduct of David. He had reason to rejoice truly, for the result of the great battle was not simply his own exaltation, but the welfare of his kingdom. But he had reason to weep bitterly, for a part of the price of his success was the untimely death of a beloved son, and he was but too well assured that Absalom was not prepared to die. David was a king, but he was a righteous king. He was a father, but he was a pious father. It is the happy influence of true religion to sanctify and to render both more binding and more tender the natural bonds of human life. "Without natural affection" is one of the marks of extreme depravity to which even ungodly men do not often reach, and from which by the farthest remove the pious mind should be distant. It is the just influence of piety to strengthen and not to weaken the relationships of life; and that man has good reason to suspect that his is a vain religion who is not made by it a more faithful friend, a more affectionate husband, a truer father, a more obedient son, a more dutiful citizen. The same God who has made these the ordinary duties of life certainly never designed that when the soul of man more truly realizes his character and is more truly devoted to his fear, it should thereby be less prepared or fitted for the discharge of other duties. The new affection—GOD OVER ALL—which in all ages fills and characterizes a regenerated human mind, does in no wise drive out of the heart a single virtuous affection nor relax a single virtuous tie binding man to man.

There is certainly no relationship of our social life that has resting upon it responsibilities and duties of more general interest and of deeper importance than belong to the estate of a parent. We do not need, indeed, to institute a formal comparison between our various ties of kindred. Yet perhaps we may venture to say that no love on earth is purer in its own nature, none is more capable of surviving the various changes of circumstances, of separation, of neglect, of ingratitude, and even of guilt, than the love of a parent for a child. We too often see that separate abodes, separate engagements and jarring interests rudely tear asunder the ties of kind feeling and interest which should bind together in bonds of closest unity the children of the same womb and the same hearth. We have even seen it true that that nearest and dearest love of human kindred, by which in the wise arrangements of God's providence two persons whose early years have been passed apart, are united together with solemn vows that death only shall ever divide them—we have seen this bond snapped rudely asunder when chilled by unnatural coldness or struck by irreparable guilt. But it requires more to separate a parent from a child, so that the heart becomes cold toward him or that he can be careless of his welfare, than to break off any other earthly affection. The parent's love shuts out every feeling of jealousy, and cannot find any object to supplant it; it grows more tender and soft, yet more strong and self-denying, when calamities have made a suffering child unusually dependent upon the parent's care, and it hopes against hope in the dark and cloudy day of a child's perverseness and iniquity. There is no earthly affection that endures through severer trials than a parent's love. It has sometimes to bear very cruel trials from the very hearts that should thankfully return it. Children are often restive under the restraints that love and wisdom throw around them; they make ungrateful returns for kindness they can never repay; they rebel against the counsels and the wishes of those that love them as they love their own souls, and by their wickedness they sometimes bring down with sorrow to the grave the gray hairs they should have held in the deepest reverence.

But we do not need to compare the strength and durability in the different relationships of life. If every principle and influence of piety tends but to strengthen the duties of life in the hold they have upon our hearts, a pious parent will cling to the children of his love and refuse to be separated. We may look then upon the weeping of David over the untimely death of Absalom, and see if we cannot learn some of those valuable lessons which it is our wisdom to put in practice as we are called to occupy those positions in life. We are all either parents or children; and here are brought before us a father and his son. Let them teach us the lessons that become the parent and the child.

Surely this is an impressive scene to lead us to study the duties of life. An aged father weeps in bitterness for the early death of a misguided and wretched son. We may lay aside our remembrance of the attending circumstances and look on the simple facts. It is not that the one was a king and the other a noble prince, beautiful in person and polished in his demeanour. It is the living father and the dead son we would contemplate. The natural order of things is for the child to weep over the parent's grave; and even where such a loss is deeply felt and seriously mourned the grief is shorter lived for many reasons. When a parent dies we feel that longer time has been given to discharge the duties of life, and it is but the anticipating by a brief period of an event that cannot long be delayed. The urgent duties of life yet press upon those that are bereaved, and they more easily lose their sorrows in new engagements; and it is the wise ordination of Providence that new ties to a rising generation take the place of those ties that are gradually severed from the generation receding from the earth. But when a surviving parent mourns over a child, it is over one whose early promise is blasted and who is early cut off from unfinished duties; the parent less readily forms new ties to take the place of those thus broken off, and the breach in the household is not easily filled up. The longer the child is spared in the household, the weightier seems the stroke that removes him from our sight. Yet these are not uncommon scenes in these our abodes of sorrow. Many a parent is called thus to grieve. To every reflecting mind it must appear that we have no times better fitted to impress upon us the mutual duties and responsibilities of parents and children than those solemn seasons when they are called to separate. Serious at any time and in any aspect, our duties seem deeply solemn in view of those separations that are the begininng of an endless state of existence.

We may look upon the weeping of David over the death of the unhappy Absalom as teaching us some of the responsibilities and the anxieties of a pious parent, and the threatening dangers of unconverted children.

The responsibilities that belong to a parent are inferior to none that men are ever called to bear, when we take into consideration the number of persons that are affected by it. The family is the smallest of organized societies; and we would not, of course, declare that the parent of any one single family has a post of superior influence to any that any man can elsewhere hold. But, in comparison with the number of persons influenced and with reference to those that are in the family, all the elements of weighty responsibility are found in the parental office, and with stronger power than anywhere else. Is it a responsible thing to be a ruler over men; to make their laws; to control their conduct; to form their habits; to direct their energies; to guide their destinies for good or evil? No king ever possessed more uncontrolled authority, ever ruled by a clearer right, ever had better opportunities for guarding his whole body of subjects, or ever exerted greater influence for good or evil, than has the parent over his children. From the beginning the authority of a wise and just parent is never disputed; his kingdom is small, but the throne is absolute; the fewness of his subjects does but place them more completely under his government; and so far as human destinies ever can depend upon a ruler's wisdom or folly, do the character and destinies of a household for time and for eternity depend upon the parent at the head of it.

Is it a responsible thing to be a teacher, and to train the minds of the young for their future duties? Of all teachers the parent is the chief. His school is small, but every member is an apt scholar. The eye and the lip and the heart are trained there as they never can be again, and whether the lessons be wise or foolish, vicious or virtuous, no pupil ever is graduated in ignorance from the first of all academies. The lessons taught by the parent begin with the feeblest dawnings of intelligence in the child; they preoccupy the mind so that no lessons subsequently learned can ever make a deeper impression; and in the vast majority of cases the sons of men are what their fathers have made them.

Should men ever carefully use the influence they have gained over their fellows? The influence of a parent is justly great, and is exerted upon those, in the first place, who know none upon whom they should depend as they do, and ought to do, upon the authors of their earthly existence. It is the influence of a friend long known and trusted, having every care for our welfare, having wiser and more mature thoughts; and surely if any man is to be relied upon, we may rely upon a parent.

It is deeply to be regretted that few parents form a just conception of the serious duties of such an office, or of the momentous bearing of its influence upon the temporal and everlasting welfare of their children. How, indeed, can any parent bear to reflect upon the solemn truth that he is himself unreconciled to God, and therefore unprepared to understand his own important duties, or to discharge them, in their bearings upon eternal things. The burden of his own soul's salvation should be a great thing to weigh upon any man's heart; but how can he who feels not for himself as he should, feel as he ought his responsibilities in reference to his children, or earnestly exert himself to discharge them? It is a very easy thing to decide that the entire face of human society would be changed and improved, that we would have a happier and a holier world if every parent felt the burden of his responsibilities, and, with the heavy weight upon him, set himself about the careful discharge of his duties. Men may be unwilling to look at their responsibility, or to acknowledge that they are under so great obligations. Yet is it infinitely better for themselves and for their families that God has so bound them; it would be a great calamity for the race if the common carelessness of parents could be justified as right. We do not magnify, we are prone rather to undervalue, the parental office. But if every parent felt as the principles of the Bible would lead him to feel, how would we ponder our obligations, and how would our anxieties be awakened for the temporal and eternal well-being of our children!

Alas! it is too late for us to feel these responsibilities when we retire to our solitary chamber, as David here does, to bewail the neglect of duties that cannot be recalled for their more faithful discharge, and to mourn over a bereavement for which there is no remedy. Yet it is wise for us, in our calm moments of devotion in the sanctuary of God to forecast the deep griefs of a day of bereavement; it is wise for us, while our children are young, while our duties can yet be discharged, to learn our salutary lessons from parents whose griefs we wish never to share, and whose errors we wish earnestly to avoid. Let us look upon the Israelitish king in the anxious waitings of that eventful day when his armies had passed out to meet his rebellious Absalom; and the yearnings of a father's heart, that could do no more now than to pity and pray for a son who had passed from his control and spurned his authority, go forth in the touching command, "Deal gently with the young man." Let us realize his anxiety as he sees the swift-footed messenger speeding across the plain, and knows not which tidings he had rather hear—the success or the defeat of his son. Let us sympathize with the weeping father, who forgets his own success in the overwhelming tidings that his son—his miserable, his impenitent son—has already passed beyond a father's efforts and a father's prayers. We need to know the revelations of divine truth, we need to feel as true piety bids us feel, before we can understand a scene of grief like this; yet it may make us more carefully ponder our duties, it may awaken our solicitude, it may save us and our families from a similar scene of hopeless sorrow, if we come with teachable and prayerful hearts to hear the mourning of this stricken father.

Let parents learn something of their deep obligations in view of such a scene. They are responsible in this, that their own characters have a great deal to do with the formation of the characters of their children; that their sentiments will be the sentiments they generally adopt; that their habits will be the habits formed by them; and that if they neglect their careful and prayerful training, they will find in this serious occasions for grief at a future day. Is it possible for parents to throw around their families too many safeguards? Is there one of those that Christian piety desires to use that can safely be omitted by any intelligent parent? Think of the judgment we would form of parental duty if now we were looking back with the grief of David in this hour of bereavement; for wisdom bids us do now just what we will wish we had done when we understand most fully the nature and results of parental responsibility. If now we felt as parents as we shall feel when God calls us to give an account of our stewardship, which of our family safeguards would we be willing to relax? Would we be less careful to bring our families to the sanctuary, and to teach them by precept and by example the value of the house of God? Would we cast down in the dust the altar of family devotion and neglect to bless our children with the parental prayer? Would we allow the cares of a passing world to crowd from our attention the chief labours we are doing for eternity?

How, indeed, should the words of David find an echoing response from every anxious parent as he sends forth his children in the world—Deal gently with the young man. We nurse them in infancy when they know little of the burdens they impose, little of the cares that wear upon our hearts, little of the deep self-denials that parental love prompts in their behalf. We see them go forth to their duties in life with joy and pride, yet with trembling as we hope that the cares and trials and griefs of life may deal gently with them. Alas! the world too often proves like the deceitful Joab, who hears the earnest words of David, but all resolved to give no heed to them, and our Absalom is slain by the hand that we have charged to protect him.

We are anxious for our children because we know that they are partakers of that fallen nature which is so prone to evil, so averse from good. No man is wise for himself or for the interests of others who denies or overlooks that sinfulness of our nature which works so much evil even against our most watchful solicitude. And when with hearts like these, unrenewed by God's grace, our children go forth beyond the watch we have given to their childhood, we are deeply concerned for them.

We are concerned to know what characters they will form and what influence they will exert for this life. We send forth our children from the parental roof to the schools and colleges where they are to receive a fitting education, but they meet with companions and temptations we know not; they are enjoying advantages which many have found of inestimable value, but which many also have abused to their miserable undoing; and they are forming habits of great good or evil. We repeat often, therefore, the inquiry of David, "Is the young man, Absalom, safe?" and we follow our children with an earnest and anxious prayer. We send them forth to mingle with the community around us. We must do so, we ought to do so, but anxiety whispers again and again, Is the son, is the daughter safe? Let no one say that these are undue anxieties. Let the eye of a Christian look over the dangers that lie in wait for the young, beginning with the insidious and seductive advances which we are almost ashamed to resist and rebuke, they seem so blameless, and which yet give us the only hope of a wise and successful resistance. It is no trifling indication of evil things in advance, that our children so early leave the Sabbath-school and form habits of inattention to the lecture-room and the sanctuary. It is a cause of solicitude to every wise parent that when our sons enter upon the business of the world as apprentices or as clerks, there is rarely any attention paid to their religious habits, and our anxieties are certainly not allayed by the frequent defalcations and frauds that result from their neglect. And when we look upon the common opinions and practices of that genteel society into which our sons and daughters are introduced; when we know that frivolous and heartless conversation and conduct are common; when we know that the wine-glass is often offered, that the card-table is often opened, that the sneer at religion is often indulged—we wish to know where all this leads. We know that drinking-saloons are always open, and that many a beloved son, unsuspected by his friends, has there become entangled in the meshes of a vice from which few ever escape, and as we see the numbers of these on every hand, we tremble for our children and say, "Are the young men safe?" We know that temptations to gaming, to reckless expenditures, to impurity, abound on every hand. We know that the fairest promise of early life has been soon clouded over by inexpiable shame, that the children of the pious are often engulfed in spite of the teachings and prayers of godly parents, and that no past care or earnestness can make amends for any neglect of the duties that still bid us watch and counsel and pray; and it is thus with constant anxiety that we ask ourselves, in view of the various temptations of life, Is the young man safe? Is he safe?

The anxieties of a Christian parent chiefly have reference to eternal things. These our children are by nature sinful—immortal beings, but rebels against the God that made them. If these our beloved ones were truly converted to God, our chief anxieties would be allayed for them. We know, indeed, that there is sometimes a profession of piety where no real change has occurred. Therefore we watch in thankful but solicitous hope even over the pious confessions of those we love. But no greater joy, after his thankfulness to God for his own hope of forgiveness, can affect the heart of a parent than that which he feels over the conversion of a darling child. How just and how deep is the anxiety that belongs to a Christian parent contemplating the thought that a child whom he has reared and caressed and loved and prayed for shall be a rebel against his God—the thought of that separation beyond a remedy that must occur when a believing parent and an impenitent child have met for the last time before the judgment-bar of God!

How deep is the anguish of the parent who bows down by the cold remains of an impenitent son, suddenly snatched away from life without even the uttering of his despairing and unavailing cry for that divine mercy he had so often spurned! We see it here, and we cannot wonder that the agonizing father would gladly have exchanged places with the lifeless son, and that he pours forth a lamentation like this: "O my son Absalom! my son! my son Absalom! would God I had died for thee, O Absalom, my son! my son!"

And it is proper to add that these anxieties of Christian parents are immeasurably increased by the serious truth that our children do not share the solicitude we feel on their behalf. If our sons, if our daughters, were as much concerned as we are, a chief cause of our anxiety would be removed. But because the youthful mind is naturally hopeful, usually looks upon the bright aspects of life, and is confident in its own capacity to discern and to resist temptation; because the young are restive under authority, are prone to be even reckless where parental love is solicitous, and easily learn to resist the kindest leadings of those who love them dearer than they love their own life; because especially the unregenerate heart finds the duties and claims of piety distasteful,—every wise parent feels that his anxieties are equalled only by his perplexities. Gladly would he do the wisest and most salutary things if he could but decide what these are. The more careless his children are, the greater is the pious parent's anxiety, yet the more difficult his duties as he would endeavour to lead them toward God and heaven.

## CHAPTER XVIII.

### *THE REBELLION ENDED AND THE GIBEONITES AVENGED.*

IT is no easy thing to restore peace and good order to an unsettled government. Rebellions and revolutions affect too many—give occasion to find fault with too many, either for what they have said or done or for what they have not said or done as became them in the time of trial; they have given license to too many things that are restrained in orderly times—to allow that the victorious party should be moderate in their triumph or that the defeated party should feel comfortable or easy in view of what has passed. When the cause of strife is removed, the effects of an array of parties against each other often long remain. Now Absalom is dead; his chief counsellor, Ahithophel, is dead also; the next in wisdom, Hushai the Archite, would not be slow in declaring his true position of loyalty; and the troops of the rebellion were no longer together. Yet David comes not back in triumph to resume his crown and his government. Indeed there seems to be trouble among the tribes, and danger that the kingdom may be divided into two parts, as it had been under Ishbosheth a quarter of a century before, and as it became permanently under Rehoboam half a century later than this.

The first matter we notice as tending to keep up this distinction is the conduct of David himself after the issue of the battle with Absalom. We may sympathize with the anguish of the heart-broken father at such a time as that. We have known perhaps periods of such strange perplexity, when our reasons for grief and for joy were at the same time so strangely mingled together, and we are not surprised that the victorious king felt no emotions of rejoicing at all to be compared with the bitter sorrow of the bereaved father. At the same time we can scarcely wonder that the people did not understand the king's conduct; we can easily see that it was exceedingly impolitic to treat thus an army who had ventured their lives to save his. And here again comes in play the characteristic boldness and energy of Joab. And here again, as in almost every instance, so far as the well-being of the government was concerned, Joab was in the right. We may not approve of language so arbitrary and of a tone and manner involving so much disrespect to his sovereign as we see here in Joab. It is in keeping with the usual character of the man, and it may be that the habit of military command had a tendency to strengthen such a natural characteristic. But apart from these improper circumstances, Joab was in the right, and perhaps even his rough way of reaching the case was the only effectual way. David's conduct was highly impolitic. His people really deserved well at his hands, and we may understand his anguished feelings and sympathize with the parental bereavement, at the same time that the ruler ought to have acted wisely and refrained from the public indulgence of his grief. The stern remonstrance of Joab had the effect he designed, and David came forth and showed himself to the people.

But the difficulties flowing from the rebellion may not be thought to reside among the adherents of David, though they were for a time disheartened by his seeming repulse of them. The part of the people on the side of Jordan where he had been were faithful to him; the chief strength of Absalom had been on the other side, and the tribes there were tardy in making submission again to the king. David perhaps, through policy and to give them the opportunity of voluntary submission, did not pass over into his former territories as a conqueror to assume again his throne. But the people there began to agitate the subject. A little delay may have been naturally the result of embarrassment, lest their overtures might be ungraciously met. Unhappily, while they delayed, David sent messengers to influence the elders of Judah, through the priests Zadok and Abiathar. It is likely he sent there, because they dwelt at his capital, Jerusalem, and it was in the tribe of Judah; and it is possible that Absalom's brief rule in the city had been attended by some compliances and festivities on the part of the chief inhabitants which made them fear for the anger of the restored king and need special assurances of forgiveness. David gave this assurance, not only in the message to them, but by declaring also that Amasa, who had been the leader of the rebel armies, should have more than a pardon. The malcontents were to be conciliated by the promotion of Amasa to the command of David's troops. This message was gladly heard in Jerusalem. Immediate answer was given and the king invited to return, while the men of Judah made their preparation to escort him over the Jordan. What is here said concerning Shimei and Mephibosheth we have before noticed, and hereafter we will speak of Barzillai, the Gileadite.

The message thus sent to the tribe of Judah was highly impolitic on the part of David, and the reason given, that they were his near kindred, was still more so. The kingdom was made up of twelve tribes, each naturally independent of the rest; and there ever will be, in such cases, some jealousy of each other's privileges and rights, and this jealousy more plainly appears in times of agitation and revolution. That David was related to the tribe of Judah would be the very reason, in view of the other tribes, why that tribe should not be too forward in restoring him to the throne. The other tribes ought to have been consulted at the least, if not in honour preferred. Yet the single tribe brought the king back, with the aid doubtless of a few of Israel, but without the presence or concurrence of all the tribes. And the matter was made vastly worse by the reply of Judah when expostulation was made. "A soft answer turneth away wrath, but grievous words stir up anger." Had the men of Judah been wise for the good of the realm and of the king, had they been kind and conciliatory in their tone, had they perceived the error and frankly avowed and regretted it, no harm might have come of it. It is very likely, indeed, that they had been as far wrong in the previous scenes as any of the other tribes; the success of Absalom seems to intimate this; their plea, then, of kindred and superior affection for David but poorly agrees with their past behaviour; yet this explains the matter more fully, for the fierce temper of the men of Judah exactly flows from their previous wrong. When men have felt and acted rightly, we may more reasonably look for a kind and conciliatory temper; but nothing more disposes a man to quarrel needlessly with other people than an uneasy heart that is dissatisfied with itself. The zeal of Judah would not have been so exclusive had it arisen from true love of David; but springing now from the effort to repair the past injury, it overreached itself, and had wellnigh produced greater mischief than before. The men of Israel expostulated, and Judah answered too roughly; an angry controversy sprung up just at the time when the land should have been filled with rejoicing, and the kindred of the king used the fiercest instead of the most conciliatory language.

Indeed the matter produced a rebellion upon the spot. This sprung up among the feeble remnant of the tribe of Benjamin, but whether it had any connection with the family of Saul we are not informed. It is not likely that any descendant of Saul was directly named, much less proposed, as king over the ten tribes; but it is likely that some memory of their previous pre-eminence may have made the Benjamites more disposed to throw off the rule of David. The leader in the case was one Sheba, the son of Bichri, and at his signal the men of Israel retired from David and refused to take any further part in the ceremony of the restoration.

This whole matter seems to have been greatly aggravated by the further impolitic step on the part of David that had promised to Amasa the command of his armies in the stead of Joab. This Amasa was a half-blood Ishmaelite (1 Chron. ii. 17), but a full cousin to Joab and a nephew to David; and if he is the same as Amasa, he joined himself to David just before the fatal battle of Gilboa, and assisted him in pursuing the Amalekites after the destruction of Ziklag. (See 1 Chron. xii. 16–22.) We are at no loss to understand why David was willing to make this exchange of generals. In the first place, it is likely that Amasa was a valiant man and an able commander. No other man would have been chosen by Absalom than one who had the confidence of the tribes, and David had known him long and well. It was no rash appointment, so far as the man's capability was concerned. 2d. We are at no loss to see that David is restive under the domination of Joab. We do not wonder at this. Though from first to last Joab seems to have acted so as really to promote the wise ends of the government, yet he is so unscrupulous and selfish and overbearing—even toward his king, he seems himself to be the ruler of the land and not a subordinate—that we cannot be surprised that David at several times tried to get rid of him. And since these troublous times Joab is more lordly than ever. Perhaps he felt it so, and perhaps it really was so, that the throne of David could not stand without him. What an advantage to Absalom if Joab—a host in himself—had declared in his favour! But if Joab felt himself of this importance, he shows it too plainly, and David is resolved at all hazards to supersede him in the command. His chief reasons now are these recent events. He knew that Joab was the destroyer of Absalom's life—that this was done in direct disregard of his orders and in violation of his tenderest feelings. Moreover, Joab had directly used toward him a conduct and language that were unbecoming the position of a subject toward his sovereign. We cannot feel surprised, therefore, that the king desired to be a freeman—that he wished to be delivered from the irksome bondage in which this overbearing Joab had so long held him.

Doubtless a third reason for this movement on the part of David was the expectation that this appointment would conciliate that portion of the people who had acted with Absalom. After a rebellion is quelled every wise government mingles conciliatory measures with the punishment of ringleaders. Now, if the very commander of Absalom's troops is pardoned—indeed, also promoted over his victorious rival—all the rest of the people may return to David's rule without apprehension.

But in this entire matter David very much mistook the popularity of Joab and the temper of the times. It is not indeed unlikely that his very mildness in punishing the rebels may have given boldness to the attempt of Sheba. It is very plain that the people did not sympathize with the change; and we can hardly wonder that they did not. They did not feel the overbearing temper of Joab as the king did. They looked upon him as a servant of David, long tried and ever found valuable; they reflected that now his greatest crime in the eyes of the monarch was his greatest virtue in the eyes of the people; and they thought it an exceedingly hard thing that for winning the greatest battle in David's reign, and for putting to death an enemy the most formidable, Joab should lose his honours, hard earned and long enjoyed. It made the matter worse that a man who had fought against the king, and whose defeat in that signal battle seemed to prove his inferiority to Joab, should be the successor of that chief; and especially after the rebellion of Sheba, when the influence of Amasa did not seem to be great enough to keep his own party from a further revolt from David, we cannot wonder that this effort to promote him proved an utter failure.

Indeed, the matter was likely to have a disastrous issue, and would have so resulted if Joab had not proved himself here, as he always proved himself, a true patriot. The king commanded Amasa to assemble an army within three days to go forth against Sheba and put down this rebellion. This Amasa was quite unable to do; he was longer about it than the appointed season, and time was precious. Let us not impute this delay to a lack of energy on the part of the new commander. It was rather the unwillingness of the people to serve under him, and he could not find the men. David was then forced to fall back upon his old friends. He commanded Abishai to move forward in the matter; and if in such a crisis Joab had taken offence and refused to do anything till his place had been restored to him, it is likely David would have been compelled to do this. But Joab acts the part of a patriot and goes forth to the conflict; yet as soon as opportunity offers, he maintains his former character, using any means to carry out his own purposes. As the army passed on, Amasa put himself at the head of it and assumed his lawful command as the chief captain. The treacherous Joab re-enacted with him the tragedy of Abner; he saluted him in a kind and friendly manner, but took the occasion to strike him one fatal blow. The shocking sight of the commander-in-chief lying in his blood in the open road struck the people with horror, but one of Joab's friends removed and concealed the corpse, and the former general immediately assumed the command. Perhaps the popularity of Joab is shown in the fact that the tribes were easily gathered after this, when proclamation was made in his name; and he proceeded to fight against Sheba.

From this time forth David seems to have made no further effort to punish the crimes of Joab. It is evident that he had no sympathy with him, and that he would have punished him had he possessed the power. For these crimes Joab was put to death as one of the first acts in the reign of Solomon, by which time the power of the throne had increased and the influence of Joab had doubtless waned. But from first to last, in David's life, the energy and popularity of Joab set him above any power that the king could put forth.

Whatever the rebellion of Sheba might have amounted to under Amasa, the name of Joab was enough to put it down. The rebel retired, doubtless with but a small force, to the town of Abel, in the tribe of Naphtali, and about ninety miles from Jerusalem. Here Joab rapidly pursued him, and began, with his usual promptitude, to lay siege to the place and to prepare for battering down the walls. But evidently the besieged had little confidence in their cause, and perhaps as little in their leader. After a brief consultation, it was agreed that Sheba should be put to death and his head thrown over the wall in token of submission, and that then the town should be spared from assault. This ended, for the present, the troubles caused by the rebellion of Absalom. Yet it is likely that the jarrings between the tribes still broke forth upon occasions that excited any jealousy. The strong hand of Solomon kept these things in check so long as he reigned, but no sooner was he dead than the kingdom was rent in two through the imprudence of his successor; and no union was ever again formed.

Not long after this there was a famine in the land that lasted three years. Inquiry was made of the Divine Oracle for the cause of this, and the reply was, that it was a chastisement for Saul and for his bloody house, because he slew the Gibeonites. Several things here are beyond our knowledge: First. We have no previous record of any attack made by Saul upon the Gibeonites. We know who the Gibeonites were. They were the descendants of that tribe of the Canaanites who had imposed upon Joshua by pretending that they had come from a distant land to make a covenant with the Israelites. Joshua and the elders of Israel, without any inquiry into their statements, made a league with them and soon afterward discovered the trick. But it was too late to draw back and treat this tribe as they did the other Canaanites. A solemn treaty had been formed with them and the oaths of the elders passed, and the lives of the Gibeonites must be spared. But, incensed at the deception, Joshua condemned this people to be hewers of wood and drawers of water for the congregation. In the space of four hundred years, we may easily judge, a great change had taken place among the Gibeonites. They had beyond doubt laid aside their idolatries; they had in all likelihood learned to worship the true God. Yet they were in the midst of Israel, still a distinct and a servile race, and apparently not admitted to the privileges often conferred upon proselytes. We need not wonder, therefore, since the Gibeonites were not a part of Israel, that their claim for revenge is rather according to the usual Oriental claims, and not according to anything else we read of among the Jews. But we do not know when Saul slew the Gibeonites. Some suppose that at the time he attacked the city of the priests the Gibeonites also were slain, who were servants to the tabernacle, but there is no mention of any slain there except those that belong to the priestly families. It is more likely that upon some occasion Saul affected a sudden zeal for pure Judaism and resolved to cut off out of the land this race of Gentiles. But conjectures are vain. This we know: Saul unjustly attacked and slew the Gibeonites.

Second. We cannot know why the famine that punishes his crime is delayed so long. We are familiar with the fact, both in the Bible and in providence, that nations suffer for the errors and crimes of their rulers. We see in this whole transaction that what is done by a nation is regarded as binding upon that nation hundreds of years afterward. But we can give no definite reason why the sin of Saul as king of Israel should pass unavenged for thirty years after his death, and then come in the reign of a righteous successor. We cannot give any reason why, in the orderings of Providence, the conscience of a sinner is often allowed to sleep long in carelessness after his deed is done, and why he seems to escape with almost entire impunity for his sin. We only know this much—that God in infinite justice will take account of every sin; that from the moment a sin is committed the transgressor is liable both to the awakening of his conscience and to the judgments of God; and that no man can ever anticipate the time or the measure of that vengeance which the divine law demands. So, a practical commentator remarks, "God's judgments often look a great way back, which obliges us to do so when under his rebukes. It is not for us to object against the people's smarting for the sin of their king, which perhaps they were aiding and abetting, nor against this generation suffering for the sin of the last. God often visiteth the sins of the fathers upon the children, and his judgments are a great deep. He gives not account of any of his matters. Time does not wear out the guilt of sin, nor can we build hopes of impunity upon the delay of judgment. There is no statute of limitation to be pleaded against God's demands. God may punish when he pleases."* Perhaps we are too prone to forget our sins that are past. As we look back upon them, we may blame ourselves for their commission; perhaps we wish we could live over again some past periods, that we might avoid some of the obvious faults we have committed; but if even we judge that we have been wrong, it is too seldom with that just idea of God's law which reminds us that we have been criminal, and that we are answerable for all the past as truly as for the present. No matter what is the date of a sin unpardoned by the blood of Calvary; it will meet its perpetrator one day, and it may perhaps bring forth upon earth its bitter fruits for his children and for others after he has passed away from time.

Third. It seems strange to us that the Gibeonites should demand this method of reparation for the injury done to them. Yet it is but carrying out the ancient customs of the Orientals, of which we

* Henry, *in loco.*

have a modified form among the Hebrews, including their cities of refuge. They would take no satisfaction except from the family of the man from whom they had received the injury. We have no reason to believe that David had any choice in the matter except that, being forced to deliver up Saul's descendants, he was able to spare certain of them and select certain others. He spared Mephibosheth, the son of his friend Jonathan, and selected others. These were taken by the Gibeonites and put to death and hanged in Gibeah. The very manner of doing this shows that the Gibeonites were not governed by Hebrew laws, but had regulations of their own. The law of Moses expressly enjoined, concerning a man that was hanged, "His body shall not remain all night upon the tree, but thou shalt in any wise bury him that day." Deut. xxi. 23. Either this was an extraordinary execution exempted from this law, or more likely it was governed by Gibeonitish laws. These bodies remained exposed from early in the spring until rain fell from heaven. No definite time is mentioned, but the fall of rain is the token of the end of the famine, and therefore of the divine reconciliation.

In this connection we have an instance of strong maternal affection. Rizpah, the daughter of Aiah, two of whose sons were slain upon this occasion, resolved that their bodies should not be torn by beasts or birds of prey. She therefore took her mournful station beside them, lay down in sackcloth upon the bare rock, but not for sleep. With an endurance which only a mother's love can show, she kept her toilsome vigils by the dishonoured bodies of her children. Doubtless she was better sustained in this because the deed had not been committed by her sons, though the implication is that Saul's house had been but too consenting to the crime. This execution took place at Gibeah, where Saul had lived, this being a plainer and more public declaration of the cause of the scene.

After this, David took measures to have the remains of Saul himself, and of Jonathan, with all three of his sons, gathered together and taken to the usual burying-place of his fathers and there interred. Then God was entreated for the land—that is, the period of famine passed away and the former prosperity was again granted.

Nothing is more plainly taught in this entire transaction than the solemn and permanent obligation of a promise confirmed especially by an oath. If the question be asked, Why was the house of Saul thus punished for his slaughter of the Gibeonites, while we hear of no punishment specially inflicted for the massacre of the priests? we may find the solution of it here. It seemed the practice of this unhappy man to be zealous in the wrong place. When God sent him to destroy the Amalekites, he spared them, and he is zealous to destroy the Gibeonites, whom he was bound to protect. The chief matter here remembered and punished is the breach of the solemn oath which Joshua had made with these men. It served in no degree to invalidate this oath that it had originally been secured by fraud. There are some oaths that ought not to be taken at all, or not fulfilled when taken. No man has the right to take an oath that binds him to a crime, or, having taken such an oath, no one is bound to keep it. The oath which Joshua made he felt bound to keep; and if fraud to secure a treaty is ever right, we may surely excuse the Gibeonites, who had no other resource by which to save their lives. But the fraud did not vitiate, nor did the lapse of time make any alteration in the obligation of this oath. Made by Joshua, it was none the less binding on Saul. Nor need we wonder, but the rather rejoice, that the Scriptures lay so much stress upon the maintenance of such obligations. It is not hard for us to understand that scarcely anything is more important for the happiness of reasonable beings than the maintenance of the truth; nothing is more sacred than a promise; few offences are more serious than a lie; and an oath is but the most solemn confirmation of a promise made. There is much falsehood, much covenant-breaking, much perjury in the world; yet all that is excellent in our social order, all that is happy, is based upon that confidence which falsehood and perjury do so much to break down. The records of history are full of the evils that have resulted from the breach of faith solemnly covenanted between nations, and our ordinary society is full of mischief wrought by falsehood between man and man. When we see the judgment here recorded against Israel for the breach of this ancient oath, we may learn how much God loves the truth. It is set forth in the Psalms as characteristic of a good man that even when his oath is injurious to himself he keeps it. A wicked man breaks his word or his oath to secure some advantage; a righteous man keeps even the promise that costs him most. What a world this would be if, in this single particular, it was thoroughly changed! A world of truth without falsehood—how different would it be from this world! We cannot too deeply impress upon our minds that God hateth lying lips, that he is a God of truth and without iniquity, and that from his blissful presence shall be cast out for ever "whosoever loveth and maketh a lie."

And if we learn in this transaction how solemn is the binding obligation of an oath, let us call to mind two important passages of the Scriptures in which the Most High God himself condescends to ratify even his declarations by the sanctions of an oath. It is hard to decide which may most call forth our wonder—the unbelief of man that seemed to render it necessary that God's word should be ratified by an oath, or the condescension of God that stoops to regard even this unreasonable requirement of our sin. But here is the truth.

Though it is impossible for God to lie, he has in two matters solemnly interposed his oath:

1st. God has solemnly sworn that every believer in the Lord Jesus Christ shall be saved. (See the whole matter explicitly set forth in Heb. vi. 16–18.) Sinful hearts fear to trust the word of God, and he condescends thus to give them every possible assurance of their safety when they flee to Christ, the appointed refuge. Let believers take the strong consolation of this solemn assurance. Let sinful men flee to this refuge, for it is impossible to find any other so excellent, so suitable or so safe as that here afforded.

2d. God has solemnly sworn that no unbeliever shall enter into his rest.

Many are the flattering delusions by which men keep quiet their consciences. They hope for exemption from the wrath of God; they hope for a future day of repentance; they hope that the Spirit of God will still strive with them; and, forgetful that death itself may come at any hour, they judge that at any time during life they may flee from the wrath to come. They have, perhaps, never noticed the serious fact that the generation in the wilderness were rejected of God forty years before the last of them died in the desert. But let this be a serious thought for us to ponder, both to show the great sin of unbelief and the increasing danger of its indulgence, that God has solemnly sworn that such shall never enter his rest. Let any one alter the apostle's strong language to suit the case of the unbeliever, and let it thus read: God, willing to show unto the heirs of perdition the immutability of his counsel, confirmed it by an oath that by two immutable things, wherein it is impossible for God to lie, they who have not fled to Christ may have the strongest assurance of their certain perdition. Will God so abhor lying and prove himself perjured? Let every sinner reflect that God or he must change. It is both impossible and undesirable that God should change; therefore turn ye, turn ye, for why will ye die?

## CHAPTER XIX.

### *THE PESTILENCE OF THE NUMBERING.*

WE are arrested in the outset of our reflections upon the next important scene in the life of King David by an apparent discrepancy in the accounts as given us by two inspired narratives. In the study of the Bible it is of very great advantage that we often have two—and sometimes even four—different narratives of the same transaction, and are able thus, by comparing them together, to get a clearer and more accurate view of the case. No book in the world comprises so much teaching in so brief a space; and the necessary tendency of so great brevity is to leave many things unsaid, which not unfrequently leaves important things in obscurity. When we have two accounts of the same thing by different writers—or even sometimes by the same writer (compare Acts ix. 7; xxii. 9)—we secure different views of the matter; what is omitted by one observer is supplied by another; it seems like two independent witnesses testifying to the same truth; and where there are diversities and apparent discrepancies—which are not contradictions when carefully and candidly examined—the internal evidence is strong that the writers were speaking the truth without collusion. When men make up a story to impose upon others, there is an artificial agreement that carefully casts out obvious discrepancies; but two independent writers, both telling the truth, will never tell it alike, will never agree in the incidents mentioned by each and omitted by each, and will always strengthen the truth of what they say by their very diversities. Every intelligent student of the Bible must pay great attention to the harmony of the varying accounts; and if he will find himself perplexed for the solution of things that do not apparently agree, he will yet discover no manifest contradictions, while he will be richly repaid for his closest investigations by the clearer views that arise from the earnest study of those pages.

The discrepancy in the narratives to which we now refer is somewhat remarkable. In 1 Chron. xxi. 1 we read thus: "And Satan stood up against Israel and provoked David to number Israel." In 2 Sam. xxiv. 1 we have this account of the same matter: "And again the anger of the Lord was kindled against Israel, and he moved David against them to say, Go number Israel and Judah." Here is a temptation presented to the mind of King David, and this is ascribed to persons so widely different as God himself and Satan.

The word Satan signifies *an adversary*.* Some

* See Matt. xvi. 23.

therefore refer it here, not to the proper name of the arch-adversary, but to some wicked person among David's counsellors. But it seems obvious that any such change would not alter in the least the real difficulty of the passage. The real difficulty lies just here: How can God be said to stir up David to do an evil thing? How can he use any inferior instrumentality, satanic or human, for such an end? To the bottom of such a mystery mortal line cannot reach. It is, in fact, the great, the most profound, mystery of Providence. How can evil enter the dominions of the infinite God. This is a mystery which we need not attempt to solve. There are some things we know. We know that evil has entered the universe; we know that evil is not of God in any such sense as to imply his approval of it; we know that in no bad sense of the word does he ever tempt men to sin, "for God cannot be tempted with evil, neither tempteth he any man." James i. 13. There are some things also we believe. We believe that God has allowed the entrance of sin into the universe for reasons of infinite wisdom; we believe he will bring forth from it his own more illustrious glory; we believe he will fully vindicate his character and his providence in due time in the eyes of all intelligent beings. But great as is the mystery and great as is the mischief of sin in the universe of God, it seems to me that I can conceive of a mystery both more profound and more disastrous to the universe than the existence of sin. Conceive of the entrance of sin into the world against the divine consent and beyond the divine control, and you have an infinite mischief that degrades God himself at the same time that it ruins his rational creation. No such mystery as this exists. It is our place to believe that God for reasons of infinite wisdom has allowed sin to enter the world—has allowed Satan to depart from his Creator and to become an adversary to his fellow-creatures, and allows us to come into contact with evil—for the evidence of these things we have everywhere around us. It is our place also to believe that sin is not of God—that he thoroughly abhors it, and that he is incapable of leading us to wrong. But it is not less essential to the divine honour for us to understand that the entire universe is under the control of God; that sins and sinful beings and every sinful act are no less so than virtue and virtuous beings and every virtuous act, and that we may truly say, even in full view of the evil all around us, God doeth his "will in the army of heaven and among the inhabitants of the earth, and none can stay his hand or say unto him, What doest thou?" Dan. iv. 35. This unquestionable truth allows us, with the teachings of the Bible, to attribute the same act both to divine agency and to created agency. We may say in truth that every event, good or bad, has its divine aspect and its inferior instrumentality. The crucifixion of Christ by the Jews, his betrayal by Judas, these were the carrying out of divine purposes, but not the less were they done by wicked hands. Our philosophy may be at loss here to explain how God governs free moral agents, and yet leaves them free; is holy himself, and yet permits such sins; controls even sin, and yet justly judges the actors according to their habits and motives; but let our philosophy do here what human philosophy everywhere else is compelled to do—let it observe and recognize the facts, and acknowledge its own inability to go farther than this. God is not the author of sin, but he is its controller. Nothing occurs, of temptation or evil, that he allows not, and he even uses the evil passions of men for carrying on the righteous and the punitive measures of his providence. This would be a wretched world if any other doctrine were true. If men can do evil, if Satan can plan mischief and urge men to do evil, and even God cannot prevent or control him, then God is no longer governor of a world that has fallen into inextricable confusion; he cannot make a promise with any certainty that Satan will not thwart it; he cannot carry out his plans; in truth, he is dethroned, for a God who must contend with plans he cannot control is no longer God. Let righteous men rejoice in the assurance that Satan is a dependent being; that, far as he may go, he can go no farther than God permits, and that he simply carries out what infinite wisdom allows. Let sinful men know that no plan of theirs can ever succeed beyond the point where it may be made to subserve God's purposes; that evil may prove ruinous to themselves, but never harmful to God; and that its indulgence is both folly and mischief to the perpetrator in every case.

There is a sense, then, in which we may attribute the temptation of David both to the providence of God and to the agency of Satan. There are certainly aspects of this subject where a man may easily lose himself in speculations both profound and unprofitable; there is a simpler solution that rejoices in the reign of God while it is amazed at the agency of evil. And after all, our simplest recognitions of the facts allow us to understand the matter as fully as the most profound inquiries. It is interesting to notice here the writers of the Bible. They simply place upon record the facts which involve these great principles, and leave them so, just as if they needed no explanation; just as the great truths of every science—of astronomy, geology, chemistry, natural history, etc.—have been placed by Providence before the eyes of men in all ages; and men are called upon to observe, to classify, to arrange them, and to deduce from long experience the hidden laws that so often seem strange and contradictory to a superficial student.

The meaning of the record is, that God allowed Satan to tempt David. The divine permission rose out of some previous sin, for we are told that the anger of the Lord was kindled against David, and out of this grew this temptation. But we are not told why the Lord was displeased with him. The temptation in this case was to the numbering of Israel. Are we to understand from this that it is a sin for the ruler of a land to take an account of his people; to reckon his resources; to mark the progress of things by careful statistics of commerce, of population, of wealth? In modern times such things have been found of great advantage, and in the United States we have arrangements under the general government for taking a careful census of our population and resources at the end of every ten years. These are published by the order of Congress, and embody an immense amount of most valuable information. When we find David and the people of Israel severely punished for taking such a census of the kingdom we ask, Wherein is the sin of the transaction? And the clear and plain answer is, There is no sin against God in this thing itself. So far from it, that we are told that God commanded Moses to take the sum of all the congregation after their families, with the number of their names; and one of the books of Moses is called NUMBERS because it contains just such an enumeration. The enumeration in itself was not wrong, but the evil must be found in its circumstances. Indeed, if we would keep ourselves from evil, we should carefully notice that Satan's most dangerous temptations have some plausibility about them. Men often start back from acknowledged iniquity, while the specious appearances of things that are not so plainly wrong deceive them into departures as wide from the way of duty. The deceit of sin often lies in its apparent innocence. There was something wrong in the enumeration which David here made of the people—so wrong that Joab discovered and pointed it out, and did all he could to prevent the execution of the king's wish. But commentators are not agreed as to the precise point of David's delinquency. It was the express command of God to Moses that when he numbered the people he should lay a tax upon every man as a ransom for his soul, that there be no plague among them. Ex. xxx. 12. Josephus says that the omission of this tax was the sin of David, but it seems strange that he should omit such a tax at the very time when he was diligently collecting money in preparation for building the temple. It is more likely that the offence of the king lay in the motives that led to this numbering, rather than in the thing itself or in the manner of conducting it. The prosperity of the tribes of Israel was doubtless greater now than ever it had been since God bade their great forefather look toward heaven and tell the stars, and had assured him, So shall thy seed be. Gen. xv. 5. It was a great thing that David should be king over such a people; a great matter that so great prosperity should be under his rule; a great matter that they held now that wide land as God had promised. Yet the increase of Israel had not been owing to David's conduct, but to the divine blessing; nor had he any just reason to indulge the vain pride of his heart, the foolish conceit of his own greatness, the miserable confidence of his own strength in view of the prosperity of the kingdom. There is no sin to which men are so prone in every land, in every age and in every possible condition as the sin of pride, for the sin will not be banished even where there seems no room for its exercise. Yet there is no sin in a servant of God which more quickly awakens the divine displeasure. God will not give his glory to another. This is a matter of no trivial importance for our notice, for we cannot reasonably question that tokens of divine displeasure are often seen in our churches because prosperity makes us proud; and in the growth of our denomination or of our Church we become conceited and arrogant, as if our hand had wrought our enlargement. Here is a thing in which we cannot be too jealous of our motives. It is not wrong to look around us and to look abroad to see the work which the Church of God has to do, but it is wrong to be proud of our zeal to do it. It is not wrong to note our progress; to mark the difference between the present and the past; to rejoice in the enlargement of Zion; but we are prone to glory in what we are, and to claim at least a share in the honour, which all belongs to God. Let no denomination grow boastful, or God will divide and scatter its numbers, and turn the energies of its members against themselves till they are humbled in the dust. Let no congregation be puffed up in a sense of superiority, or the displeasure of the Lord will be seen upon the very matters of its pride, and this sin will bring every hurtful curse. Let no pastor be proud of his preaching, or God will make it profitless. Let no Christian think of himself or of his attainments or of his doings "more highly than he ought to think," for the blessing of the Lord maketh rich, and his blessings he will not give to such as rob him of his honour.

The numbering of the people went on in spite of Joab's remonstrance, but it was not cheerfully done nor fully done, and David, after all, was disappointed in the end he aimed at. Different numbers are recorded in the two accounts; perhaps because some were omitted in the one case and included in the other; perhaps because the incompleteness of the returns affected these reports of them. Before the matter was finished, David saw his error and bitterly lamented it; but the sin was now done. We need not stay now to ask, Why the land should be smitten for a sin that seems to belong peculiarly to David? The Judge of all the earth does right even in cases where we cannot discern it. We know that often the nation suffers for the sin of the ruler, but we know also that there are ever reasons to justify the divine dealings to them. It may be that the sin of the nation in supporting the rebellion of Absalom, or other sins not recorded here, may fully justify the severities that find but their occasion in David's transgression.

The messenger to David is the prophet Gad; he is directed to offer the king his choice that by one of three things God should punish this sin. The choice lay between three years of famine, three months of defeat before his enemies, or three days of pestilence. Here again there is a difference of the numbers stated. In 2 Sam. xxiv. 13 it is seven years of famine; in 1 Chron. xxi. 12 it is three years. The Hebrew method of writing numbers makes it not at all surprising that many errors should creep into their books, nor need we regard such errors as proofs of mistake in the original writers. Any one who looks at the two Hebrew letters signifying three (ג) and seven (ז) will feel no surprise that one copying the sacred writings should mistake the one for the other. Yet there is this conjecture which might make both right: The *additional* years of famine might make seven years in all in this way. There had been three years for Saul's sin against the Gibeonites; if the next year after these was a sabbatical year, in which the Israelites neither sowed nor reaped, and at the end of this a new famine should begin for three years, such a judgment might properly be termed a famine of either three or seven years.

This message of the prophet threw David into a

distressing perplexity. He knew something of all these evils. None of them are light, and by each of them does Divine Providence punish the sin of man. David had but recently passed through three years of famine; he was a man of war, and knew too well the severity of that scourge, and it is possible that he had some idea of the fearful ravages of pestilence. It was a sad strait indeed. The famine would be the longest. Happily, in the kindness of God's providence toward us, we know very little—nothing, indeed, by any national experience—of the miseries that spring up from the prevalence of famine. But we have read the authentic and appalling accounts of its deplorable ravages elsewhere. The wretchedness brought upon Ireland by a time of famine is yet fresh in the memory of us all. Of the ravages of war we have all read; yet perhaps few minds are not more appalled by the dreadful march of a pestilence than by any other evil that ever comes among a people. The more dreadful severity of this is marked in the prophet's offer by the brief space of time allotted to it. Three *days* of pestilence are placed as equivalent to three *months* of the horrors of war or to as many *years* of the slow wastings of famine. We are told that seventy thousand men died in Israel during the prevalence of this plague, and even then the hand of the destroying angel was stayed in mercy before he had done all he might do. Some think that David made no choice in the case, but referred it back to God. But it seems evident rather that he makes choice of pestilence not because he thought this in itself a higher evil than the others, but because more explicitly it is in the Lord's hands and is apart from human instrumentality. In war, human passions are enlisted; and though nothing can occur without divine permission, it greatly aggravates our griefs that fierce and hostile men inflict them. A famine is more directly from the divine hand, but the avaricious and selfish passions of men do much to increase the sufferings of such a time; for food is hoarded to secure larger prices and violence is committed without remorse to appease the cravings of hunger. A time of pestilence is not without its evidences of human depravity; all experience shows that men become hardened in iniquity when death is nearest in its most hideous forms, and many a wretched deathbed is forsaken by those that should lavish there their kindest attentions. Yet the silent march of the pestilence is more directly under God's control, without the semblance of human instrumentality, and David desires to fall into His hands from whom he could hope for mercy. It has been remarked that this choice was noble on the part of David, because thus himself and his family were placed upon a level with the rest of Israel in exposure to the coming evil. If he had chosen *famine*, the standing and wealth of the royal family would sufficiently protect them from suffering; if he had chosen *war*, the people had already forbidden him to go forth to battle, and therefore it involved no personal exposure. But to choose pestilence made his family as liable as any other in the land. Yet let us not overlook this great lesson, that they who best know the Lord have the largest confidence in his tender mercy. David had great reason to know the Lord's justice, but he had large experience of his forbearance, his forgiveness and readiness to pardon. But it is easy to see that in the depth of David's feelings of grief and concern for his people he has no personal selfishness. He recognizes himself as the chief culprit, and with the elders of Israel he humbled himself before God and supplicated his mercy. It would seem that the disease began at one end of the land and rapidly passed toward Jerusalem. We are familiar with the progress of the cholera from one point to another, so that its march can be easily indicated. In this case it would seem that an angel became visible as the plague approached Jerusalem, and a drawn sword in his hand denoted his destructive errand. David and the elders hastened to meet him—not at all as braving his power, but not deterred by their fear of him from their post of duty, that they might pray for divine deliverance. The angel stood by a remarkable spot. It was the threshing-floor of Ornan or Araunah the Jebusite. By the Jews it is supposed to be the place where

Abraham had been stayed by divine interference when about to sacrifice his son Isaac. David was directed by the prophet Gad to erect an altar upon this spot. We may admire the spirit of both David and Ornan. The owner of the land came forth nobly to present the land to the service of the Lord; as a king Araunah gives to the king; but David will not serve the Lord with that which costs him nothing. He wishes the offering to be at his cost, not at the cost of Araunah. Two prices are mentioned here, and they are very different. Fifty shekels of silver bought the oxen and the threshing-floor, 2 Sam. xxiv. 24; but six hundred shekels of gold were also paid, and this, it is likely, was for a larger place. It is likely that David now or soon after understood that the temple was to be built upon this spot, and by the larger sum he bought ground enough for this purpose. The Lord accepted the sacrifice at that time by kindling the fire upon the altar (1 Chron. xxi. 26), as he had done upon the altar of Moses in the wilderness (Lev. ix. 24), and as afterward he did in Solomon's temple (2 Chron. vii. 1), and upon the altar erected by Elijah upon Mount Carmel. 1 Kings xviii. 38. Thus David not only recognized the divine acceptance, but knew that in this place, where Solomon afterward built the temple (2 Chron. iii. 1), would the Lord be pleased to hear the prayers of his people.

## CHAPTER XX.

### *PREPARATION FOR BUILDING THE TEMPLE.*

WE have had occasion before to speak of David's earnest desire to build a magnificent house for the worship of God. The very conception shows his zeal for the Lord; but here is a lesson on record for all ages of the Church, that our offerings for religious purposes are a favour to us, and not to him, and that they must be so rendered as to glorify him or they will not prove acceptable. The Lord approved of David's wish to build a house for his name, but he was unwilling that he should do this. The temple itself he accepted, and in the succeeding reign it was built, but a man of war from his youth seemed not a fit builder for a house devoted to the God of peace. God does not allow us to do all we desire to do for him. It may not be for a reason so definite as this assigned in respect to David, yet for wise reasons he does not give us the privilege of seeing his work prosper according to our desires. In this case, if we feel as we should, we will imitate the conduct of David. He could not build the temple, but he could make such preparations for it as would enable his son and successor to proceed more rapidly in the work and to prosecute it with ease. Because he could not do all he wished, he did not conclude that therefore he would do nothing. So no man ever reasons whose heart is really interested in any work. When men are influenced by ambition or pride, or any other selfish prompting, they are unwilling to bear an inferior part where they wish to be conspicuous; but when men are truly interested in the progress of any work, they will cheerfully do the part which Providence assigns; they will do all they can here, as zealously as if they were made more prominent. The man who loses his interest in the Church of God because he fills a place of little influence, would not do the most important things in a proper spirit if he had them to do. Hardly anything in his history makes David appear in a more honourable light than his humble acquiescence in the divine will when told that he should not build the temple, and his diligent care, after this, to make all possible preparation for its subsequent erection.

After the plague had ceased, David bought perhaps the entire possession of Araunah the Jebusite, that upon this ground his son should build the house of the Lord. This temple itself, when afterward built, was one of the most costly and magnificent buildings that man has ever framed, if indeed it did not surpass all others in splendour. If we are disposed to wonder how a house should be planned on so grand a scale in an age like that, the solution of the matter is very easy. As when Moses built the tabernacle God showed him in Mount Sinai a pattern of all things, so David was instructed by the Spirit of God to plan the temple and the orders of the priests to serve there. 1 Chron. xxviii. 12. So he declares: "All this the Lord made me understand in writing by his hand upon me, even all the works of this pattern." 1 Chron. xxviii. 19. In undertaking any service for God, it is of chief importance that we are guided by the divine will; and though it is true under every dispensation, especially in New Testament times, that many things are left to our voluntary action without specific directions of measures to be adopted, yet the great principles by which we are to be guided are explicitly given, and we are accepted in our cheerful desires to advance the glory of our God when mindful of his teachings.

The preparations made by David were on a scale of great magnificence. When we read of the thousands of talents of gold and silver, of the immense weight of brass, of the precious stones, we are surprised at the wealth of his kingdom. We may readily suppose that much of his wealth was gathered through his wars with the neighbouring nations, but we may justly consider that David devoted to this great enterprise the chief part of his riches. He says: "Behold in my trouble I have prepared for the house of the Lord a hundred thousand talents of gold and a thousand thousand talents of silver, of brass and iron without weight, for it is in abundance; timber also and stone have I prepared." 1 Chron. xxii. 14. It is difficult to estimate in modern value the worth of ancient money. And it is impossible to make accurate statements on this subject. We are not certain how much the Jewish talent was; we know that the value of money itself varies from one age to another, and that the relative value of gold and silver has changed within our own memory; and for these reasons we can have no definite idea of the value of David's offering.

Besides the munificent offering made by David in preparation for the temple, he used his influence to induce the people to offer freely their contributions to the same end. Indeed, it would seem that not only did he appropriate to this purpose treasures that had previously been laid up by men now dead, but that some of the living who had taken spoils in war consecrated them to this purpose. Especial mention is made of the veteran Joab, whose long career of victories without a reverse must have thrown much wealth into his hands, and of this he also makes his offering. A certain man, named Shelomith, was appointed treasurer, and this record is made of the contributions: "Shelomith and his brethren were over all the treasures of the dedicated things which David the king, and the chief fathers, the captains over thousands and hundreds and the captain of the hosts, had dedicated.

Out of the spoils won in battle did they dedicate to maintain the house of the Lord; and all that Samuel the seer, and Saul the son of Kish, and Abner the son of Ner, and Joab the son of Zeruiah, had dedicated, and whosoever had dedicated anything, it was under the hand of Shelomith and of his brethren." 1 Chron. xxvi. 26–28. But all the people were also now called upon by the king to make their free-will offerings, as Moses in constructing the tabernacle in the wilderness had called for the voluntary offerings of their fathers. And if a noble example had then been set before them, the people now had reason to follow such a precedent, and were heartily disposed to do so. The king explained to them that the work now undertaken was no ordinary enterprise, nor designed for mere human purposes—it was a palace for the Lord God. He urged upon the principal men of the nation that God had given them rest on every side, had made the people of the land peaceful and subdued the country before them (1 Chron. xxi. 18); he told them of the preparations he had personally made, and of an offering of special love which he had consecrated to adorn the house in some specified particulars (1 Chron. xxix. 3), and reminded them that the transfer of the sceptre from the hands of age and experience to the tender hands of his son made it the more needful that they should give him a hearty co-operation. To this call to consecrate their cheerful offerings to God the princes and people freely responded, and a large amount both of money and of materials for building was received at their hands. Great joy filled the hearts of the king and of his people in this ready service.

And we have reason to judge that in these free-will offerings the king and the people of Israel were actuated by holy and proper principles, as much as the mind of man can ever be. There may have been offerings made from ostentation or vanity, as in our holiest services we find cause to lament how deficient we are in upright motives, and as mingling with those that truly fear God there are ever in the earthly Church some whose hearts are not right before him. How hard it is to bring home to our darkened minds the reasonable and salutary conviction that we gain nothing before God by services that are insincerely made! Surely the impressive description which our Lord Jesus gives of many of the religious acts done all around him should warn us from copying the things that are done "TO BE SEEN OF MAN;" and his solemn declaration, "*Verily, verily, they have their reward,*" should make us long, far in preference to such a reward, for the approbation of our "Father who seeth in secret." If we did but keep in mind that no service can be acceptable in his sight unless it is rendered out of regard to him, that all inferior motives mar our own enjoyment as well as our acceptance, that he knows the entire workings of our minds, and that really his smile is the richest reward his creatures can enjoy, we would more carefully strive to put away from us every earthly motive and truly endeavour to glorify him. And it may be well for us to notice that scarcely any of the duties enjoined upon us do more truly exhibit the temper of a pious mind than the contribution of our substance to the service of God. Scarcely any duty, perhaps, gives more perplexity to a mind truly conscientious than the duty of benevolence. It is ever found a hard thing to decide what proportion of his substance a pious man should give. In many matters the path of right is plain. In speaking the truth not a word or shade of falsehood can be allowed; in honesty not a trifle of fraud can be admitted; no thought of impurity or of hatred must the upright heart entertain. But the line of division between benevolence and covetousness is not so plainly marked. There are objects of apparent benevolence where it is hard to decide whether the Christian should give or not give; it is harder to tell what proportion should be given here or there, and still harder to decide in what proportion of his receipts or his possessions he should contribute to objects like these. These practical difficulties all tend to make this very thing—the contribution of our substance for the glory of God and the honour of religion—one of the most valuable tests of personal piety that we can find in all the varieties of Christian duty. The very fact that these are FREE-WILL OFFER-

INGS; that the amount is not designated by any express terms of a divine statute, but left to a cheerful heart; that the worldly standard is so low that we are but little tempted to give too much lest our good name should be reproached; and that the smile of our Father is the chief approbation we can expect,—all these things tend to make the benevolence of a man a most important test of personal piety. A man may be honest and truthful without piety, for his conscience and his reputation lead him to these things, and in benevolence doubtless many are liberal far beyond others by natural temper and education. But in benevolent matters a man may come so much farther short of his duty without reproach either from his conscience or from the world—it is so much more a matter of free-will, left so by Providence designedly, that we can see the inclinations of the heart more plainly here than elsewhere. How easy is it to do those things on which the heart is set, and what pleasure we find in doing them! Yet let me not be supposed to mean by this statement of the matter that benevolence is not a duty in the Church of God, or that the conscience of the Christian has less to do in this than in other matters. I would rather say that nowhere is it more needful for a man to have a conscience, as well as a heart, to lead him to the performance of a most important duty, than in this very thing—consecrating his property to the service of religion. The reputation he desires to maintain in the community will lead many a man to speak truly and deal honestly, while yet he is regardless both of truth and honesty. But in a matter like this the community may still retain its confidence in one who is very far from being liberal in the sight of God, and the man may form a high estimate of his own liberality, because even the divine law itself has made no definite proportion of his property, his duty for benevolent contributions. Perhaps in this matter the deepest source of wrong and of injury to the cause of religion lies in this—that each man, being made the judge in his own case, is led thereby to regard his own estimate of duty as the correct one, and considers himself as liberal because he gives all he thinks he ought to give. This would be true, provided this man has given due care and pains to find out what he ought to give. No man ought to be considered as truthful who tells a story which he *thinks* is true while yet he has taken no pains to discover whether it is or is not. Every conscientious man in paying his debts is willing to find out how much he owes, as well as willing to pay the full amount. Now why should not this as truly apply to the duty of benevolence?—and indeed so much the more just because this duty is so peculiarly referred back to ourselves and made to rise from the cheerful service of our hearts. It is true, indeed, that when we give any sum that our circumstances will permit for the promoting of the cause of God, we but render back to him of that which he has given us. In everything we must be infinitely inferior to God in our imitations of him. But perhaps no man ever comes nearer the character of God—the GREAT, and, indeed, the ONLY, GIVER—than he does who cheerfully consecrates his property to secure large blessings upon the souls of men—it may be upon men he has never seen, or souls that have been or are thankless for all the efforts that can be made for their salvation. If it is the wonder of Christ's grace that he gave so freely and with such self-denial, the apostle urges our knowledge of his grace who for our sakes became poor that he may prove the sincerity of our love. 2 Cor. viii. 8, 9.

We return from these thoughts to say again that David and the people of Israel seem to be influenced by righteous principles in the large free-will offering now made to God. The king makes acknowledgments for them that all these things, which they now cheerfully render to his service, they had but received at his hands; to him belonged the greatness. Riches and honour came of him, and they had but rendered back his bounty. "Who am I and what is my people that we should be able to offer so willingly after this sort? For all things come of thee, and of thine own have we given thee." 1 Chron. xxix. 14, *seq.*

Besides making these preparations of materials and of means for erecting the temple of the Lord,

David made further arrangements for its building. As we find afterward that the stones of the temple were hewn at the quarries before they were brought to the place where they were to be used, and as thus—so complete was the plan and so competent the architects—everything at the temple went on quietly till all was done, so it is likely that many of the stones were cut out and prepared during the lifetime of David. We have instances of large public buildings in this country that have occupied many years in their construction, but our experience is nothing in architecture. The cathedral at Cologne, in Europe, was three hundred years in building. David seems to have made a law for employing the strangers in the land as masons to hew the wrought stones. 1 Chron. xxii. 2. Who these strangers were is explained afterward. When the Israelites conquered Canaan they were not able wholly to drive out the old inhabitants, but the descendants of the Amorites, the Hittites, the Perizzites, the Hivites and the Jebusites remained there still. It may be that their idolatries were put down, but they seem never to have been incorporated with the Israelites; and upon them was laid much of the harder service in building the house of the Lord. 1 Kings ix. 20.

In still further preparation for the service of God in the temple, David made arrangements for the duties of the Levites toward the house of the Lord. He divided them into four great classes: twenty-four thousand to set forward the work of the house of the Lord, six thousand officers and judges, four thousand porters, and four thousand musicians. These seem to have been subdivided into smaller divisions, so that they took turns in their various duties. For example, we are told how many of the porters were to be employed as watchmen on the different sides of the house—each man's post and his time being so understood that no spot of the sacred ground should be without its guards. It would be easy of course to provide amply for the services of the temple, both in resources and in men, when there was but one consecrated place for their most devout services for the entire nation. The great multitudes of Levites, in comparison with the population, doubtless offered temptations to this tribe to forget their sacred character, but if this body of men had zealously devoted themselves to the interest of education and religion, no people in the world ever had arrangements better adapted to instruct the masses than we find among the Jewish people.

These offerings of David and his people were either made upon a day of solemn convocation, or such a day was held in thanksgiving for the success of their efforts in collecting means. It was a day of many sacrifices made to God after the manner of their worship. At David's exhortation the people joined in solemn worship to God, and the solemn second coronation of Solomon as their future king in the stead of David closed the impressive scene. These things seemed to have occurred in the seventieth year of David's life; and he soon afterward sunk into a state of imbecility, from which he seems at times to have rallied before his death.

The dispensation of the Church to which we belong is so entirely different from the one in which he lived that we are often struck by the contrast rather than with the similarity between them. There may spring forth from the matter that has now been before us an instructive line of thought to remind us that we are in circumstances not so widely different from the position of David, and that in every matter of comparison the advantage is upon our side.

It was in the mind of David to build a house for the Lord God. This desire sprang not forth from any special command which he had received from God, and yet it was well pleasing in his sight. As for us, our God has commanded us to build a temple to his praise, and our duty is thus laid upon us, so that we cannot innocently turn away from it. The house that David had it in his mind to erect was to be exceedingly magnificent; the fame of it was to fill all lands; and we cannot doubt but that many a blinded pagan came, in after years, into the city of Jerusalem to view the splendours of that building, who there learned, it may be, the greater glory of that God for whose name it was built. But the temple of God there was but little to his glory in comparison with the temple we are to erect to his praise. Our temple is the living Church of the living God himself. It is no forced or unnatural analogy that compares the Church of God to a temple. It is used again and again by the inspired writers—one fitly used and one easily understood. The God we serve "dwelleth not in temples made with hands," and no house which man's wealth or wisdom can erect is so magnificent and so worthy of his abode as the humble and the contrite heart.

In building this temple for the living God we are permitted to bear a part. He himself has planned the building; he himself superintends its erection; he has laid in Zion its sure foundation-stone, even the Lord Jesus Christ himself; to him shall be the glory. This temple is long in building. Its foundations were laid in Paradise in that dark and gloomy day of Satan's first triumph over man, and its top-stone is to be brought forward with shoutings of grace just before the final sounding of the trump of the archangel. We stand and see the raising of this glorious house of God. As Solomon's temple was built without the noise of a hammer or plane, so the kingdom of God cometh not with observation. Much is done now, and much is to be done in preparation for the building which is to go on after we are dead.

The Church of God, as we are allowed to promote it, is far more for his glory than the temple which David desired to build. If he would have reckoned it the chief honour of his life to build such a house, how thankful we should be for the privilege of building the Church of God!—how joyful in the assurance that against all our efforts the gates of hell shall not prevail! We may look at the Church as to her principles and as to her power, and we may rejoice in the prospects before her. These great truths of the word of God are to be spread abroad in all the earth; we are directly commanded to use means to give them the widest dissemination, and they are certainly to fill the whole earth. The triumph of these principles we are certainly assured of by the word of the Lord. This does not mean that every soul that hears the gospel shall embrace its precious truths and find its great salvation. Neither the word of God, nor the past history of the Church, nor our own experience would lead us to look for such results. But the triumph of the gospel shall be great. It shall never be preached without success. It shall never be received by a single soul without great benefit to himself and great glory to God. The transforming power of this gospel, the precious fruits of holy living, the earnest exertions of benevolence which it calls forth—all these honour God more than all the gold and incense of the temple of Solomon. Our temple is built not of hewn stones, but of living stones. These are the souls of men, taken from the quarry of corrupt human nature by the choice of the Great Architect himself, and built by him into his spiritual house. 1 Peter ii. 5. Our ornaments are not gold and silver and precious stones, but hearts filled with love, meekness, peace and humility, which are in the sight of God of great price. Our great Sacrifice has been for us offered once for all to reconcile us to God, and our incense is the pure and humble utterance of our prayers and thanksgivings in the name of our Lord Jesus Christ.

And now why may we not look upon ourselves as called upon, as truly as were David and his people upon that day, to build this temple for the Lord of hosts? This Church of God shall certainly be built; we are called to bear our part in it; this privilege we should not wish either to avoid or to lay aside from our sight. May not the question of the king of Israel be seriously urged upon each of us as one of personal interest—as one claiming legitimately our serious and prayerful thought? Who, then, is willing to consecrate his service this day unto the Lord? The call is for willing hearts. Who will come?

## CHAPTER XXI.

### *THE DEATHS OF SHIMEI AND JOAB.*

AGE and infirmities now led the mind of David to consider his approaching death, and to make those wise provisions which were needful for the welfare of his kingdom after his departure. It would seem that the law of the kingdom of Israel did not demand that the eldest son should succeed to the throne of his father; or if this was the general rule, and the expectation of the people (see 1 Kings ii. 15), yet this government was so specially under the rule of God that the succession was arranged according to the divine will. Although Solomon was a much younger man than some of his brothers, we are told that his promotion to the throne was from the direction of Jehovah. So David says, "Of all my sons (for the Lord hath given me many sons), he hath chosen Solomon my son to sit upon the throne of the kingdom of the Lord over Israel." 1 Chron. xxviii. 5. How fully this may have been published—if published at all before Solomon's coronation—we do not know, but the expectation of the kingdom had filled the mind of another of David's sons. This was Adonijah, the son of Haggith. He is described as a very goodly man, but it gives us no exalted estimate of the family training of David's household when it is added, his father had not displeased him at any time. Parents lay up for themselves trouble, and for their children even greater trouble, by undue indulgence. No man ever learns to govern himself except by first learning to submit to government, and he who is expected also to govern others most of all needs this earlier discipline. Had Adonijah been better governed in his father's prime, he might longer have survived his father's age.

The ambition of the young prince follows too closely in the fatal steps of Absalom. Taking advantage of the feebleness of his aged father, and perhaps supposing that his end was near, Adonijah made his preparations to secure the crown. Among those who joined him in the undertaking were Joab and Abiathar the priest. It is not necessary to aggravate their treason by supposing that they knew that Solomon was divinely chosen for the throne. This knowledge would indeed make their sin much greater, but there is crime enough in any hasty movement of this kind to condemn the actors. To presume that a man ought to be king, to take measures to make him king, and this during the lifetime of another monarch, without taking pains to consult him, and to the especial slighting of some whose counsel ought certainly to have been asked, betrays more than inconsiderate action. No man may presume to put forth his hand to sovereign authority without so just a right that he is willing to risk his life upon the maintenance of it. The plot of Adonijah had gone in the very track of Absalom so far as to adopt the honour of chariots with men to run before him, and further a sumptuous feast was prepared perhaps for his coronation. The guests were assembled at En-rogel, which, though outside the walls of the city, is very near Jerusalem, and between the walls and the brook Kedron to the south-east. But these preparations did not escape the attention of David's experienced counsellors. Measures were immediately taken to secure the interference of David. The prophet Nathan visited Queen Bathsheba, and arranged with her that she should first visit David to bring the matter before him, and that he would follow, as if without design, to corroborate her statement. The king was feeble, but it appears he was capable of being roused to exertion on needful occasion. Bathsheba reminded him of the oath he had given to her that her son Solomon should succeed him on the throne, and then informed him of these proceedings on the part of Adonijah. She called his attention to the fact that his decision in the case would be regarded as settling the matter before the eyes of the people, and, as excusing her zeal, she plead not simply her concern for Solomon, but the danger of both herself and her son if a different hand held the sceptre. The king had no time to make his reply before it was announced that the prophet Nathan was desirous of an interview. Bathsheba, therefore, retired until Nathan came in and reported, as if unconscious of the queen's visit, that Adonijah and his friends were carousing as if for a coronation. Hearing these things, the mind of David was fully aroused, and he acted with a prompt decision needful for the occasion and worthy of his best days. Recalling Bathsheba, he filled her heart with joy by renewing his solemn oath that Solomon should indeed be his successor upon the throne. Immediately after her departure he called for Zadok the associated high priest, and Nathan the prophet, and Benaiah the captain of his guards, and ordered that without delay they should take the usual measures to proclaim Solomon king. In this measure there was great wisdom and propriety. It is not uncommon for a younger person to be associated with an elder upon the throne—for a reigning king to be virtually dethroned by his infirmities; and monarchs, even in their prime vigour and in the tide of successful rule, have been known voluntarily to resign the crown and sceptre to others, and to throw off the cares of royalty. After the experience of trouble from his own family already felt by David, especially perhaps as other sons besides Adonijah may have been too much accustomed to have their own way, it would have been most unwise for David to leave unsettled the question of his successor until after his decease. An open question like this might have thrown the whole kingdom into discord.

The officers appointed by the king hastened to do as he commanded. They placed the young prince Solomon—now perhaps about eighteen years of age—upon the royal mule, and proceeding to Gihon, on the opposite side of the city from the assembly in favour of Adonijah, and also without the walls, the priest Zadok took a horn of oil from the tabernacle and solemnly anointed Solomon king. Then returning to the city, and passing through the streets in open procession, the proclamation was made for a new monarch before the people knew what was going on. The summary settlement of the matter, which perhaps may already have awakened an anxiety for coming troubles; the popularity, it may be, of Solomon, whose wisdom, already apparent beyond his years, may have excited affection, though his tender age may have created apprehension; the stately march of the royal guards, the sound of the trumpet and the unwonted ceremonial, called forth the great crowd of inhabitants, who received Solomon with loud acclamations and passed with him from street to street with every demonstration of joy. The noise of the uproar—especially the trumpets' stirring notes—reached the ears of the revellers that were with Adonijah. Joab was the first to notice the matter. Nor were they long in doubt of the meaning of it. Jonathan, the son of Abiathar, came in from the city, and gave them a full account of the coronation, of David's satisfaction in the case, and of the actual occupancy of the throne by King Solomon.

The entire scheme of the conspirators was thus at once completely foiled, and they saw themselves not only defeated, but put in the utmost peril. They had begun a thing whose defeat subjected them to the charge of treason. The banqueters therefore hastily dispersed in dismay, every man consulting for his own safety, and chiefly anxious that his presence there might not become publicly known. Adonijah, fearing for his personal safety, fled to the tabernacle and caught hold upon the horns of the altar, and refused to leave until Solomon had given his oath that he would not put him to death. The young king showed the greatest dignity and wisdom as well as justice in the case. He declined to give his oath, but simply passed his word that so long as Adonijah behaved himself properly he should be in safety. When he was brought before him and saluted him as king, he bade him go to his own house, which was equivalent to a dismissal from all public services—as light a punishment as could well be laid on one who had aspired to sit upon the throne.

The temporary revival of David's vigour gave him an opportunity to give certain charges to his successor respecting his conduct upon the throne of Israel. We may pass by for the present the deeply interesting charges, considered as the words of a pious, dying father to his beloved son, and simply notice now those that have reference to certain matters of public duty. We do not follow the order of the narrative.

He urges upon Solomon to show kindness to the sons of Barzillai the Gileadite. This venerable and wealthy man had shown great kindness to David in the time of his distress, and he had then made offers which showed his gratitude. That now the sons of Barzillai are mentioned, and not Barzillai himself, may intimate that his life was already ended. This would not be strange, as he was older than David then ; yet, because at that time he had declined any personal favours, the mention of his sons now will not prove that he was dead. It is likely that this charge of kindness to his family was not forgotten by Solomon.

Another very grave matter in the last words of David to Solomon is the injunction made upon him concerning Shimei the son of Gera. It will be remembered that this man met David as he left Jerusalem upon the approach of Absalom and heaped grievous curses upon him. Even then he would have been put to death but for David's interference, and afterward, at the restoration, he made early submission and the tender of his aid in quieting the kingdom. Then David gave him a pardon, and swore to him that he should not die. It has therefore been laid as a serious reproach to David that upon his dying bed, and almost with his latest breath, he should remember the offence of Shimei, not only now passed, but also sealed with an oath of forgiveness. We are accustomed to feel that the dying couch, especially of a believer, should be a place sacred from the intrusion of unworthy thoughts, and that no unworthy motives are more unsuited to a time like that than those of revenge. When a soul, conscious of his numerous and aggravated transgressions, is about to pass into the presence of the great Judge, when its only hope of acceptance there is in the pardon of God graciously given, he ought to be more ready than ever to forgive the offences which his fellow-men have done against him. It is no part of our duty, in considering the life and conduct of David, to vindicate his motives, whether right or wrong; neither is it any part of our duty to judge harshly that he is in the wrong, when perhaps he may not be. Here, as elsewhere, the feelings and doings of pious men are no criterion of right, except as they accord with the holy principles of the word of God; yet let us judge calmly what are the best teachings of each historical scene.

Dr. Kennicott urges that according to the usage of Hebrew writers the "NOT" of the 9th verse (1 Kings ii.) should be rendered also with the latter clause: "Hold him not guiltless, yet bring not his hoary head down to the grave with blood." He cites such instances as these: Ps. i. 5, the Hebrew reads literally, "The ungodly shall not stand in the judgment, *and* sinners in the congregation of the righteous." The plain sense is, "*nor* sinners in the congregation," etc. So Ps. xxxviii. 1: "Rebuke me not in thy wrath, *and* chasten me in thy hot displeasure;" the sense certainly is, "*nor* chasten me." So Isa. xiii. 22; xxii. 4; Ps. ix. 18; Prov. xxix. 12; xxx. 3. The sense, then, would be, "Hold him not guiltless, but do not put him to death." And it seems true, certainly, that Solomon respected the oath of David to Shimei, and did not put him to death for this crime. But Shimei was a man of considerable influence. When he made his submission to David, he was at the head of a thousand men, yet he seems to have been a troublesome and dangerous, as well as a presumptuous, character. King Solomon therefore thought it best to put a check upon his proceedings, and impose terms upon him, by keeping which he should live. Shimei understood and assented to these terms, and had he kept them he would not have met with a violent end. His death, then, though connected certainly with his former deed, was the result of his renewed transgression against Solomon.

Yet with the understanding that the oath of David was respected, so that the life of Shimei was not taken for that offence, there remains behind a feeling of surprise and regret that David should recall such a matter at such a time, and counsel his son to watch the movements of Shimei. The only possible vindication, and perhaps it is sufficient, must be found in the official position of David. It is not through the impulse of private feelings, not through the actings of revenge, that he utters these advices. He is leaving in the hands of a very young son a kingdom that has lately been in great distraction, and he needs to put him upon his guard against seditious persons. Whatever hopes he may have had in the wisdom of Solomon, he could hardly then anticipate his future eminence, and it was needful to give him prudent forewarnings. Even if we understand him to advise the death of Shimei, if we read the passage as it stands in the English Bible, it may still be true that the impulse of David's feelings formerly had done a public wrong which he is desirous of correcting. It may have proved so that he had improperly bound himself to spare Shimei, and now he charges his son to devise means by which the oath might be kept and yet the ends of public justice secured. But in the worst form of the matter, Shimei's life was safe except against his own folly.

There is but one additional remark on this matter. We cannot but see in the close criticism to which everything in the sacred volume is subjected the disposition of men to scrutinize the Bible more closely than any other book, and at the same time the most convincing proof that these are indeed lively oracles of divine authority. Any vindication we make of the Bible is apart from the conduct which its principles clearly disavow. If David here is in the wrong, we need no more apologize for him than for his former sin against Uriah. If this was a case of revenge, it is not only contrary to the eminent excellence of David's long-continued demeanour toward Saul under great provocation, but expressly contrary to teachings both of the Old and New Testaments. But apart from this solution of the question, it is obvious that if plain and unquestionable objections could be brought against the moral teachings of the Bible, cavillers would not be driven to pick out such as this. Oftentimes we can tell the good character of a man from the fact that his enemies and those who are prejudiced against him are compelled to draw their objections from the most trivial things. We are sometimes led to think, "These matters are beneath the notice of a candid mind; if his enemies can say nothing more than this, he must be a good kind of a man." Yet we do sometimes become prejudiced against persons for matters which, if true, are of very minor importance. But we judge of the Bible, not only from the trifling nature of the cavils made against it, but also from the assaults it has so frequently endured without evil. If we were called to decide the strength of some strong fortress, we might decide that it was impregnable by viewing its battlements or by considering the attacks it has already withstood. A fort that has been attacked by every kind of fire and is still unconquered, may well command our confidence in its strength. No volume in the world has ever had the attention directed to it that has been bestowed upon the Bible. This statement is far too tame. When we consider that the chief literature of the world is among Christian nations, and that books upon religious questions are so abundant and so widely circulated, we may venture the assertion that more than half of the books of the world have sprung forth directly from the Bible, and that this sacred volume has been the subject of more criticism than all the other volumes in the world combined. It is *almost* proving its divine authority to establish the simple fact that it has been deemed worthy of so much reading and so much investigation. Certainly no other volume making claim to inspiration could stand up for a single century against the storm of attacks to which, if at all possible, it would be subjected, or against the contempt which feeble pretensions would excite. Yet here is a volume written through the course of eighteen centuries by fifty different writers of various intelligence, treating upon the most important of all subjects, yet touching also upon every subject of human thought. Now it is undeniable concerning this book that it has been closely scrutinized not only in its general character, but in every page and in every phrase by the best-educated and keenest intellects of the world; that every variety of motive that could quicken men's minds to vehement action has urged them to its study; that every new light of history and of philosophy and of science has been used to search the claims of a book that has older history and older philosophy and older science than any in the world. Now what has been the result? What is the state of things in the world now? There is a great deal of skepticism and infidelity among men? And this Bible could not be true if these evils did not exist and even abound. It gives us such ideas of man's depravity and opposition to God that we never expect the clearest evidences to be admitted by the sons of men in reference to a divine revelation. No good man lives without his enemies, and the best of books will never lack its cordial haters while time lasts. But the result is, among the crowd of flippant skeptics, very few first-rate minds have ever been infidels. A very intelligent gentleman—himself very far from being a Christian, and better acquainted with the opponents of the Bible than with its friends—once suddenly surprised me by asking if I could give the names of any first-rate men who were infidels. I named La Place, and neither he nor I could go any farther with names that we were willing to admit among the first class of gifted and educated minds. This is a most remarkable thing, when we reflect that prejudices and depravity have so much to do in forming men's religious opinions. Further, the result is very few *serious* minds in the world are infidel. Pride, vanity, ignorance and love of sin often lead men to avow infidelity who give little attention to it, and indeed from various causes are incapable of profoundly investigating any subject; but serious and thoughtful men, who really weigh the evidences and claims of the sacred volume, are not so easily led to throw away the only teaching which really points us forward to immortality, and gives us the needful preparations to secure its blessings. And the result further is this undeniably: let the men who have any just acquaintance with the Bible be separated into two classes. Range on the one side those who are really acquainted with the volume, who read it constantly, who know the contents of it, who carefully compare it with the teachings of nature and providence around them and within them, and on the other side those who are careless of the evidence in its favour and careless of its influence. Of these two classes, infidelity will be found very rare in the first and abundant in the second. The chief opposers of the Bible know the least about it. Separate again. Put the honest men of the world, the sincere searchers after truth, the diligent students of the earth, into one class, and in another the reckless and dishonest, and it is easy to decide where the lovers of the Bible will be found. The result is, that men can oppose this sacred volume without sustaining for themselves any reputation for truth or morality, and the more depraved men are, the more certainly may we expect them to oppose it, while we ever expect the good men who know the Bible to love it more the more they know of it. Naimbanna, an African prince, gave as his simple reason for receiving the Bible as the word of God that he saw good men so regarding it and bad men disregarding it. A shrewd native on the African coast used to offer tracts to the traders he met. If they received them respectfully, he knew he could trust them; if they rudely rejected them, he found it necessary to guard against their dishonesty.

But David further charged Solomon to remember the crimes of Joab, and to bring upon him the punishment he so well deserved. We have before seen that Joab escaped the punishment of his crimes only because David had not the power to execute the laws against one of so great influence. It must be seen that there is room for suspecting that David felt the influence here of his private resentment, for he had not received from Joab the treatment due from a subject to his sovereign. Yet it would be harsh to impute this as the controlling motive, when we can see reasons of public importance demanding that the laws should be vindicated against one who had violated them with impunity. A mischievous influence must have been exerted in the kingdom now for many years by the unpunished crimes of Joab. He had slain two public men in a treacherous manner, and the result in each case had been not punishment, but promotion. We are willing to give due credit to Joab for all his active and successful efforts to built up the power of the kingdom. His energy and success as a commander, his fidelity as a friend, his loyalty until the day of Adonijah's feast as a patriot, are all commendable. And it was just because he was the idol of his soldiers that thus long he had braved the authority of the law. But we say that all these matters form no apology for the wickedness of Joab, and were no reasons for allowing him to be unpunished. We say, rather, that more mischief is done to society, as well as greater injustice, in fact, by allowing the escape of powerful, and—if you so please to term them—*respectable* criminals, than by failing to punish those whose influence would be less. It is a very common reproach of the law—a reproach, as we suppose, urged in every land and age, but more justly urged at some times than at others—that criminals without money and without friends are easily convicted, but that those who are rich and of influence in society escape even against the clearest proofs of guilt. Certainly, the reproach should never be true. The law of the land should know no man above its authority, and no man beneath its protection. The poor and the weak should be safe in all their rights and privileges; the strong and the rich should be liable to judgment for every wrong; and while no man should be condemned for a crime without a fair and impartial trial, the law should know no respect of persons. The poor man must not so excite the sympathy of a judge that he will acquit him for his poverty's sake, nor the rich awaken his fears or his cupidity or his prejudices for either too great severity or too great leniency because of his circumstances. The ancient heathen represented the goddess Justice as holding aloft a pair of scales, and as being blind to show her impartiality. It is easy to see that more evil is done by acquitting one rich and powerful offender than by the escape of many minor ones. The crimes of Joab were aggravated by his standing in society and by his other services rendered. The apologies which sometimes belong to other crimes he could not plead. The nation had a right to expect that a man in his position should regard the laws, and his impunity must have brought great reproach upon the government that was confessedly too weak to punish him. The maintenance of law for the punishment of uncommon offenders is of the utmost importance. A very important criminal case occurred in England during the reign of George III. A forgery was committed by a clergyman, who had been one of the most popular preachers of London and a chaplain to the king. Immense exertions were made to secure a pardon, but the king stood firm, and perhaps the law has never been more fully vindicated than when Dr. Dodd was executed at Tyburn for his crime. So, a few years ago, a distinguished professor in one of our highest institutions of learning was convicted of murder, and it would have been a very great public calamity if the governor of Massachusetts had yielded to the petitions that were got up upon his behalf, and had spared his life. Dr. Webster's execution was due to the law, and was of more importance than the execution of a hundred whose characters were less exalted and whose crimes were less known.

It is a sufficient apology for Joab's escape hitherto that David had not the power to punish him, but this only made it the more righteous that a stronger government should deal with him. It belongs rather to the reign of Solomon than to that of David to speak of the execution of the sentence, yet the account would be unfinished if we did not go through with all that is given us.

After Solomon was firmly settled upon the throne, he began to execute the counsels of his father. The death of Adonijah and the fall of Abiathar warned Joab that his time had come. He fled to the tabernacle of the Lord and caught hold on the horns of the altar. We have seen already that Adonijah had once before sought refuge there. It has been questioned whether the altar of God was ever properly made a sanctuary of refuge for the criminal. It seems plain that Adonijah and Joab, with others mentioned in the

Scriptures, fled to the altar to find protection, and the law of Moses intimates that it would be a protection in some cases. Ex. xxi. 14. But it is very certain that the altar of God under the Jewish law was not a protection to any criminal so as to defeat the righteous sentence of the law. The altar of God was not a *sanctuary*, as that term has been used in later times. Among the ancient heathens there were certain temples and altars consecrated to the safety of those that fled there. So sacred were they that a criminal was safe there, no matter what were his crimes, nor how important that he should be punished for them. This privilege of sanctuary was retained in the Romish Church; and until very lately, under papal rule, if a criminal fled to the church, his crime was changed from a civil offence to an ecclesiastical one, and the Church, and not the civil law, took cognizance of it. This threw great power into the hands of the Church, and criminals often escaped by the payment of sums of money as the priests decided. Under English law, if a man committed any crime (treason and sacrilege excepted) he might flee to any church or churchyard, and within forty days confess his crime in sackcloth before the coroner, and take an oath to leave the realm. He saved his life if he went with a cross in his hand to the port assigned to him and embarked. The entire privilege was taken away in the reign of James I. It is easy to see that the result could only be to encourage crime.

A criminal should have no protection from law. Let him have protection from mob violence and from hasty proceedings, but not protection against the very claims of justice. The only thing at all like this in Israel, which has been mistaken as similar, is essentially different. The cities of refuge were established not to protect the guilty, but to protect the innocent. According to the Oriental law, the man who sheds blood—no matter what his motives or the manner of the deed—was liable to be killed by the nearest kinsman of the deceased whenever or wherever he could find him. But if a man fled to a city of refuge, time was given for investigation and discrimination. If it was found that the deed was an accidental, a justifiable homicide, he was safe there; if it was a crime, even the city of refuge was no protection.

Joab seems certainly to have expected safety at the altar. But Solomon did not understand the law of God as ever throwing the shield of impunity over crime. The sins of this man were too many, and his approach as a supplicant now to the place of mercy was too late to allow that his appeal should be successful. The command, therefore, was given to Benaiah not to tear him away, but to execute him there, as if to show that the altar itself had no protest to enter against his death.

## CHAPTER XXII.

### *DAVID'S DYING WORDS TO SOLOMON.*

WE were introduced a little while ago into the chamber of mourning, where a pious father grieved for the untimely death of an ungodly son. Common as it is for the young to die before the old, it is not so natural. The scene to which we now pass is the natural result of the present state of earthly things. An old man lies upon the couch of death; and we see here that no regard is paid by death to station, or character, or usefulness. Here is the deathbed of a king, but it differs not, because of this, from the death of any other mortal. We may approach it as we approach the couch of feebleness in our own abodes, with quiet seriousness, to receive profitable instructions. It is a solemn thing to die; sometimes it is deeply painful. Suffering makes it painful; delirium and insensibility, which shut us out from the last exchange of thoughts with beloved ones, make it painful; indifference to religion makes it painful; above all, the opposition of the soul to that God before whom it must soon appear, makes death an event inexpressively painful to every rightly-thinking mind. But solemn as death is, it has other aspects. God himself says, "Blessed are the dead;" but the voice from heaven adds, "who die in the Lord." And we use, it may be, the language of David himself when we say, "Precious in the sight of the Lord is the death of his saints." Friends may stand by a dying bed with calm composure, with entire resignation. Men may lie upon such a bed and look forward to all to which it introduces them with more than calmness; they may arrange thoughtfully all the worldly affairs they leave behind; they may counsel the children from whom they must be separated; they may speak of the duties which appear now in a clearer view than ever; and they may look forward to say of that which lies before them, in the language of David, "As for me, I will behold thy face in righteousness; I shall be satisfied when I awake with thy likeness." Ps. xvii. 15. Far above these calm thoughts rise the raptures of the dying believer at some favoured time when God allows the clear light of the coming world to shine upon his soul. It may not be denied that men may depart calmly without the hopes of the gospel; but in full view of all that belongs to the question of our immortal life, the only desirable departure from earth is one sustained by the principles and hopes of that sacred volume in which alone is revealed the eternity before us.

This great subject is common, but can never be

uninteresting to a serious mind. Providence brings it before us many times in the history of our lives; its lessons are deeply impressed upon us as we part from friends dearly beloved; and, if we are wise, we will yet more frequently turn our solitary thoughts to the same topic. For the truth should never be forgotten—we too are to die. The narrow pathway trodden by so many we all must tread, one by one, and a personal interest bids us mark the closing scenes of life.

If it is not as a king but as a man—not as a man but as a believer—that we take an interest in David, now drawing near to death, there is also a sacredness about the scene when we regard it as the counsels of a dying father addressed to a beloved son. This indeed is the special aspect which we have here presented. We have before considered some of the matters of more public interest upon which David addressed Solomon. Here we have just such charges as a father in any case should wish to impart to a son, and of course just such as every son should desire to receive. Whatever differences exist among men, from position, education or age, all alike possess a reasonable, moral and immortal nature, and the substantial interests and duties of all are alike. Especially let every young person hear the counsels of aged piety to the young, and while he ponders let him resolve to obey these important teachings.

First in this matter let us reflect upon the

touching circumstances in which this advice was given. A man of age and of piety speaks from his dying bed his last counsels to youth and inexperience. By confession of all, the dying hour is one peculiarly marked by truth. We do not understand by this that then men never deceive themselves nor wilfully deceive others. We have no question that men are deceived and are wilful deceivers in every profession and condition of mortal life, the last solemn hour of earth not excepted. But we mean that at that last solemn hour there are special reasons why a man should feel and speak in all sincerity; that the mask of hypocrisy often falls before the eyes of men just before the soul passes to stand before its God; and that men who are insincere at other times are shocked into truthfulness by the solemn thought of an opening eternity. But if there is any sense in which we may truthfully say that the dying hour is one of honesty, what a testimony is it to the value of piety that all the testimony of the last hours of men have been in favour of it! Men have mourned over many things when they came to die. To say nothing of the execrations heaped on the infidel and ungodly companions who have ruined the unhappy soul by their seductions; to say nothing of the disappointments of thousands who have been honourably occupied in the engagements that are profitably held for this world; to enumerate nothing of the variety of hopes and fears between these wide extremes,—it is a great matter that we are able to say of true piety that no man has ever regretted that he had known too much of it when he came to die. But when we have said this much, when we have claimed that religion is our best friend in life and our best support in death, we have fallen greatly short of making a just impression on the subject. We may justly say that the more a man has of piety the more reason has he to rejoice in the final earthly hour. Piety and its engagements only seem of greater interest the more thoroughly a man is acquainted with them and the longer he has practised them. Nor is this all. It is well worthy of our consideration that no men ever have as much deliberate thought upon the subjects of duty, and especially of death and the eternal world, as pious men have. It is a very rare thing to see an ungodly man calmly look death in the face, reflect seriously upon its approach, converse collectedly of what lies beyond it and counsel wisely the friends that remain behind, in view both of earth's duties and of eternity's prospects. In all the range of English literature I know no more lamentable evidence of the weakness and folly of irreligion and infidelity than the account of David Hume's dying hours, as given in a letter from one of his most intimate friends. Let any one read that account and Dr. Mason's remarks upon it, or let any one compare the last thoughts and words of the ancient David, a believer, and of the modern David, a skeptic; let him see the one rejoicing in his God and the other whiling away the declining hours of life with a game of cards and with affected jesting upon the ancient heathen mythology, and he can easily decide upon which couch—that of the infidel or that of the believer—he would wish to stretch his dying limbs.

But the circumstances of the scene before us are further rendered impressive by the fact that here are not only the counsels of aged piety to youth, but the affectionate advice of a father to a son.

It is not needful here to urge that no relationship of life calls forth more of the warmest respect and affection of the human heart than the parental relation. We can see that this is natural and reasonable, and the cases are rare where men justify any departure from filial obedience. Among some barbarous and degraded tribes, indeed, it is the custom to put aged parents out of the way when they become a burden to their children, but even heathenism often teaches lessons far superior to this. With few exceptions, a father is a sacred character in all the earth; we reverence and respect him during all his life; we are deeply impressed by his dying counsels, and we cherish his memory after his departure. It gives a sacred interest to the words with which David now addresses Solomon when we judge of them in this light. The speaker and the hearer stand in this tender relation to each other. The experience of the aged parent now seeks to guide the young and tender heart of his beloved son.

And let us not forget that the counsels of aged piety from the father's lips are more deeply impressive because they are among his last utterances.

We are accustomed to treasure up the last words we have heard from beloved lips. Though the words themselves may have been uttered when we did not know they would be the last; though they may be unimpressive and insignificant in themselves, compared with many that we have heard from the same lips; though sometimes they are words whose remembrance we would wish to banish from our minds for ever,—there is something deeply affecting in these last utterances, upon which we dwell with interest frequently recurring. But especially when the last words of friends are deliberate and important; when they teach us lessons that are only more valuable the more we reflect upon them; then such counsels sometimes have the effect to influence the life ever after, and, indeed, their influence is transmitted to subsequent times. This is emphatically the case in the present instance. We may judge that Solomon was led by David's words, if not to the choice of piety, yet to its more diligent prosecution; and we now, at the distance of nearly three thousand years, sit reverently to read the dying counsels of the believing father.

Notice then, *first*, in these counsels, that David urges Solomon to know the God *of his fathers.*

We cannot, of course, say that any religious views are binding on us peculiarly, simply because our fathers have held them before us. That the Chinese have been idolaters for ages is no good reason for a native of China in the present day to continue those practices of heathenism which ages have rendered no more true than they were at first. If a man's parents have been in any degree unmindful of duty or ignorant of truth, he is not thereby justified in his disregard of the duty that belongs to him. No man of us refuses to avail himself of the growing improvements of science because his fathers never rode on a railway or saw a steam-engine. Errors do not become venerable by age, but as soon as discovered we should discard them, and nowhere sooner than in matters so important as religion. Where God's favour and our salvation are involved, we cannot be too desirous of knowing and following the truth. But though it is true that error does not become more venerable through age, it is equally correct to say that truth does become more venerable by its years. Principles which our fathers have tried, and which never have failed them in the severest straits, we too may rely upon. The history of piety becomes almost a part of piety itself. When David urged his son to know the God of his fathers, he directed his youthful eye backward down the pathway of the history of the Church, and filled his soul with stirring recollections of the great things which Jehovah had done for Israel.

The expression, "the God of thy fathers," might carry back the thoughts of Solomon to the darkness and idolatry that covered the earth when this God called forth Abraham from Ur of the Chaldees and established in his household the altar of his worship and the home of piety. Following down the train of thought through nine eventful centuries, it would place him by the door of Abraham's tent, and bid him look up to the innumerable stars and hear the promise, "So shall thy seed be." It would place him on Moriah's top to see the angel holding back a father's hand from the sacrifice of Isaac; by the slumbering Jacob gazing upon that wonderful scene when heavenly messengers were passing up and down between earth and heaven; by the Red Sea when the delivered hosts were passing through the divided waters beneath the protection of the pillar of fire and cloud; and under the summit of quaking Sinai when God spake to his people his holy law and gave them his commandments for their guidance. We need not fill up further the stirring thoughts, of which these are a few, that hung upon the expressive words of David, "The God of thy fathers." Everything of interest and of value that belonged to Jewish history was from his hand. And we too should rejoice to think of the God of our fathers; and this all the more because we are not of the stock of Israel; because our fathers, less than nine centuries back, were as idolatrous as now is the heathen world; and because from the darkness of corrupted religion God brought our fathers forth, and through their efforts and sacrifices and toils and martyrdoms has handed down to us the precious legacy of our faith. It is right for us to awaken our hearts by recollecting our fathers. Their successes and their defeats, their preaching and their suffering, equally endear them to us; and when we trace the wonderful dealings of the providence of God with respect to them; when we see how he led them through the wilderness; when we understand for how much of our present advantages we are indebted to what they did in his service and what he did for them, we are led to glory in the Lord God of our fathers, and to say, with all our hearts, This God shall be our God for ever and ever. He will be our guide even unto death.

Secondly. David urges Solomon to know the Lord his God. We will not now stay to show that the knowledge of God is the foundation of piety. Ignorance is the mother of superstition, but the devotion that is due to God from every humble heart will be increased by his knowledge of him. But it is doubtless the true meaning of David in this instance not to urge his son to study the character and ways of God so much as that he should love God. The word *know* in the Scriptures is often used with this meaning. When we are told, "The Lord knoweth the righteous," it means more than his acquaintance with the righteous and their ways.

In this sense God knows both the righteous and the wicked, but the meaning is, the Lord *loveth* the righteous. David uses the word in this sense, and calls upon Solomon to love the Lord God of his fathers. Already had he been trained somewhat in this way, to know God, but the essential demand is that he must yield his affections to him. Without the love of the heart, all mere knowledge of God but aggravates our sin; and if the heart is right it is easy to go on and secure an increasing knowledge of him. This love will lead to the service of God which David now inculcates upon Solomon.

Thirdly. We may notice the simplicity and sincerity which David commands.

He urges him to serve God with a perfect heart and with a willing mind. A wide and palpable distinction may justly be made between perfection of design and desire in what we do for God and perfection of accomplishment. The pious men of all ages have mourned over their shortcomings, have lamented that in many things they have offended, and have sought the divine pardon for the defilement of their holiest things. Yet they have not been hypocritical, but sincere. There is a sense in which the righteous have been both perfect and imperfect before God. They are imperfect and ever will be during this life. But they do not harbour willingly any evil thing. They are perfect in this respect—that they sincerely desire to know and love and obey God. Nothing short of this can God accept. The truly pious man often fears that he is harbouring sin; he fears he does not know himself, but he desires to be freed from every iniquity and his prayer is, Search me, O God. And David suggests here a thought which no worshipper of God should ever forget, and which should teach us the utter folly of all insincerity before such a God. We may sometimes seem to gain something in our dealings with men if we withhold something from them and attempt to impose upon them, for they may believe our falsehood, and we may get credit for professions that are not true. But this is not so in our dealings with the Most High. "The Lord searcheth all hearts, and understandeth all imaginations of the thoughts." No man should attempt to serve God at all that serves him not in entire sincerity. No professions that answer not to the real state of the heart can in any wise deceive him. If there is scarcely any more impressive thought than God's infinite knowledge of all we are and of all we do, yet it is a great comfort to every mind really sincere, The Lord knows.

Fourthly. David encouraged Solomon to this cheerful service of God: "If thou seek him he will be found of thee."

The gracious willingness of God to hear and answer when we call upon him is much insisted upon in the Scriptures. Nor does his willingness to hear at all conflict with the sovereignty of his grace toward many who wander far in sin. That Saul of Tarsus was arrested by divine grace when he thought not of it, is no reason why he should not thoughtfully reflect and humbly pray for divine acceptance, but the rather one of the strongest reasons why every guilty sinner should. The striking words of a judicious commentator—"God is *sometimes* found of them that seek him not, but he is *always* found of them that seek him"—are scarcely strong enough to express the force of the truth in the case. If God is sometimes found of those that seek not for him, *much more* may we expect that he will be found of them that seek him. And this *much more* rests not only upon his own character, not only upon the full and rich promises by which he is pledged to give when we ask, but also upon the truths that our prayers, prompted by the secret influence of his grace, are not inconsistent with his sovereignty, but may display it as truly, if not as remarkably, as the case of Saul; and that Saul himself and every other trophy of grace are led by that grace to seek God. David utters in the ears of Solomon a truth which any sinful soul may hear: If thou seek him he will be found of thee. Especially let every young person listen. There are special considerations addressing these gracious words to youthful ears. To such they were at first directed, and the teachings of providence, of Scripture and of grace are all alike. They that seek me early shall find me, is their united teaching.

It is, however, a matter of no inferior moment that we should consider how we are to seek God that we may find him. We are to seek HIM, and seek him as he has directed, if we would expect to find. If any man approaches the presence of an earthly king to ask his favour, yet with a studied or a negligent disregard of the rules of the court, he need not wonder to find his access denied and his suit rejected. When God calls us to seek him, he calls us to ponder those teachings of his holy word which tell us how he is to be sought and how we may expect to secure his blessing. We must come to God; we must plead for those blessings which he authorizes us to expect; we must put away from us those things that are grievous in his sight; we must ask in the name of Jesus Christ; and we are to wait patiently for him if for any reason he seems to delay in granting our petitions. We often mar an acceptance by indulging sin, unbelief, impatience. We should never forget that the true cause of our failure to secure the divine acceptance lies in ourselves. The plain promise is, "Seek and ye shall find." But we are so prone to act upon mere impulse and at the mere prompting of our fears, rather than according to the principles we should feel, that the prophet Jeremiah changes the form of this promise: "Ye shall seek for me, and find me when ye shall search for me with all your heart." Jer. xxix. 13. And so it is said of Judah: "They had sworn with all their heart, and sought him with their whole desire, and he was found of them." 2 Chron. xv. 15.

Fifthly. David solemnly warns his son against departing from God: "If thou forsake him, he will cast thee off for ever."

It seems a wonderful thing that men do not more fully recognize that all the gain of piety belongs to us, and that our departure from God is but mischievous to ourselves. Each of us may say, "My goodness extendeth not to thee." We can do ourselves infinite harm, but no harm to the immutable majesty of God, by our folly and sin. "Look unto the heavens and see, and behold the clouds which are higher than thou. If thou sinnest, what doest thou against him?" See the whole passage, Job xxxv. 5–8. We cannot afford to depart from God. Should we forsake him, his throne would remain yet firm for ever, his character spotless, his happiness infinite; but should he cast us off for ever, what immeasurable woe belongs to such a thought!

Let us fear to neglect God—much more to forsake or reject him. Above all other sinners may we fear, for God has granted us mercies so large that to rebel against them is great provocation in his sight. Those who rebel against mercies have greater reason to apprehend his early displeasure, and should especially fear to presume upon the forbearance of the Lord.

These are some of the thoughts that arise in view of David's dying charges to his son Solomon. But it is the excellency of such teachings that the more carefully they are pondered the richer they prove to be, and that each mind may see new beauties as it carefully dwells upon the thoughts. It is interesting to associate such teachings with the last words of an eminent believer, but it is profitable to remember that the real value of these counsels lies not in the circumstances, belongs not to the age in which David and Solomon lived, and is not confined to the experience of the youthful king. We may receive all the profit from it as well as he. And these inquiries may arise in view of these words to Solomon.

1st. Do those of us that are parents feel the same solicitude for the piety of our children that David here exhibits? It may be true that the dying bed shows out more plainly these affectionate desires. We have too much reason to fear that David was not as careful in the training of his household as he should have been. It is sad to reflect that though he says, The Lord hath given me many sons, we read much of the wickedness of his children, but are not told of the piety of any except Solomon. It may be that his dying advice is the more earnest because during his life he had too much neglected a pious father's duty. But how poor a compensation for long-neglected duties to a large family would a charge like this be as given to a single son! Let it be our wisdom to reflect upon the constant importance of holy principles, righteous examples, pious affections and earnest exhortations as given to our families during our lives and sealed by our latest teachings when we come to die. We cannot too deeply study our duties toward our families, nor be too much impressed with the value of our present opportunities for training them to love and serve the God of their fathers.

2d. Do we personally adopt the principles here urged upon the youthful Solomon? This is an inquiry irrespective of age or position. Let the aged ask; let the middle-aged reflect; let the young consider these things. No man can give too careful or too early attention to them. He who neglects them while in life and health shows thereby how little his heart is really interested in them, and the longer this neglect continues the more he puts in peril all that is valuable for this life and the life to come. Men too seldom understand that religion is our most valuable possession for this life; they too seldom realize that every year lost in the neglect of piety is an important loss of happiness and of usefulness, even if it should not result in the final loss of the soul. But the unhappy truth is, much as men hear about their duty, they will not seriously consider—they will not humbly pray.

Finally we have the record that David, the son

of Jesse, "died in a good old age, full of days, riches and honour."

So pass away the generations of men. Seventy years seem a long time for any man to live. A much shorter time than this is amply sufficient to give every opportunity for life's most valuable purposes. The chief usefulness of most good men, and the chief end of most wicked men, are over before they reach so mature an age of life, and the character of each man for his everlasting life is usually fixed at an early period. But long as the period seems of seventy years, it is but a moment in the lifetime of the soul, and no words can express the folly of the man who has spent his early years without preparation for the eternity beyond. If we had no record for David except of his years, his riches and his honours, what are all these worth when life itself is gone? "Call no man happy until the day of his death," said one of the most profound sages of ancient heathenism. Man here is subject to so many changes—this year rich and the next poor; now honoured and now despised; now happy and now wretched; now innocent and now ensnared by temptation; now surrounded by friends and now bereaved—that we may call no man happy till we know how he has passed through the various trials of a changing world. "The day of death," says the inspired wise man, "is better than the day of birth." Eccles. vii. 1. And yet the apothegm of the heathen sage looks not far enough for those that are well read in the volume of divine revelation. "Call no man happy except in view of that eternal state which succeeds the day of death," would rather be the serious thought that should fill our minds. What are the years or riches or honours of any man if his soul is unreconciled to God, and his life on earth has not been in the service of his Maker?

## CHAPTER XXIII.

### *CHARACTERISTICS OF DAVID.*

WE propose in this closing chapter to take a general review not of the incidents in the history, but of the character of David as we may view this in four particulars:

1. David as a man.
2. David in his public relations.
3. David as a type of Christ.
4. David an instructive exemplar in religious experience.

In the first place, David deserves a high place when we consider him as a man.

We have no reason to suppose that his early advantages were anything in advance of other Jewish children. We find him at first the least esteemed in his father's family, and his place is that of a humble keeper of the sheep. These things, perhaps, merely betoken his youthfulness when his name first occurs on the sacred pages; but even his youth would not have placed him so much in the background if his father had discerned in the child any tokens of his future eminence. But that shepherd-boy was a poet and a musician whose fame and influence were never to be surpassed, even in more polished ages. David was unquestionably a man of taste and genius; and as he rose to power and wealth, we have rarely found reason to question the wisdom of his counsels or the vigour of their execution. We have previously considered more fully his firm and faithful attachments as a friend; we have seen reason to commend his patience and forgiveness toward unprovoked injuries; his patriotism even against the ingratitude of his king and people; and his persevering energy in the most discouraging circumstances. Let us not therefore magnify the faults which appear in this great man, so as to lose sight of the sterling, excellent qualities which belonged to his character. There is this thing that ought to be said concerning any man's faults—that we ought rather to judge of him by that which comes after his errors than by the errors themselves. When we find a man boldly denying or carefully covering up his faults; when we find him vindicating as right injurious and wicked conduct; when no sign is given but that he is of the same mind still as when he committed his sin,—then we may judge of him according to the full wickedness of the offence. But when, on the other hand, no man more openly and directly condemns the transgression than does the transgressor himself; when he humbly and penitently confesses and renounces his sins and bears meekly the consequences that result from them;

when thus there is every reason to believe that he entertains a far different mind from that which has allowed him so to offend against God and man,—we ought to form quite a different opinion of his entire character. We do not still place such a man upon the same level with one whose life has been unstained by crime. Yet there are some thoughts of special interest gathering round the life of one restored from dangerous sins. There is joy in the presence of the angels of God over one sinner that repenteth, and this more than over ninety-and-nine just persons that need no repentance. We cannot omit the faults of David in a just view of his character—his own penitent confessions of them are as severe a condemnation as any enemy can make—yet we may see and acknowledge that he had many virtues. We rank among his accomplishments a vigorous intellect, a cultivated taste, a ready discernment of times and measures, fearless bravery in battle and a facility of adapting himself to his various changes of fortune. We rank among his virtues a high regard for truth and justice, yet marred by gross instances of falsehood and injustice; a warm attachment, especially as exhibited in his friendship for Jonathan; an enduring faith, tried by many changes at different periods of life; an earnest zeal for the service of God, which was specially shown by his desire to establish and maintain public worship, and by the large and magnificent preparations he made for the building of the temple; while the Psalms, of which we will speak again, give evidence that the warmth of devotional feeling in David ranks among his great excellences. The character of this man, as a whole, fully justifies the high esteem in which he has ever been held in the Church.

II. We may next consider David in his public relations.

1st. He was an able and victorious warrior.

As we first find him upon the sacred pages he was a mere youth, yet he is willing to go forth against the giant of Gath. To form a just idea of his military capacity, we need but consider the state of the kingdom at that time, and compare it with its flourishing condition when Solomon ascended the throne. We have seen that the desire of the people to have a king arose from their oppressed and scattered condition by the power of the tribes around them. But the reign of Saul was well-nigh a failure, and would have been so entirely but for the sterling patriotism and the steady valour of the very man whom he persecuted, oppressed and drove into exile. Even the successful battles he fought against the Philistines he knew not how to use; the kingdom during his reign was brought into straits as great as ever before; even while David was in his army the enemy occupied the very gates of Bethlehem, and the last effort of the unhappy king was the desperate struggle on Gilboa, that completed the ruin of the house of

Saul. But from the moment that David reigned in Hebron his name was a tower of protection for the tribes of Israel. We hear no more now of the victories of the Philistines. The progress of the kingdom was steadily onward and upward. The lands that had been wrested from the feeble tribes since the first conquest of the land by Joshua were recovered, and the boundaries of the kingdom made as wide as the promise given by God to Abraham. The power of his arms had made his throne respected by the nations all around him, and few would care to provoke a king who had been a warrior since his youth and had never lost a battle. Whether we look at the energetic counsels, the personal valour or the restless energy of David; whether we consider his success in gathering about him brave and able commanders, or in winning the affection of his soldiers, or in impressing his enemies with terror of his name; whether we consider the zealous patriotism of every movement, the evident aim to promote the well-being of Israel, or the moderation that marked his triumphs in all this great success,—we may declare that this king of Israel was one of the best examples in the earth of a man of war. Without ambition in the bad sense of the word; seeking no conquests for conquests' sake; keeping himself within the boundaries which God had placed for his kingdom, or passing beyond them only to chastise unprovoked insolence; aiming in all things at the peace of his people, and securing peace to their great benefit,— David may not be ranked among the ambitious conquerors of the earth, while he may be placed high in the list of warriors. We would have no wars if all men were like David, for he gave no needless provocation to foreign power; but so long as wars rise out of man's lusts, the storms of human passion need to be guided and controlled by the wisdom and valour and patriotism of such warriors as this king of Israel.

2d. David was a wise and righteous ruler. It is not needful for us now to speak of the laws of the kingdom, except to say that they were given to Israel by divine wisdom; that even those parts that seem peculiar and strange to us are to be understood in connection with the peculiar state and circumstances of the people; that in all respects they were largely in advance of the nations around them, and that modern nations of the highest civilization have paid this compliment to Jewish jurisprudence, that the best principles of modern governments find their original expression in the laws of the first great Jewish lawgiver, Moses. But in order to wise rule we need far more than righteous laws. The same law stood upon the statute-book of the Jewish commonwealth in the days of the Judges, when every man did that which was right in his own eyes; in the days of Saul, when the monarch played the despot; and even in the days of Ahab, when the very laws themselves were used to oppress the subject. Righteous rulers are as important as righteous laws. The reign of David had its exceptions, as when the king was unable to punish the crimes of a powerful criminal like Joab, or as when the monarch himself stooped so low to deeds of shame and crime. Yet David was a righteous king. In the one hundred and first Psalm we have the expression of his purposes as a righteous ruler, and the principles of that Psalm may well be pondered by every conscientious magistrate. The prosperity of the kingdom in every respect, both internal and external, during the rule of David, except as disturbed by the rebellion of Absalom, proves the wisdom of his government; and it is deeply impressive to observe that we read of no internal troubles under his government except those that sprang out of his great sin and were subsequent to it. Yet in the main, David was a wise and righteous ruler, and in his reign the kingdom was firmly established. Under him first they had a fixed seat of government; by his care the lawful arrangements for public worship seem first to have been carried into full effect; and even the splendour of Solomon's reign owed its chief glory to the great preparation which had been made for him by his father—a preparation that had as much regard to the civilization and education and government of the tribes as it had to the collecting of money and materials for the building of the house of the Lord.

3d. David is the chief devotional poet of the Church of God.

No part of the worship of God is more delightful than singing his praise; and we may easily believe that a service so natural and so excellent has prevailed in the Church from the earliest ages. The use of instrumental music seems ever to have accompanied it. The harp and organ were invented before the Flood. When the Israelites passed through the Red Sea the people sang the praises of God; and in the organization afterward for public worship express and full provision was made for this part of the service. But David is the chief Psalmist of the Church from his time onward. Only one psalm of the entire Book of Psalms is expressly referred to an earlier period, and nearly one-half of the whole bear the name of David, while many others give internal proof that they were composed by him. It is, then, within the bounds of sober truth to say that no poet since the world began has been the favourite of the people compared with David. The simple truth that every Sabbath-day for centuries back, with a wider spread in each succeeding generation, the Psalms of the Hebrew poet have been the basis of praise for thousands of worshipping congregations, and that every day millions of voices use them in the family for private singing, make it easy to say no writer has ever exerted more influence than he. His Psalms are the special delight of pious minds.

"He who has once tasted their excellences will desire to taste them again, and he who tastes them oftenest will relish them best."

III. We may next consider David in a still more public relation—not to his kingdom alone, but to the Church of God; not simply to the Old Testament times, but to us also. David was an eminent type of Christ.

The promise of the coming of Christ had been so renewed from age to age as to point out more and more definitely in what line he should be born. To Abraham, Jacob, Judah and David the promise was successively made. With David particularly God made a covenant by which he was constituted the great type of the Messiah as a king and a prophet. This was recognized by the ancient Church, so that there was no difficulty in deciding where Christ should be born, whose son he should be and whose throne he should occupy. But the character and the throne of David were but faint emblems of the greater person and kingdom which they symbolized, as the shadow of anything is greatly inferior to the thing itself. Upon the ground of David's greatness our Lord argued when he would convince the Jews of the superior character of the Messiah. David himself called him Lord, and he perplexed the short-sighted Pharisees with the pertinent inquiry, How could he be both Lord and Son?

David was a type of Christ as a king. There

were imperfections in the kingdom of David such as may not be found in the kingdom of the Messiah; yet so much is the kingdom of Israel like the kingdom of Christ that the promise runs, "He shall sit upon the throne of David." In the eighty-ninth Psalm especially, we have a prediction that in its highest meanings can apply only to the great kingdom of Christ. As the kingdom of David was established by the power of his arms, so the Messiah was to go forth as a conquering Prince. In the special promises made to David by the prophet Nathan, when he announced to him that he should not be allowed to build the temple, many interpreters suppose that express reference is made to the Messiah and to his kingdom. So David acknowledges with thankfulness: "Thou hast spoken of thy servant's house for a great while to come." And the seventy-second Psalm speaks of the reign of Solomon, but in language that belongs in its largest meaning to the greater Son of David. Even the high-flown language of Persian flattery could scarcely speak of a less kingdom than that of Christ as enduring for ever and as extending from the Euphrates to the ends of the earth.

David as a prophet sets forth in the Psalms predictions of the coming Christ, and exemplifies in his own person many of the sufferings of the coming Redeemer. There seems this remarkable thing in many of the predictions of the Scriptures, that they so fall in with the designs of Providence as to find their fulfilment at several times even when chiefly referring to one great event. Thus the outpouring of the Spirit spoken of by the prophet Joel found its chief fulfilment upon the day of Pentecost, but is repeatedly further fulfilled in the experience of the Church at various times; the raging of the kings against Christ, spoken of in the second Psalm, was fulfilled when Herod and Pilate and the Jews put our Lord to death, but it has again and again been fulfilled in the persecutions the Church has subsequently met. The promised gathering of the Jews from among the nations, though once accomplished, shall be yet more gloriously fulfilled. The prophecy of our Lord respecting Jerusalem's destruction has evident regard also to the judgment of the final day. So in the Psalms we have many predictions of Christ's sufferings under the figure of the sufferings of David. The most remarkable of David's complaints which in the highest sense can apply only to our Lord is Psalm xxii. It is harder to understand how the words of this Psalm can apply to David at all than to see how wonderfully they set forth the sorrows of Christ. So the sixty-ninth Psalm sets forth his griefs as our Redeemer. Other portions of the Psalms are quoted in the New Testament as applicable to him. The malice of the kings, the treachery of Judas, the matchless grief of the sufferer, as well as the glory of the

Church, the exaltation of the Messiah and the wide spread of his kingdom to all the earth, are given in various forms that can be fully appreciated only by the careful exposition of each Psalm that may be justly esteemed Messianic.

IV. We will consider David as an instructive exemplar in religious experience.

In vain for us are all the lessons of the Scriptures, unless they are brought home to our personal experience. It is easy for us to see that in all the history of the human family there is no man whose inmost thoughts are more fully set before us than those of David. Of other believers we have records that others have written of them—truthful indeed, but still not giving us the workings of their hearts. Of David we can compile a history from his own confessions at every age of life. As a shepherd-boy we hear him sing in light-hearted piety as he watches his flocks by night; as an exile, we hear him mourn his absence from the altars of God; as a king, he resolves that he would be a just ruler over men, ruling in the fear of God; as a penitent for a great iniquity, he teaches our burdened hearts how to pray for divine renewal; and we listen to his tremulous voice in declining years, pleading that when he is old and gray-headed he may not be forsaken. It ought to be for serious profit that we have passed through the history of such a man as this; and though his spiritual history, as recorded in the Psalms, has not received special attention, yet we have not failed to point out many lessons of spiritual advantage. Let us now briefly notice such matters as these:

1st. David teaches to love the worship of God. We have no example of spiritual piety more fully brought before us. He had his times of dejection and discomfort and absence from the sanctuary; and he shows us that he envied the very sparrows that could build their nests within sight of the altars of God, and longed to be a doorkeeper in the tabernacle rather than an honoured guest in the tents of sin. No man had ever shown in all the Church greater zeal for public worship. None before him had ever spoken of building a temple for the Lord; and, though the privilege was denied him, he had all the credit of the desire, and his magnificent preparations for its future erection show how sincere and earnest he was. Let every believer imitate the zeal of David for the public worship of God; let every one long for access to the sanctuary as he did; let every one of us show that he esteems a day in God's courts better than a thousand in the tents of sin,—and the influence of the sanctuary would be wonderfully increased. And if David did so much to establish the worship of God, how ought we to maintain the ordinances we have already established among us!

2d. David teaches us the deceitfulness of sin. We have freely spoken of his faults. We have specially spoken of the great transgression that marked his later life. We should remember that he was overtaken by grievous sin at the very time we would least expect it. He was a man of mature character, he had received many favours from the hand of God, he was full of honours and prosperity, when he fell so low to sin. David should impress upon us the lesson of a later prophet—"The heart is deceitful above all things and desperately wicked." No lesson of piety do we need more fully to understand—no lesson are we more prone to forget than this.

3d. But David teaches us the true nature and exercise of piety.

Let us not forget that he teaches us how wide open is the door of return for the penitent sinner. Penitence is not a reparation for guilt; and no true penitent but mourns that he ever stooped to the committing of iniquity. In no sense does David teach us to sin that grace may abound. But we may be thankful that as sinners we are permitted to use such a model of prayer as this penitent has given us in the fifty-first Psalm. Let us learn from it that the same language of grief and repentance suits the lips of the backslider who has tasted the Lord's grace and yet gone away from duty, and the humble confession of one who for the first time is deeply impressed by a sense of his sins and prays for God's mercy in his forgiveness.

It might easily be shown further how fully the

evangelical sentiments of David agree with the great teachings of the gospel in the New Testament Church. Though he lived so long before the clear light given by God to the Church after the coming of his Son, the principles of piety as set forth by him are the same as those proclaimed by the prophets and apostles of our Lord. Sufficient proof of this is given in the use of his Psalms by the pious men of all later times, and by the fact that the most eminent Christians have most relished their teachings. Here are lessons of hope and of resignation in trial; of patience and forgiveness under injuries; of justifying faith that relies only on the righteousness of God; of enduring faith that believes his promises in the darkest hours; and of triumphant faith that delivers the soul from oppressing fears. Here is joy in God greater than the world can give; here is love for God that many waters cannot quench; and the fruits of his piety are peace, truth, justice and righteousness.

4th. But there is this FINAL THOUGHT of practical interest to which our minds may be turned in the close of these chapters. We are again and again assured in the Scriptures that God made a covenant with David—an everlasting covenant, ordered and in all things sure. This covenant had reference to public matters—to the establishment of his kingdom and the coming of the Redeemer through him. In regard to these things we will now say nothing further. This covenant had its private aspects. It had regard to the salvation of David personally. Between him and God there was a covenant. A covenant differs from a law. A law declares a man's duty, and obliges him to do it, with or without his consent. A covenant is a mutual contract made between parties, who by the covenant imply their peaceful agreement. God, whose law man has violated, condescends to enter into covenant with man. He covenanted with David. On the part of David was stipulated love, faith, repentance, obedience to God; on the part of God, forgiveness, grace, life eternal, and such guidance and chastisements of providence as seemed needful to infinite wisdom, with a distinct pledge that David should never be forsaken. This is the great matter of all we have considered that should engage our thoughts. Every soul of us is under the law of this God—as fully bound to obey as we can be, and as transgressors subject to his wrath. God graciously offers to change the form of our allegiance—to bring us under a covenant rather than under the law. This is a privilege of unspeakable value. He blessed David; he will bless with the very best mercies he gave to him. He says by the prophet: "Ho every one, come. Incline your ear and come unto me; hear, and your soul shall live; and I will make an everlasting covenant with you, even the sure mercies of David."

www.ingramcontent.com/pod-product-compliance
Lightning Source LLC
LaVergne TN
LVHW021120110826
845150LV00005B/902

* 9 7 8 1 4 2 5 5 5 2 1 6 9 *